Going Against the Grain

Going Against the Grain

When Professionals in Hawai'i Choose Public Schools Instead of Private Schools

Ann Shea Bayer

University of Hawai'i Press
Honolulu

© 2009 University of Hawai'i Press
All rights reserved
Printed in the United States of America
14 13 12 11 10 09   6 5 4 3 2 1

Library of Congress Cataloging-in-Publication Data
Bayer, Ann Shea.
  Going against the grain : when professionals in Hawai'i
choose public schools instead of private schools / Ann Shea Bayer.
    p. cm.
Includes bibliographical references and index.
ISBN 978-0-8248-3273-5 (hard cover : alk. paper)
ISBN 978-0-8248-3339-8 (pbk. : alk. paper)
  1. School choice — Hawaii.   2. Public schools — Hawaii.
I. Title.
LB1027.9.B39   2009
371.010969 — dc22   2008048774

University of Hawai'i Press books are printed on acid-free
paper and meet the guidelines for permanence and durability
of the Council on Library Resources.

Designed by April Leidig-Higgins

Printed by The Maple-Vail Book Manufacturing Group

To all the parents who so
graciously participated
in this study

Contents

Preface

I have attended both public and private schools, and I feel that I have learned important lessons from each. However, the most useful information came from my public high school experience. I grew up in a small town in Maine in the 1950s. There were three elementary school options at that time — the public elementary schools, one Catholic school for French-speaking Catholics, and a second Catholic school for all others. I attended the latter for eight years. I remember being curious about the kids who attended the other schools, especially the public school students. How different were they from me? My curiosity was soon satisfied because all the students from these three small school systems transferred into one public high school, with the exception of a few who went away to boarding school.

While there was some ethnic and socioeconomic class diversity in my Catholic school, I found much greater diversity in the high school. It might seem strange to some to consider ethnic diversity in a small town in Maine, but in those days one could find citizens who were first-generation (including my father) and second-generation immigrants from Italy, Ireland, Scotland, Lithuania, Poland, and Canada, including French-Canadians, as well as long-time residents. Everyone in town went to this public school, whether their parents were farmers, doctors, paper mill workers, lawyers, teachers, garage mechanics, or business owners, so the socioeconomic diversity was broader as well. And, for the first time, I went to school with students of other faiths. There was nothing remarkable about any of this. It's just what we did.

My experience within this diverse context had a significant impact on me, though. While my high school provided me with the important academic foundation I needed to pursue higher education, thanks to the dedication of our teachers, it also gave me the opportunity to recognize the similarities rather than the differences between my classmates and myself. This perspective has been beneficial in my adult life.

Because of my appreciation for what I received from my public school education, basic and unadorned as it was, I have always been an advocate for a strong public education system in a democracy and have always been interested in the public schools in the communities in which I have lived.

It is because of this perspective that I became curious as to why many in

Hawaiʻi (and on the mainland) do not share this view. I wanted to know why private schools in Hawaiʻi have higher status than public schools and why, then, the professionals interviewed for this study chose to "go against the grain" of their peers and send their children to public schools. I connect these findings to a discussion about what, if any, are the broader implications for the civic and economic health of a community when there is not community-wide support for a strong public school system.

I wrote this book for audiences of parents contemplating private or public schools, teachers, administrators, legislators, school board members, policy makers, members of the business community, and social science researchers.

Acknowledgments

I have many to thank. I so enjoyed and appreciated meeting the parents in this study. They were willing to be interviewed at their places of work, at restaurants, at the university, or at just about any mutually agreed upon location, both in Hawai'i and on the mainland. They were willing to share their beliefs about school choice, their children's school experiences, and their suggestions for improving schools, as well thoughtful ideas about the role of public schools in a democracy. And they shared with openness, reason, and, in many cases, a degree of fervor. I learned something from each and every one, and I walked away with enormous respect and a sense of optimism.

I want to thank my colleagues Betsy Brandt, Ron Heck, Ernestine Enomoto, Tracy Trevorrow, and Fred Bail for their encouragement and support. I would also like to extend my appreciation to the reviewers whose careful reading of the manuscript provided the guidance I needed to make my revisions. And thank you, Eileen Tamura, for providing excellent insight into the history of schools in Hawai'i, as did Jeanne Keuma. Jeanne was also invaluable to me for her patience and expertise in assisting me with the many tasks needed to prepare the manuscript for submission. Darrell Asato, in turn, provided the necessary technological know-how for the map showing the geographical locations of the public schools. And, needless to say, I most appreciate Bill Hamilton, director of the University of Hawai'i Press, who conveyed a sense of calm and wisdom throughout the publishing process. I am most appreciative for Ann Ludeman's professional guidance, and for Susan Biggs Corrado's excellent editing and stylistic suggestions.

Lastly, I want to show my appreciation for Stacie Odo, administrative professional extraordinaire, who works with me and supports me in myriad ways each day, as do our wonderful student workers. I am grateful.

Note on Hawaiian Spelling

Throughout this book, for accuracy and consistency's sake, all Hawaiian words are properly spelled with the macron (known as the *kahakō,* or a line above long vowels) and glottal stop (known as the *'okina,* or the Hawaiian letter denoted by a single open quote mark before a vowel, indicating the letter pronounced as a stop, much like the stop in "oh-oh").

Notes on Research Procedures

This is a qualitative interview study. This research design was chosen as that which best matched my intention to understand an important social issue in Hawai'i, namely school choice. I wanted to study the reasons professionals in Hawai'i chose to "go against the grain" of their peers and send their children to public schools rather than private schools. I wanted to know the support or the barriers they faced when making such a decision, their children's experiences in public schools, and their thoughts on the role of public education in a community. Interviewing provides the means by which it is possible to "understand that about which little is known" (Strauss and Corbin 1998, 11).

The parents were selected initially through a technique called "snowballing," where one participant leads to another (Bertaux 1981, 55). I considered this technique to be reasonable, as I needed contact with professionals who made this alternative choice in favor of public schools, versus the typical choice of private schools. A participant in the study often would recommend several other professionals who were sending their children to public schools. My decision as to whom I should contact from these recommendations depended on my attempt to reach a maximum variation sampling (Patton 1989), meaning I wanted as representative a sampling as possible of the professional population, gender, ethnicity, and location (neighborhood). I continued to conduct interviews until saturation occurred in that that no new information was being introduced (Strauss and Corbin 1998).

All interviews were audiotaped and transcribed. The transcriptions were analyzed and coded to determine common themes. The transcriptions serve as the primary database for the study. The printed excerpts of the transcriptions were edited to protect confidentiality. As a result of this initial analysis I realized that the parents' inclusion of the history of Hawai'i's schools and the role of newspapers in framing the community's perceptions toward private and public schools were important. I conducted further research by reading primary and secondary historical documents, consulting with a local historian, and analyzing the headlines related to public education during 2004–2005.

1 Introduction

It wasn't long after I arrived in the islands that I started to hear what one private school parent calls the "incessant conversation" about school choice in Hawai'i. It came up in the classes I was teaching at the University of Hawai'i. It came up in the corridors of my workplace. It came up at social events. It came up when I was exercising at the gym. It was everywhere, constant, and negative toward the public schools. And I was told many times that professionals send their children to private schools, especially to the elite private schools, so a "class" issue seemed to exist as well.

I couldn't figure it out. As part of my work as a professor, I visited or conducted workshops in a number of the 284 public schools and a few of the 135 private schools. I soon learned of problems related to the state school system bureaucracy and the poor conditions of some of the public schools, but I also observed many well-maintained and highly successful, functioning public schools.

I remained surprised and confused about the extent of the negativity toward public schools. This attitude was not part of my personal experience on the mainland, where I taught in middle schools in several states over a twelve-year period. And the notion that professionals in Hawai'i wouldn't choose public schools didn't seem accurate to me. After all, 180,000 of Hawai'i's children attend public schools versus the approximately 35,000 who attend private, mostly small, religious schools. Surely middle- and upper middle-class families were represented in that public school population.

So I set out to find some of these families. I was looking for professionals who had the option (in terms of finances and children who via tests, interviews, etc., could qualify) of sending their children to private or public schools and for those who chose the latter. I used a technique called "snowballing" to select these parents (Bertaux 1981; Seidman 2006): This is the case when a parent in the study referred me to other parents or when colleagues who heard I was conducting this study referred me to possible participants. I attempted to include as much variation among the participants as possible. I considered gender, occupation, ethnicity, and geographical locations.

I interviewed fifty-one parents, forty-two of whom were identified by colleagues as professionals who sent their children to public schools. I also included five parents identified as having chosen private schools for their children. Since the public "incessant conversation," or narrative, is so widespread and viewed as an accepted community-held belief, I didn't believe I needed to have an equal number of private school parents in the study. The reasons for private school choice are repeated over and over in the community narrative. But I did want to hear from these parents to see if their reasons for choosing private schools confirmed the typical reasons given in the "incessant conversation." And I hoped to elicit a deeper understanding.

I also interviewed parents from the mainland, representing three urban areas, because I wanted to compare school choice in Hawai'i and the mainland. The number of mainland parents interviewed is small; however, they are all active in school choice coalitions, so I thought their perspectives would be knowledgeable and representative.

The occupations of all of the parents comprised physicians (including one dentist), professors, attorneys, military officers, teachers, legislators, business executives, business entrepreneurs, bankers, administrators, media management, and nonprofit executives.

In Hawai'i I interviewed twenty-seven men and twenty women, typically at their places of business. Their ethnicities included twenty-eight Asian Americans (Japanese, Chinese, Filipino, and Okinawan), seventeen European Americans (Irish, German, Scottish, French, Scandinavian, and English), one Native American, and one Latino. On the mainland, I interviewed one man and three women. Three of these parents are of European American ancestry, one of Latino ancestry.

The majority of Hawai'i's participants live on the island of O'ahu, which has the densest population, including the urban area of Honolulu. Five of the parents, however, live on three of the neighbor islands. All four mainland parents live in or near urban cities.

The children of these parents attended sixty-five public schools, located throughout the geographic locations indicated on the map.

This book is the parents' story. I have told their story more or less in the sequence of questions asked during the individual interviews.

Chapter 2 provides discussions with professionals in Hawai'i who talked about why they chose public schools over private schools. These parents saw public schools as a means of providing "the best for their children." The phrase is the same used by parents who chose private schools.

Chapter 3 reports the findings related to the children's experiences — both

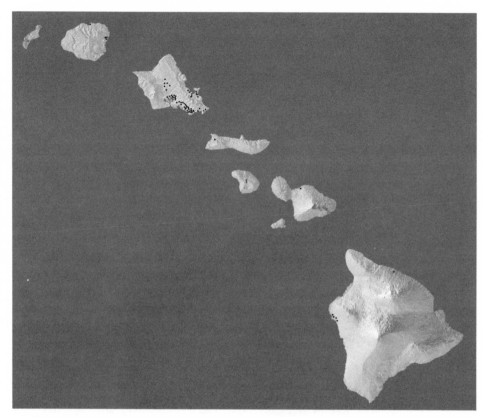

Geographical locations in Hawai'i of the sixty-five public schools attended by the children of the interviewed professionals who chose public schools instead of private schools.

positive and negative — while attending public schools. From the parents' conversations emerged a concept of a "good public school"; parents also talked about opportunities available at the public high schools. Several mentioned that their children were accepted into the same colleges as the private school graduates. This chapter also includes a list of these colleges and universities.

Chapter 4 discusses what I discovered about the reactions these parents received regarding their decisions to send their children to public schools. In general, many others expected them to choose private schools. I wanted to know what the parents' professional colleagues, as well as their neighbors, families, and friends, had said. The parents talked about the type of feedback they received, including from their children's public school teachers.

Chapter 5 examines more closely the community-held belief regarding public and private schools in Hawai'i, and the negative impact that this prevailing opinion has on parents. It is important to understand this belief system and how both newcomers and local residents are exposed to it, because the system works to constrain or facilitate parental decisions about schooling. I asked public and private school parents how newcomers to Hawai'i come to learn about this perception of Hawai'i's schools. It was during these conversations that I also found out how this belief is reinforced among local residents.

In chapter 6, I stepped back from the parents' interviews in order to examine the possible interconnections among the typical reasons given for the existence and acceptance of the community-held belief regarding public schools in Hawai'i. This analysis included an examination of the role of Hawai'i's history, the role that the "incessant conversation" plays as a means by which this historical belief is passed from one generation to another and to newcomers to the islands, and the role of the headlines related to public schools in the two mainstream newspapers and one local magazine.

After unpacking some of the reasons the citizens of Hawai'i have become predisposed to favor private schools, chapter 7 returns to the parents' conversations. Specifically, this chapter includes their suggestions for changes they believe would make the public schools stronger. I added changes that are presently occurring in the public school system.

The final chapter addresses the question, "Why should we care whether a community's or state's public school system is well respected?" The parents' responses to this question were connected to issues of our democracy and our economic well-being. The parents are concerned that two-tiered schooling fragments the community and contributes to an apathetic and unengaged public, as well as a lack of identity with a cohesive community in which a populace works toward common goals, both civic and economic.

In the past two decades this pulling away from support of public education has also occurred on the mainland. In his well-known and defining work *Bowling Alone* (2000), Robert D. Putnam documents the broader change in America from the civic behavior of its citizens during the first two-thirds of the twentieth century, when Americans became increasingly connected to each other and to community activities, to the continuing reversal of this behavior beginning in the last third of the twentieth century.

What to do? The last section of the final chapter includes a discussion of what Putnam and others refer to as the social capital needed for healthy communities and strong public schools, as well as how to increase that social capital. Communities with high social capital usually have strong support for public education, whereas, as David Matthews explains, "Schools are seen quite differently where public life is failing. People talk about them as being detached from the community. The dominant concern is 'taking care of my child' rather than educating every child. In this atmosphere, public schools find it virtually impossible to garner the support they need to be successful" (quoted in The Harwood Group 1995b, 4).

This book is about passion, advocacy, and the parents' willingness to "go against the grain" of one's professional peers. It is about professionals choosing public education for their children in a state that adheres to the commonly held belief that "Public schools are failing. Private schools are succeeding. Send your children to private schools." The results of this study suggest that this belief is inaccurate. A more accurate narrative would acknowledge that both public and private schools vary. There are excellent choices in both types of institutions.

2 Professionals Choosing Public Schools

When professionals move to Hawai'i and ask their colleagues about where to send their children to school, they are likely to be told that they should be sent to private schools. These colleagues, like the private school parents in this study, typically assert that private schools have a higher status, are more academically challenging, are safer, and have more resources than public schools. If this description is accurate, why would some professionals then decide to send their children to public schools? In this chapter, these parents explain their reasoning. Their thoughts are similar to those of Dr. Loren Yamamoto, a pediatrician who wrote in *Tidbits on Raising Children: Making Our Most Important Job Easier by Doing It Better,*

> The quality of education that my children have received has been outstanding. . . . There is less stress on day to day life since the neighborhood school is a three-minute ride down the street instead of a long stressful commute. My children attend school with neighborhood kids. Their friends are from the neighborhood. . . . It is a personal preference of course, but I feel that there is a benefit to let my children grow up with the wide spectrum of neighborhood kids of the public school. . . . It teaches them at an early age about the diversity of people. (2000, 148)

Much like Yamamoto, the parents in this study talked about choosing public schools instead of private schools as a means of providing "the best for their children." Their definition of what constitutes the "best" includes not only a good academic education, but also an educational experience that will help their children become well-rounded individuals through exposure to diversity in the public school populations in Hawai'i. Viewed through the eyes of these parents, student diversity is reflective of the "real world," and the experience of going to school with those different from oneself (whether ethnically, socioeconomically, or resulting from special needs) is an opportunity to learn life lessons that will benefit their children as adults. This was a strongly held value for many of the parents in this study.

Nonetheless, school choice typically involved more than acting on this belief alone. Parents included a number of other factors as they weighed the variables in their choice between public and private schools. And for the majority of these parents, a decision in favor of private school would have meant one of the elite private schools in Hawai'i. Many of these parents also value the idea of having their children attend the neighborhood school with the added benefit of avoiding a long commute, with its potential negative impact on family time. For this reason, a number of parents conducted research on the public schools in order to determine where they would purchase a home. Some parents also believe it is important to advocate for public education. One obvious way of doing so is to send their children to the public schools. And although the majority of parents in this study could afford private schools, for several it would have been difficult. For them, the benefits of a private school education did not outweigh other uses of their money.

To help them make their school choice, many parents conducted research on public schools with a "good reputation" and neighboring schools that were less well known. They visited schools, talked to principals, searched the Internet for public school information, and talked to friends and colleagues whose children were attending these schools.

The Value of Diversity: "The Real World"

For all the parents I interviewed, a good academic education for their children was a priority. However, they also talked about why they value the diversity found in public schools. They often mentioned experiencing diversity firsthand when they were in public school and wanting that same experience for their own children. Below, one attorney recalled an example from his own personal public school experience when personal contact with a classmate with a disability had a significant impact on his life.

Attorney: Way back in third grade, the teachers had mainstreamed a student. I don't know what his problem was. Whether he had cerebral palsy, or whether he was mentally retarded, I don't know. All I know is that he couldn't walk well. He couldn't speak very clearly. And I was the only one who could understand what he was saying. So I had to kind of translate what he was saying to the rest of the class. He only stayed with us for a few months and then, either they moved him into a special school or something. But I thought that was a really valuable experience.

I kind of wish more people had this experience, where teachers would mainstream some of these kids so children would have that opportunity to understand people as being—I didn't see him as being disadvantaged as much as just difficult to understand. And being the one who could understand him made me feel good. I don't know that you get those experiences in private school. I just don't know.

A photographer also talked about how those kinds of school experiences helped him when he moved to the mainland, where he lived and worked with different cultural groups.

Photographer: Growing up in a plantation camp . . . we didn't have too many Japanese in the camp. So we went up to the gulch and swam in the river with Portuguese and Filipino friends. We played baseball and played in the park, climbed mango trees, had guava fights. And it was fun. It was a lot of fun.

Later on, though, as I think about it now, [that experience] did really help me adjust when I went to school on the mainland. I was able to draw on experiences of being with [people of] different ethnic backgrounds, where I didn't have any perceived prejudices, except those that were kind of inferred by my parents, of course. But by the time I was in college, that didn't matter anymore. My parents were my parents, and I had my own ideas and ideals. [Being on the mainland] was a culture shock for me. I had never been among so many white people before. My personal experiences helped me to adjust to understand that I should not judge people. I should just see them as they are and try to understand them, and become friendly with them.

Other parents articulated their belief that the opportunity for their children to go to school with children different from their own socioeconomic and ethnic groups promotes empathy, respect for difference, and flexibility —traits they believe will continue to benefit their children as adults when interacting with diverse groups in their personal and professional lives.

Nonprofit Executive: I view the inclusiveness of public schools as being a vital part of why public schools have the opportunity to be a much better education—a much more lifelike and realistic experience for children. The reality is that we live in a world, especially here in the United States, that is quickly being integrated with a multitude of different cultures, races, religious backgrounds, and unfortunately, that's something that's often missed in private schools—obviously missed in a sectarian school.

If you took a school that was Catholic-based, or a Christian-based school, they certainly don't see the children that come from Hindu, or Buddhist, or other backgrounds. Often, many of the minorities, because of their recent immigration, don't have the socioeconomic base to afford private school. Of course, there are exceptions.

You also don't see a lot of children who have disabilities—both physical and mental disabilities—in private school. Why? Because private schools aren't equipped to take them. They choose not to take them. They have that ability to say, "Well, we don't want your child because he comes with dyslexia, or because he comes with a behavioral disorder." The reality is, in the world, you're going to deal with people like that, and so I think that public schools offer us the opportunity to be exposed to more real-life situations.

And you also gain the—I hate the word "tolerance" because it's not to gain tolerance—but to gain a real appreciation for people's background and cultures. I have a real appreciation for the Hawaiian culture. And I'm not sure that I would have embodied that if I, personally, had not exposed myself to it somehow in the real world. I was not exposed to it naturally. So it's not just about tolerating a culture, it's about celebrating it, and not to celebrate just one culture, but to celebrate many.

Q: And you're saying these are life experiences that will benefit your children as adults as they will be able to move back and forth among different socioeconomic groups, and deal with different ethnicities comfortably?

Nonprofit Executive: Absolutely. Without a doubt. And that's one of the great advantages that public school has. I also think that it tends to put a greater value on society as a whole.

A husband and wife talked about valuing diversity as well as other factors and how those values contributed to their decision to send all four children to public schools. They are public school advocates, they both attended public schools, and the mother was a public school teacher. These parents also considered their family finances and decided that public schools would allow the mother to stay at home—a decision they favored—and give them the option of sending all four children to college on the mainland.

Public School Teacher: [My children] all went to [public] schools in our area, which would be the neighborhood elementary, intermediate, and high schools. I'm a public school teacher, and while I haven't been teaching in a long while, we're committed because we both went to public schools—as long as the children were challenged. And they were as far as we could tell.

It also enabled us to meet our goals of sending them to college on the mainland. With four, if we sent them to private schools here, that would really be tough. And the other goal was for me to be at home, so I could be at home with the children. So I think we accomplished all of those goals.

CEO: And we liked the idea of our children mixing with other socioeconomic groups, even in our neighborhood where there are usually upper/middle income families. There were pockets of people that were not upper/middle income that went to these schools, so we wanted them to have the diversity.

Q: They had friends that were outside of their socioeconomic group?

CEO: Yes.

Q: And could you talk a little bit about why you felt that that was important?

CEO: Basically, that's the real world. The real world is diverse with different peoples from different walks of life that you are going to have to deal with. And I wanted my children to have that kind of exposure early. I wanted them to be able to deal with different kinds of people. And I felt that the private schools didn't have that. Mostly the [elite] private schools were oriented toward the upper-income socioeconomic class.

Public School Teacher: To add to that: it validated where we came from too because we did not come from an upper socioeconomic group growing up. And we wanted our children to know that, and to understand where they were in terms of other kids that are not advantaged.

And being a teacher, I don't feel that a child's brain is an empty brain, and you pour all this knowledge in it. I think children really need to be exposed, and the public schools give a bigger exposure in terms of the teachers as well as the students. I think you get a bigger environment to live in.

Parents explicitly connected this opportunity for "real world" experiences in public schools with benefits to their children as adults in their careers. The professor quoted below believes that public schools provide his children with the opportunity to become "well-rounded" individuals who can communicate comfortably with individuals from different groups. He thinks this is the case because children have more experiences in public schools that encourage them to "look at things from different perspectives," helping them to become better persons. He views this skill and ability to communicate comfortably with individuals from different groups as valuable in the workplace.

Professor: One of the reasons why we were comfortable sending him to public school is that he comes from a family — particularly his parents — that are post-graduate graduates, so the kind of stimulation we think he should have intellectually will be supplemented at home. So what we want out of school is not only intellectual stimulation — and we've had lots of soul searching about this — but having our kids mixing and being with different kinds of people. . . . We want our kids to be able to participate in the world, and the world is made of up different kinds of people from different kinds of backgrounds.

We think that being able to deal with different kinds of people is a skill and an experience that benefits one as one grows older, and enriches one. I don't mean that solely as an economic benefit. I think that as a person it benefits you.

I think that the economic benefits are indirect in the sense that if one is a well-rounded person who is able to communicate with different kinds of people, that is a skill that employers and/or clients value. Being able to negotiate in different kinds of social settings is a social skill that could, in many occupations and fields, have some value. I think that, on a personal level, to be able to look at things from different perspectives makes one a better person. And I think the experience of growing up with people from different backgrounds and/or experiences helps people do that. I don't think that's the only thing that it does, but I do think that it helps.

I want my kids to know that people who may not have their background and who may not have their economic background are good people. And I cannot teach them that in the abstract. That's a value that my wife and I feel strongly about, and if we have that value, then we're going to live it. And because I think that by saying you have the value but not living it, well, kids learn by what you do and not what you say.

A banker talked about his friendships in public schools with individuals from communities different from his own. These relationships, he believes, allowed him to develop the ability to look at people without categories and without making assumptions — traits that he believes help him to be a successful executive today.

Executive Banker: I remember one of my closest friends in high school in the ninth, tenth, eleventh grade years was Korean-Japanese. His father and mother sort of struggled. And we were very good friends and I'd go over and stay the night. And I guess the first morning I woke up and looked out my window and was looking straight into the projects, which would otherwise be a very intimidating place for me to be.

I remember going to a party, and a bunch of us getting out of the car and walking to the party, and four or five guys walking up towards us clearly wanting to fight with us, and then the leader recognizing me. He had been an eighth grader who had been kicked out when I was a seventh grader, but he and I had been good friends with each other on the playground side. So as soon as he made the connection to me, all the tension went away, and we ended up going to the party together.

There was this range of people there at the public school and clearly some of them would not have been admitted into a private school. It was kind of neat what people brought in from their own neighborhoods that reflected what they thought was important. Like a guy living on the plantation coming in to the school with a whole different set of [perspectives about] what mattered in life.

When I look back on the experiences of my life that have allowed me to be a manager, a lot has to do with being able to look at people without categories and without making assumptions about them, and just trying to read them and understand where they're coming from. Only as I've gotten to my forties and began to look back did I begin to realize how important some of the values that were true for me in grade school and high school and even in my twenties were connected to that school experience. What I value in management has a lot to do with your ability to put yourself in other people's shoes and to be able to accept people without making a whole lot of assumptions about why they're doing what they do.

A second banker shared a similar belief about how her own experiences in public schools help her today in communicating with individuals whatever their background. She also mentions the ability to feel empathy, an important value in her work.

Executive Banker: [Being educated in public schools] just gave me the ability to be able to communicate with people no matter what their backgrounds were. And I think to have some empathy for them, which in my job is very important.

A physician summed up the impact of his experiences with diversity in public schools by saying, "It just becomes part of your life." As an internist who sees a diverse group of patients, he definitely sees the connection between his experiences and his work.

Physician: I think that there's always an advantage in having heterogeneity available to you as you're growing up, even if you're, as I was, relatively oblivious to it. It just becomes part of your life, and so I think you are much more accepting of different ethnicities, different lifestyles, and different abilities. It definitely helps me as a physician.

Sheltered Environments versus Real World Environments

The following three parents attended private schools or a small, homogeneous public school without much diversity. They talked about those experiences as "sheltered." They felt it limited the perspective through which they viewed the world. Their personal experiences led them to want something different for their children. These parents pointed out that, as children, their sheltered private school experiences were not negative, but upon reflection as adults, they realized it was not the real world.

As with the previous group of parents, the next parent makes a connection between his public school experiences with diversity and his current work as a legislator, mentioning his ability to understand and to have empathy for others.

Legislator: Well, I think that in terms of elementary private school, one of the most positive aspects is the personalized attention that's given. Whenever problems came up, they were able to deal with it on a one-to-one level, and I know they called parents.

I think on the negative side, the experience was basically very sheltered, but maybe that's positive too? We were all very sheltered in terms of what we were exposed to. Most of the students were of Japanese ancestry. There wasn't much diversity (in the student population), which was something that I was sort of curious about because most of the children in the neighborhood were from various ethnic backgrounds. I think that was one of the reasons that I was willing to transfer to the public school . . . so I could see what the real world was like.

Q: And how did that work out?

Legislator: I thought it worked out pretty well. I think in some ways it was more difficult because you don't have the personalized attention anymore. You're just one of many. But in terms of making friends and expanding my horizons, personally, I think it was a greater benefit.

Well, I think it's important to understand different values, and different ways of thinking, different lifestyles, and especially understanding that other people may not have as much as your family. They're not necessarily middle class, but lower income. And it's interesting to make those comparisons, and to understand that the world can be seen differently from other perspectives. I think that it influences even what I do as a legislator — to understand, to empathize, to have that compassion for others.

A vice president also talked about attending a small, homogeneous private school with students from similar ethnic and socioeconomic backgrounds. Positive aspects of that sheltered environment, he believes, are that the students became close and that they had similar academic aspirations. The negative aspect, he believes, is that their sheltered environment prevented them from recognizing that other groups had different perspectives, ones they did not learn to understand.

Vice President: It was a really small school. Our class had only ninety-nine kids. But it was basically middle or upper-middle economic backgrounds because you had to pay to send your kids. The good thing about it was that — besides [the fact that] it was small — we lived together. We got very close. The bad thing about it was we were stuck with a certain group of people. I would say, at that time, it was about 80 to 85 percent Japanese — a few Caucasians, a few Filipinos. I don't think I had anybody from Hawaiian ancestry in my class. So it was a very select few.

It was a lot of fun in high school. I made some very good friends.

Basically the difference between private school and public school was you didn't have the trouble you would have in public schools from the standpoint of, you know, you have a certain group of kids that don't want to be there. In a private school setting you wouldn't have that. The kids that don't want to be there are kicked out. So basically we're there with a small group of people who want to learn, and they come from backgrounds that are actually, you know, a little higher standard economically. I think the kids have higher expectations out of life. And you don't have the kids that say, well, you know, "I want to work for a store" or "I want to be a big power worker." Basically everybody wants to be a professional, everybody wants to go to college, so I guess the setting is very different.

The disadvantage was that it was a very small school. And I think we lived a very sheltered life. We kind of lost sight of the views that you would have from a lower economic standpoint. We couldn't understand how people didn't want to strive to get ahead. So it was different. We kind of looked at the world through colored glasses. Yeah. I mean we used to think everybody must think like us, but most of the world didn't think like we did. That was a disadvantage.

Finally, a mother talked about how much more difficult it is to learn life lessons about diversity and different worldviews as an adult.

Attorney: Looking back at that time, I didn't know it. I think that the diversity of the student population could've been a little bit more diverse. And the reason — I only know that now. I didn't know it then, right? I didn't feel it then. I just thought, "Well this is the way the world was." But I did have other experiences outside of the school, but they didn't take me to a range of diversity. It was still upper-middle socioeconomic experiences that I had. I look back on it now and there are certain things I didn't develop as a person in terms of understanding about groups of people. It's harder to learn that as an adult. I want to learn it, but it's really hard to get yourself into that situation, number one, and once you're there, it's like because you're dealing with adults, they're not as open to the whole dynamics of it. So I feel that's sort of missing. That's only in hindsight.

Q: So an advantage of having children experience ethnic and socioeconomic diversity is being more at ease with members of these groups? If you don't have those experiences, then as an adult it's . . .

Attorney: It's much more difficult to cross those bridges.

"The Neighborhood": Community, Commuting, and Finances

The parents who wanted their children to attend school in their neighborhood believe that the local public school provides children with opportunities for "real world" diversity experiences and provides the family with a sense of belonging to a community. It also decreases the amount of family time spent commuting.

For example, for the following mother and father, this option not only met their goals of a "real world" education, but also allowed them to feel part of a neighborhood and to save their funds for their children's future college education.

Physical Therapist: Right about the time that our oldest would be going into elementary school, we had to move, and we had to look for a new place to live. First of all, we had to decide which area we thought would be good to raise a family, and also what area of the island had good public schools. We actually had our kids in [private school], which is very Japanese, and (*laughs*) not very diverse in backgrounds of the kids. Although we felt the education that they got there was very good, it was such a lopsided view of what the real world was like. We felt we wanted to give them more of an opportunity.

And also in the decision making, of course, was the issue of finances. We had to go look for a place to live. And with a mortgage to pay, we thought, "Well we'd check out an area with decent public schools and try it out." Financially, we felt that we would much rather try to save for their future education rather than trying to put money into private school right off the bat.

Photographer: We're both products of public schools and we thought we came out all right.

Physical Therapist: We felt that we wanted to get to know our neighbors and the neighborhood kids. We wanted our kids to be friends with them, so they might as well go to the same school. We really felt like we would be a part of the neighborhood. I know some kids that live in the neighborhood but [who] go to school elsewhere. They feel a little bit isolated because they don't really interact with the [neighborhood] kids at school. So that was important to us also.

Q: You valued the idea of a neighborhood school?

Physical Therapist: Right. Because we felt we didn't really know anybody there, and we wanted to get to know them through our involvement with the kids in their outside sporting activities. We've met other parents and families who also send their kids to the schools. We're finding that we know more and more people in the neighborhood, and it's a very comfortable feeling and really like home. We're getting more and more involved.

Although the majority of parents in this study had the financial means to send their children to private schools, many considered the expense of private school in making their decision. For these next parents, the benefits of private school education did not outweigh other choices. The father below, for example, talked about the long discussions he and his wife had about school choice. They involved their children in these discussions as well. The result was the decision that, for them, by eliminating the cost of private school, they could move into "a better neighborhood" and not have a long commute. Interestingly, this parent's spouse observed that her friends who had attended private schools appear to be no happier or more successful in life than public school graduates such as herself.

Vice President: Well, I think economics has a lot to do with it, too. I mean, if you have a lot of money and it doesn't really make a dent in your budget, I think families probably send their kids to private schools. I mean we could have afforded to send our kids to private school, but we felt that, you know, it was a big financial decision to do that. The amount that we would be paying versus the amount we would have to adjust our lifestyle — obviously there is a trade-off. For the family, we thought it wasn't worth it because we would have to give up certain things.

Q: Like what?

Vice President: Well, we wouldn't be able to move to a [new neighborhood]. We bought a brand new home. In fact, we had a family meeting about this thing. We brought the kids together. They were able to understand this is a big decision. We said, "You both can go to private school, or we can move to a better neighborhood." And they all voted to move to a better neighborhood. I guess there are families [whose] supposed income is so high it wouldn't even matter to send them to private schools or not. Private or public, they would probably send them to private school if their kids could get in.

Q: You also mentioned it was important to you for your children to stay in the neighborhood with their neighbors.

Vice President: Right. You also give up a little bit, too, because, as I said, in private schools you don't have to mess with the kids that don't want to be there.

Q: So each side has some pros and cons?

Vice President: Oh, definitely. I think you have to go back and look at your values. You have to look at what is really important. For my family, the family is very important. My wife's family is very, very close. We get together for all the holidays. So we believe that the family unit is very strong. It wasn't a very easy decision to send them to public schools versus private schools, especially since they went to private schools as very young children. But my wife and I had long discussions. She comes from a public school background, and she had a lot of friends who went to private schools. And today, there's really no difference as far as how successful or how happy they are or anything like that. So we felt, well, why spend the money, basically.

We felt also if they went to a public school, they wouldn't have the trouble with commuting. All the private schools are in urban O'ahu. And it'd be really hard for us to take them, so they would have to catch the bus and get up at 5:30 in the morning. They would have problems participating in after-school activities because they would have to commute back, or somebody would have to pick them up.

We felt, all in all, for our family that that was the right decision, and we still feel that way today. My daughter's finished with high school. She's off to her first semester in college.

Using the equivalent of what she would have paid for private school tuition for her two children, this next mother decided to pay for private tutoring for a three-year period, with the option of using other monies for enrichment.

Executive Banker: Now, one of the things that I did was that I decided that I can spend twenty thousand dollars on private school, or I can take twenty thousand dollars and use it for enrichment. And so I hired a private tutor for my children after school. Because in my mind, I knew they'd get the social stuff. I knew they'd get the artwork and the creativity in public schools. My big concern was math and English. So the tutor's instructions were to make sure that they could do math in their sleep and that they could spell anything. And so basically for three years they had a private tutor. And that set a foundation that now everything else is kind of new and interesting, but they have this really solid academic foundation.

Keeping the Faith: Advocates

Parents who work in public education feel that it is important to show faith in the system in which one's professional life resides. This question of advocacy for public schools came up in parents' interviews in several different contexts. The following excerpts serve as an introduction to this subject, but it will be explored in greater depth in later chapters.

The first excerpt is from a mother who states her comfort with her belief in public schools to provide a good education for her children. She also states that she wasn't going to rely solely on her colleagues' opinions that she should send her children to private school. Instead, she would rely on evidence that her children weren't receiving a good education in public schools before she sent them to private schools.

Q: When your son was five and you were making the decision about where to send him, how did you make the decision to send him to a public school rather than a private school?

Professor: The short answer is that as a state employee, I didn't want to take my child out of the state educational system for no reason other than rumor because I basically had no personal contact with the public schools. He was going to go to the public schools until I got to the point where I felt that being there was compromising his education in some way. So I wasn't going to put him into a private school just for the sake of putting him into a private school until I had some kind of evidence that that was my only alternative other than my colleagues telling me that.

What this mother is referring to is a common practice among professionals: colleagues tell colleagues to send their children to private schools.

The next three parents all spoke of their desire to model their belief in public education. One of the issues in the educational community in Hawaiʻi is that there is a high percentage of public school teachers and administrators who send their own children to private schools. This statistic leads to discussions about how committed these educators are to public education. A Department of Education (DOE) administrator spoke first. He defended his colleagues who made the decision to send their children to private schools, but he said he himself could not do it.

Q: And why did you choose to send your children to public school?

DOE Administrator: Well, there are at least two reasons. Number one is that I'm a public school educator. Couldn't see myself working in the area of public education and sending my children to private school. I know that there are a lot of people who choose to send their children to private school who are working in the public school sector. I know that. The criticism of them is that they are less committed to public education [and that] is not true. I know several people who have sent their children to private schools, and they are as committed as I am to public education. So to me, that's a false assumption. But the personal choice that I made was that I couldn't reconcile it in my mind — to be a public educator and to send my children to a private school. That's the first thing.

A state legislator made the point during his interview that it's hard to be an advocate for public schools when you send your children elsewhere.

Legislator: I really wanted her to go to public school, partially because of the work that I do. It's hard to be able to promote and support the public schools and send your children elsewhere.

Many professionals who do send their children to public schools send them for elementary school only. At the end of sixth grade, these children often transfer to private schools for their secondary education. When I asked the following mother what made her and her husband decide that their children should remain in the public schools when so many of her children's friends were transferring to private schools, she talked about the principle of believing in the system you work in. For this parent, believing in the public school system means that your children go to public schools. And she added that she wants to serve as a model for public school advocacy.

University Administrator: I think I just trust the system to do well for my children. And I'm a public educator myself. And I just can't see that you work in a system and you don't have faith in it. I'd like to model that for others, too. I don't feel I'm depriving my children of a good education. I think it served my husband and me.

Choosing *the* Public School: Doing the Research

Investigating and moving to neighborhoods with reputations for good public schools is one strategy that parents used once they decided to send their children to public schools. The parents in this study were typically involved and proactive in gathering information that would help them decide which public schools they wanted their children to attend. And by "good public schools" they meant not just those schools with well-established reputations, but also "undiscovered" neighborhood schools and others with emerging strengths, such as new leadership, excellent new programs, or small classes. For many, the desire for and choice of good neighborhood schools was a way of becoming or remaining engaged in their communities, a way of getting to know the families of their children's friends, and a way of cutting down on commute time.

How did they find good neighborhood schools or other public schools of interest? Many parents conducted some form of research on the various public schools to provide themselves with enough information to make reasonable decisions. This research included talking with real estate agents, searching the Internet, and visiting the schools to meet the principals, observe the teachers, and take note of the physical facilities. They also talked with other colleagues who had enrolled their children in various public schools.

As a result of their research, some families were happy with their neighborhood schools, and, as previously mentioned, bought homes in those areas.

Others made different choices, including applying for geographic exemptions and considering schools whose reputations had changed for the better as a result of new administrations and more involved communities.

This first parent talked about the decision-making process and mentioned the peer pressure to get his child into the right private preschool.

Professor: It started with the idea [we were told about], that you've got to get into the right preschool. We felt like kids develop at different rates, and some kids are going to do well academically at an earlier age than others, but those things are very easy to make up. Different things click into place at different stages, and . . . it really wasn't going to make a lot of difference if one school had a kind of an intensive academic program while another school didn't. Because in the fourth grade, if you just happened to get a good teacher, you'd catch up right away. We didn't feel like it was that big of a deal.

We also trusted [the selected public school] to be a very good . . . elementary school. The trust came from knowing people who had sent their kids there, primarily — kids who were sons and daughters of people we knew. We just felt like this was a very good school, and there was absolutely no reason for us to apply elsewhere. We didn't even apply to the private schools when she was going to kindergarten.

Later, when his daughter had completed fifth grade, he and his spouse decided to send their child to a public middle school for sixth grade. This middle school had a "bad reputation" in previous years. They made this decision based on the research they conducted. They visited the school and found it to be well maintained in a beautiful setting with a small student population. They met and liked the principal and the teachers. They also personally knew one of the teachers.

Professor: We weren't sure we wanted to send her to a private school in the seventh grade. A lot of students, when they leave public elementary school, they'll enter the private schools. They assume all along that that's what they're going to do. And this middle school really scared a lot of parents away for years because it had a reputation of being a dangerous school. It's back in the middle of a housing project. We said, "Well, let's try [this middle school] and see how it is." We did investigate the school. We found that it looked like a very good school. We thought, actually, it would be a better sixth grade for her than the elementary school.

[My daughter's elementary public school] has a reputation of being a very good school, partly because they always are near the top with their test scores. And this middle school has had a reputation of not being good partly because the test scores are low, towards the bottom end. But we looked into it, and we thought it looked like a very good school. We liked the principal. We liked the teachers. We thought it would be good for our child to have more than one teacher, to get into middle school and have the different teachers for different subjects. We went in to find out, "Well okay. Is this school really a place to be avoided, or really a place that we might want to keep her in?" So we thought let's try it in sixth grade. She was ready to switch.

Q: You actually went to the school and you investigated? And would you say that's typical [of other parents]?

Professor: Well, in this particular case, our child and a friend of hers were the first two kids to go to this middle school from her elementary school for the sixth grade. Nobody had done it before. But a lot of the kids have started going there from seventh grade in the last two years. It was maybe five, six, seven years ago that no kids from the elementary school were going. And now, a lot of them are.

Q: What do you think is causing this shift?

Professor: Well, there are a couple of big things that happened. One is that the school changed from being a junior high to a middle school. So it changed from being just seventh and eighth grades to sixth, seventh, and eighth grades. Another thing is that the population at the school went way down. At one time, it was a school of almost a thousand students and now it's only about four hundred students. Back when it was a great big school, there was gang activity and violence and there were some real problems there. But those are not there anymore now, and so gradually the bad reputation that it had ten, fifteen years ago has worn off. I think, say, maybe four or five years ago, some kids from the elementary started going there in seventh grade, and they've basically all done well. So part of the reason we had for looking into that middle [school] was word-of-mouth testimony. We did know some kids who went there, and they liked the principal.

Q: So the principal mattered?

Professor: Yes.

Q: The size of the school mattered?

Professor: I didn't find that out until after I went over and visited. We also know a teacher over there. One of the first things that got us interested was when my wife had to go over to the school to give something to this teacher. She said, "Wow, it's a really nice looking place." It's in a beautiful spot . . . in the middle of that valley. And yeah, it looks well maintained, and it's quiet, and spacious. Well, you know, there are so few kids there now, and the facility is really nice, attractive, and comfortable. So that was something that got us interested in it, too. We knew this teacher, and so we knew that if our child stayed, she'd have a good English teacher.

As part of their research, this next father and his wife visited their neighborhood school as they contemplated enrolling their children in it. They also talked to their neighbors, who have children in the school.

Vice President: Well, we visited the elementary school when we moved there. It was touted to be one of the most advanced elementary schools from the standpoint of computers — very high tech. The classrooms were very clean. All the classrooms were air-conditioned, and there was carpeting. The teachers were, I guess, handpicked. It was a brand-new type of school that they were going to set up, and we were very impressed with the school. We were very impressed with the teachers, and we felt that this is a setting that was as close to being private school, so we said, "Why don't we try it out?"

Q: So when you say the school was touted as being one of the best, who was saying that?

Vice President: Oh, we heard it from the neighbors.

Q: So they were sending their kids to this public school as well?

Vice President: Yes, they were. It's a brand-new neighborhood. The school was only two years old.

Q: Not only was the physical condition impressive, but also the classroom teachers were impressive? Did you have a sense that they would have high expectations?

Vice President: Yes.

A physician also talked about visiting the neighborhood school with his wife to help them decide whether or not to keep their children in private school or switch them to public schools. After the visit, they transferred to public schools. When asked why they initially chose private school, he said it was because of the reputation of the public schools as portrayed in the media.

Q: Why did you choose to enroll your children in public school?

Physician: We didn't initially. My daughter, the oldest, went to a little private school in kindergarten through second grade, and then our son went there to kindergarten.

Then we pulled them both out of there and sent them to public school the next year. We looked at the cost, and we weighed how much more we were getting out of the private school.

And we went to the public school that they would go to the next year, and we asked to visit some classrooms. We did that, and we met some teachers and observed them in action, and decided that that looked fine to us. And so we just switched them.

Q: When you made your first decision, why was your first decision private school?

Physician: Because of the media reporting on the public schools here. Reputation.

Looking for public school data was a second strategy that parents used to conduct their research on public schools. Before they moved to Hawai'i, a military officer and her spouse used available data from the Internet to help them decide which neighborhoods had schools that appealed to them.

Q: And why did you choose to send them to public schools?

Military Officer: We were stationed overseas before we came to Hawai'i, and we heard horror stories about the schools from people who didn't even have children in the schools. We were a little suspect when we asked, "Well, where did your kids go to school?" and they said, "Our kids didn't." So we did a lot of searching on the Internet, and did a lot of comparison of standardized test scores. I found a lot of information. We found that there were a lot of areas that we definitely would feel comfortable in living and putting our kids in the public school system. And so that's what we did. When we got here, we looked in those areas for a house that we wanted to live in, and it was an area where we were comfortable with the schools.

Q: What kind of information was on the Internet? What was available?

Military Officer: There's a wide range of information out there, if you're willing to dig for it.

A fairly typical dilemma is shared by this next parent, a legislator, and occurs when one parent favors public school and the other favors private school. In this family, as a way to resolve the predicament, both parents agreed to conduct research on the public and private schools before making a decision.

Legislator: Once the kids were getting close to being enrolled in school, all I asked of my wife is that we would spend as much time learning about the public schools in our community as about the private schools. So we did go and visit the schools. We met with the principal. We did take a tour of the public schools in our community, at least the ones that were close enough that we were able to get to. We did ask about test scores, and the performance, and achievement in the public schools in the area, as well as private schools. As a parent, all you're trying to do is provide the best opportunity for your children that you can, and my wife really believed that a private school would do that for our child, and I really believed that a public school would do that for her.

Q: That's interesting. So before you made a decision, you spent as much time researching the public schools in the neighborhood as you would research the private schools? Do you think that that's typical that people do that?

Legislator: (*Bursts out laughing.*) No, I don't think so! I don't think that that happens too often. When we called the school to ask to visit and to tour, it was like we were the first people to ask for that in a long, long time!

Q: Are you planning on sending your children to public intermediate school?

Legislator: Well, that's the next challenge because that's the next decision point. And my child, right now, is in the sixth grade, and so my wife wants to have the option of private school, and we're doing the same thing. I'm asking her to do the same thing that we did at the elementary school. We should spend an equal amount of time investigating and looking at what options that we would have in the public school system, and find out what they do, and what their curriculum looks like, and all of that. I do knows that from my wife's perspective, she's much more concerned about security and safety at public schools, and she definitely believes that private schools are safer, at least in her mind, and that's a bigger issue, as my children get older, in her mind.

Why Do Mainland Parents Send Their Children to Public Schools?

I also went to the mainland to interview parents who are professionals and who had the option of choosing private schools for their children, but who chose public schools. I wanted to find out if the reasons for school choice would be similar or different from those that public school parents in Hawai'i shared. I conducted interviews with four professionals who live in three mainland cities and who send their children to public schools. All four parents talked about the value of exposing their children to ethnic and socioeconomic diversity and their belief that such exposure is more likely to occur in public schools. They also believe that their children can get a good academic education in the public schools. And where possible, they wanted their children in neighborhood schools. All of these reasons are similar to those given by parents in Hawai'i.

One difference on the mainland was the significance and impact of funding for public schools. Stable and adequate funding sources positively affected professionals' decisions in favor of public schools. If the funding for public schools became unstable or inadequate, parents were more likely to consider private schools. This funding issue is related to tax issues and to the entire community's commitment (or lack thereof) to good public education.

Mainland Public School Parent: My son went to a private kindergarten but he's been in public school since. My daughter's been in public school the whole time. The [city] public school system's been a very high-priority school system, and it exposes them to greater diversity than they get in the private schools. And there isn't much motivation to go to a private school except for the problem of inadequate funding, which would cause us to think about it. My daughter was thinking about possibly going to a private high school next year, but the tax measure passed. It sort of ended that discussion.

Q: Whether or not the government tax measure passes will influence parents' choices?

Mainland Public School Parent: Absolutely. It'll influence a lot. Actually, we have friends who have decided just because of the uncertainty to transfer their children to private schools. I think as a parent, the first thing you want is a quality education for your child, so if the public schools can't measure up to that, then we'll be more likely to choose a private school.

I really believe my children need the diversity in order to develop. I know when I went to the university, during my freshman year, there were two kids in my dorm who'd grown up in [sectarian] schools and then, all of a sudden, were thrust into the university, and they really struggled. They did not fare very well because they had been so sheltered. They had no concept of how to deal with the diversity that they were suddenly faced with.

People [in our community] really believe that there's a strong moral obligation to provide a good education for all of our citizens. And it's important for the continued success of our community. I feel that way. And people continue to vote for more money for public schools, and continue to send their kids to public schools. I don't think you could call it uniform, but there's definitely been strong support from the wealthiest parts of our community to say we've *got* to close the achievement gap within the city's public schools. And we don't want to do it by "dumbing down" the top end. We've got to figure out how to bring the low-achieving students up. So if you're just concerned about your own kid, that wouldn't be on the radar.

Q: Do any of the upper-class families have children in public schools?

Mainland Public School Parent: Yes.

Q: That's not unusual that they would be sending their kids to public schools?

Mainland Public School Parent: No, it's not unusual. Now, they tend to be concentrated at a few schools. The very, very wealthy are often at the private schools. But there's, I think, in this city, an unexpectedly high percentage of very wealthy people in the public schools.

The second parent I interviewed was from the same city, and she and her husband send their children to the same urban public school system as the previous family. She talked about diversity as well the importance of the neighborhood school.

Mainland Public School Parent: I have two children — an eighth-grader and a fifth-grader in the public schools. I have always been a very strong believer in public education because, I think, from a neighborhood and a social perspective, it's critically important to children and to their development. And I think part of that comes from my own background and my own educational experience. I went to religious school up until eighth grade, and at that point, I refused to go to the religious high school. And I think it was mostly that I felt that it was a very stifling atmosphere. You know, we had the same thirty kids that I was with from basically first grade through eighth grade. And I had just had enough.

Now when I switched over to public school, it ended up being a real eye-opening experience because all of a sudden I was around minorities. I was around kids who [lived in extreme poverty], I was around different kids with different religious backgrounds, and I was in this very large environment all of a sudden. I really was lost for about a month or two. But once I kind of got my feet on the ground, I think that what that experience gave me was life experience — being in this kind of whole mix of different cultures and religions and economic — socioeconomic — backgrounds.

So I think for me my private school experience was fine, but it felt a little stifling. And [the] public school experience I think just opened up the whole world to me. So when we moved to [this state], my intention always was that they would go to public school. And, in fact, we moved here in part because we knew that the public schools in [this city] were very good. And certainly as we looked for housing, what we were looking for is the best public school within a *great* urban school district.

So for me, public school is always what I've wanted for my children, mostly because of the neighborhood and life experience that I think it would give them.

Q: When you talk about the neighborhood experience, how is that important?

Mainland Public School Parent: I think from my social perspective, I wanted my children to have easy access to their friends. When you go to a private school, you're typically going to end up driving quite a bit farther to see friends and to do stuff after school or on weekends. The ease of my kids being able to get together with their friends was really, really important to me. But I really wanted that sense of neighborhood and if you come to my house, you'll see that. I mean, we are set up as the kid house in the neighborhood. I want my kids' friends at our house.

So that's really important to me. Now if we were in a private school, we could still have that at some level. It would be very different because of the lack of ease of access, socially, for the kids. I mean, kids just drop over at our house constantly, and it's because they know each other — because they go to the same school.

Q: So members of the professional class typically send their kids to public schools?

Mainland Public School Parent: Close to 90 percent of families send their children to public schools. To some extent, it may depend where in the city you choose to live, but I would say, in general, that a large percentage of professionals send their children public schools.

In the second mainland city, one mother talked about the opportunity for diverse experiences that public education provides for her children. She also discussed the importance of being part of the community, and her value of wanting to work toward a good education for all the children and not just hers.

Q: You mentioned that this provides your kids with a real-life education. Why is that important?

Mainland Public School Parent: I want them to be comfortable no matter where they are. They're going to be encountering a variety of people throughout their life, and I want them to be comfortable with people who are different than who *they* are. My husband's clinic is in the district. It's predominantly Latino, and the community that we chose to have *our* office in is the district which is predominantly African American, Chinese, and Latino. So, you know, on a regular basis we can touch base with communities that are affecting our schools, and he can touch base with the community that's affecting his patients.

And then we live in the neighborhood that is right in between both communities. And so for our kids — I mean, that's what they live. They see their parents doing work in the community. They have friends from all different backgrounds, and they hear seven different languages on any given day. And that's what we want them to be exposed to.

The mentality that my husband and I have is that we're going to have our kids in the public school, but it's not going to just benefit our kids. We're going to really work to make the school a strong school so that all of the kids are achieving. And, you know, again, we're with a group of like-minded families who are at the school. And you kind of have to go in with that mindset, knowing what the demographics are of the school. The whole idea that we're recognized by the state as an underperforming school, you have to go in with that attitude. You can't go in thinking that you can go into a school that's underperforming and only your child can succeed. We want to bring everybody up.

The fourth mainland parent was a professional who actually was in Hawai'i doing business when I interviewed her. She lives in the third urban city represented by the mainland parents in this study. Her reasons for sending her children to public schools center on advocacy for improving public schools and a willingness to be involved in the community. Like many of the parents in Hawai'i, she and her husband bought a house in a district in which they wanted to live. They "were not overly concerned about sending their kids" to the district's schools, although this city's school district has a negative reputation.

Mainland Public School Parent: Both my husband and I are in school reform work. So we have been in teacher education and in some kind of K–12 and higher education work for twenty to thirty years between us. And, when we moved to this city and talked about buying a house, we talked specifically about whether we could manage the public school piece because this city has a national reputation for being one of the worst urban school districts in the state. I don't know about nationally. But it has a very bad reputation.

And at the same time, my husband's work was taking him into that district for his outreach work, and I was applying for a position that had to do with work in the district even though it was a private nonprofit and not the actual district. So we were not overly concerned about sending the kids to that district because if we had been, we wouldn't have bought the house! (*Laughs.*)

So we did talk about quite a bit. And probably the single most important piece in terms of our work is that we felt if we were committed to school reform, and we were doing the work in our day jobs, we should also be committed to doing it by way of our community involvement. So we saw those things as linked.

In sum, what emerged from these conversations is the public school parents' definition of "wanting the best for my children." What is "best" includes a good academic education within a public school — a neighborhood school, if possible — and one that provides their children with opportunities to develop into well-rounded individuals through exposure to the diversity in the public schools' student populations. These parents also want a safe environment for their children, but the topic of safety did not appear to be a major concern for them, given their children's public school experiences.

In addition, a number of public school parents are public school advocates. Several of them work in public education, and they believe they need to "model" faith in a system in which they are employed. They themselves went to public schools, which allowed them access to an education that, in turn, allowed them to be successful in life.

The next chapter will discuss the public school parents' children and, more specifically, their experiences in public schools.

3 Children's Public School Experiences

Public Elementary School

The children of this study's participants attended thirty-seven public elementary schools in Hawai'i. The major category that emerged from the interviews was the concept of the Good Public School. When talking about their children's positive experiences in a Good Public School, parents typically referred to the following characteristics.

- A Good Public School employs good teachers.
- A Good Public School is academically challenging (e.g., students exhibit high test scores, staff and faculty have high expectations for students, the school employs a strong academic curriculum, and classes are available for the gifted).
- A Good Public School employs effective administrative leadership.

Several parents also mentioned the following characteristics.

- Positive peer groups.
- Small schools or small classes.

There was also some mention of the benefits of diversity at the elementary-school level, but that benefit is addressed more explicitly when parents talk about their children's middle and high school experiences, when diversity increases.

A major category that emerged from the data across all grade levels is Involved Parents. The parents in this study are/were involved in their children's education. It is a significant finding throughout the study.

By way of introducing this section, we hear next from a parent who was also a principal at one of the public elementary schools that fits into the Good Public School category. In this profile, this parent discussed his philosophy as a principal.

A Principal's Perspective

Principal: I was principal at an elementary public school. I spent fifteen years there, never thinking that I would leave. In the fifteen years I spent there, we were able to move in different directions. And everything was student driven.

People think that [the school's location in an upper-class neighborhood indicates that] we service different clientele because it's middle class and upper middle class. People forget that the city also built a homeless shelter in our district, and there are forty units. They called it a transition house, and people thought it was going to include transition for students. And lo and behold, it became a transition for the homeless. And as we met with our parents and staff, we realized that the clientele that we served for the first, maybe, ten years that I was there, was changing. Now how do we meet the needs of all the kids who would be in our school? There were special education students, and now we have homeless children.

Our parents are really supportive in terms of, you know, what is needed to meet the needs of our kids coming in. Our PTA board members were ready to support us in any endeavor that they felt that we needed to do, knowing that most of these kids would not have had a very stable background [because] they're homeless and their parents would have to have a job or [attend] school in order to [qualify for] transition housing.

Q: What is the percentage of the population of homeless children?

Principal: It varies. We might have ten kids from there, maybe twenty. They can stay there only two years, so it's always changing.

Q: What was the total student population?

Principal: Well, about 540 kids. We always had a part-time music teacher to work with all our kids and a part-time PE teacher. And what we did was bring in art. We felt that if these children were struggling academically, then art could be another medium in which they could find success. And our PTA helped sponsor our teachers to [allow them to] attend art courses at the art academy during the summer time. And through grants, we were able to bring artists into the school to work with all our teachers.

Q: Who wrote the grants?

Principal: Teachers.

Q: How much flexibility does a principal have at a local school regarding issues related to curriculum, grant writing, etc.? Because some of the public perception is that of an over-arching state bureaucracy that has a lot of control over what can get accomplished at the school.

Principal: Yes, they do, they do. However, as the principal of the school, you are in charge of the school. And in terms of flexibility, you just have to go out there and do the research. Find people who are willing to take the risks and write grants.

Q: And the principal has to be a leader in the sense of taking initiative and being creative and establishing partnerships?

Principal: Right, right. The other thing is that, you know, principals are deemed to be the curriculum leaders at the school. However, with the scope of our principal's responsibility — if you look at a business sector, there you have a personnel person, you have a business person, you have facility person, etc. At the school level, everything falls on the principal. And how you govern your school determines the success of your school. I realize that I need to surround myself with people who are also leaders and who are also willing to take risks.

Q: Can you hire?

Principal: As a principal? Whenever there are vacancies, and normally, teachers at this school do not transfer. They retire. But when there are people retiring, I look at who I need to bring in, and I will look at their strengths. If I need to have a real strong science person, or a real strong art person, and I have a position that I have to fill, that will be one of the strengths that I will look for in all of the applicants. Because I want to be sure that I have curriculum leaders on my campus.

Q: And what if the applicants come to you, and not one of them is strong in science?

Principal: Then we look at the second priorities in terms of a teacher, and what would be my second priority that I'm [seeking] for the school.

Q: But you can't go outside of that pool?

Principal: Yes, but they have to apply. So from the people who apply to the school, I choose from that pool. I will look at all of their strengths.

The first thing that I look at when they sit across me in the interview, the first question I think about, is, "Would I want that teacher to be my child's teacher?" If the answer is "Yes," then they pass the first test.

I've always felt that you have to treat teachers as professionals. Content can always be learned, but once you walk into the interview room, that's what you have. And being an elementary school, I look at the warmth. I look at the smile and the demeanor of how they speak because the kids are going to pick it up. Parents are going to pick it up. But of course, you have people who are very good interviewers, and this is why I look at the other aspects of being a team player. Are they willing to work with others? Are they willing to train with others?

I [hired] a woman who had been a teacher who couldn't find a job. She went into the business field as a secretary and moved all the way up to the vice president of the company. And she also worked in loans and things like that. And one of the areas of expertise that she had was video technology. And all those years as a principal, I was looking for someone like that. I had people who were calling me to recommend her, and with the warmth that she had, she passed the first test. The other thing that she was able to do was to write grants.

As I said, when the transition-house kids came in, we realized that we had to do other projects, so we started doing project-based writing. Also, the university dance people called us about joining with them to include dance [at the school]. And so I discussed it with my core team, and we thought that it would be a great idea. Plus, the dance group was going to write the grant. We had to monitor all the money and do all the evaluation, but . . .

The other thing that I believe is that you have to take the time to talk to people about public education in their school. It's like a business, in a sense. You have to sell your school. You have to promote your school. We don't tell parents that we're the best school. We tell them what we have and what we can offer. And of course, parents will say, "Your test scores are always high." And I will let them know that, number one, we are a public school. We are not a prep school for private school.

Number two, testing is only one part of your child's education. For example, last night, I went down to Camp Erdman after 7:00 p.m. when I left here because our sixth graders spent three days at Camp Erdman. Our sixth grade worked with the Y program, and they had trust building. And of course, it's not only for students. We also had ten parents that wanted to go along as chaperones.

The fifth grade class goes to Turtle Bay. Schoolwork and initiatives are included in this field experience. They also had a formal dinner to learn etiquette on dressing and on dining. We also had experience with taking them to Kualoa Park, where they do canoe paddling. They have an aqua farm that raises prawns, and they have the opportunity to catch the prawns by throwing nets. And, when fourth grade goes to the Big Island, they get to see different parts of the Big Island, travel. Everything is organized in such a way that there is a booklet that they have to follow with writing assignments.

Q: And this is funded by grants?

Principal: They pay their own way, and we have fundraisers to raise money too. Sometimes the parents decide to just pay. Through the grants, we were able to provide a disposable camera for every child. Through another artisan school grant, we bring in a professional photographer. We teach the kids how to take pictures, and rather than just taking any-kind pictures, they have to know the lighting and how to set your main subject in the frame.

They have to do a lot of writing, both reflections and narratives on the pictures that they take. So if they have twenty-four shots, they have fifteen that are determining what the subject area would be. So these are all the things that are included as part of their program.

Now we hear from a parent whose child attended this principal's school. The parent described how this principal's leadership developed a positive school culture. This parent also explained that he didn't always have to agree with everything the principal did to recognize and appreciate the principal's strengths.

Professor: [My] younger child goes to a public elementary school, and the other one goes to a public middle school.

Q: What role does the principal play in setting up and creating and supporting that kind of positive school culture?

Professor: You know, I don't know if my wife and I had a great agreement with the elementary school principal about his educational philosophy. . . . Where I thought he made a difference, and a huge difference, was that he was there all the time. He was the guy who was sweeping around the school. He's the guy who was at every single parent event. He's there. He was there constantly doing everything—all the little jobs that most people don't even think about. He's watering the plants. There's nothing he's not doing. And I think setting that kind of tone means that it's very difficult for you [as the parent] or as the faculty to say, "I'm not willing to do that," because he's setting the tone by example.

He's a lot more traditional than maybe we would be. I think his commitment was exemplary, and I think that that's the reason why that school is so successful—because he was there for everything. No job was too small for him. Nothing was beyond him. He's not saying, "It's not my job." I think it makes a huge difference.

Public Elementary School Experiences

By and large, the discussions about children's experiences in public elementary schools were positive, clustered around the Good Public School category that includes good teachers, an academically challenging curriculum, and effective administrative leadership. Note also how parents describe their involvement in the schools.

The first excerpt is from is from a couple introduced previously. They talk at some length about the school's curriculum, the teachers' expectations, and parental support and involvement in the school, including their own.

Physical Therapist: We've been extremely pleased with the school. The teachers have been outstanding. The extra activities that they have for the children are very unique. I don't know how much you know about this school, but it's been in the news quite a bit because they have an excellent computer resource teacher. She's actually their computer teacher, and one of their teams actually won first place in a national contest for a Web site. Our son has been involved with her in the past year or so as one of the techies that works on the computer maintenance, as well as being one of the children involved in the development of the Sue T-Rex Web site for Bishop Museum and Meadow Gold. So we're just really excited at the opportunities.

They have also an outstanding music director. We have both of our children involved in the music ensemble, which is like a children's choir, and they put on at least one performance during the school year. This year they performed at Ala Moana Center Stage, and they'll be performing in the local parade. So I think it's those types of things, as well as the parent and family involvement in the community, that really makes the school very special. I think those parents that we've talked to that also send their children there feel the same way.

Q: So are you both actively involved in the school?

Photographer: Yes.

Q: What kinds of activities do you participate in?

Photographer: Well, I'd like to go back to talk about our feelings about the school. I guess for me it was like buying a home. You find that home that you're comfortable with. You walk into a place and then all of a sudden it's, "I feel like I'm at home." And that's how we felt about the school. We walked in and we felt very comfortable. The staff was very nurturing.

The school is very community and family oriented. They have activities for kids and parents. For instance, they have an Internet night for parents. We're computer illiterates, and it was very fortunate that they had this event. At least they were trying to introduce us to the Internet system because the kids are on it, and we need to answer their questions. When the kids come home and ask questions, we need to be able to answer them. They also have some fun activities like pumpkin-carving contests. . . . Families bring their pumpkins and sit there and carve them, and they have a contest later on. They have a karaoke night.

Physical Therapist: They have math night.

Q: Do you think the principal is a good leader, or is it more the faculty involvement that makes the school so strong?

Photographer: It's a combination.

Physical Therapist: I think it's a combination because there actually was a change in principals. But there's such a strong parent support group, and the faculty is strong. I guess, you know, even down to the cafeteria manager and librarian, who get involved in all these other activities. There's just a very strong involvement.

Q: What makes the parents in your community stay so engaged with your school?

Photographer: Well, I think the parents are very interested. I'm sure that it's prevalent all over, but our community is really like a bedroom community. There are quite a few stay-at-home parents. They do have the opportunity to get involved with their children in their school. I, for one, am very interested in what our children are learning and doing in school, so we do get involved.

You asked about our involvement. The current principal is very strong in reading. Or I should say her emphasis is on reading. And the rotary clubs have a "Read to Me" program in which Rotarians go to the classroom and read stories to the kids. They can even tutor the kids. And I'm involved with that. I got our Rotary Club involved. Oh, I'm also helping with this [event] parade.

And this is the first year that the school is getting involved with the parade. It would be kind of difficult for the children to walk and sing at the same time, so we felt a float was more appropriate. We take turns getting involved with the school.

Q: It sounds like the community is really engaged with your school.

Photographer: The teachers have been very good about keeping us up to date as far as what our children are learning, or not only learning, but how they're doing in class. I'll give you a good example. Last year, our daughter did rather well. This year, however, it was very much of a roller coaster ride for her. By the third quarter, she went down below a B average, and that was a rude awakening, I hope, anyway, for her.

Physical Therapist: For all of us.

Photographer: For all of us, yes. We felt that was fortunate that that happened because she needs to understand that she's not being graded against her peers, but she's being graded against herself.

Physical Therapist: And so the teacher would always challenge them to do better for themselves. She took the time to explain that to us at our parent-teacher conference really well. She said, "So far it's been easy, smooth sailing, but from now on I really want to make each child be the best that they can be and really challenge them to do their best in their abilities."

Q: Are the classes heterogeneously grouped or do they have a class for the gifted?

Physical Therapist: Well, they do have a gifted program. However, it's been decreased in size over the years. Before, it started in third grade and now it starts in fourth grade and there are two students per class that are selected for that. This particular class, though, that our daughter was in, the teacher had told us that she felt that she almost got the cream of the crop for that grade. Of course, there were a mixture of kids, but she had more of the gifted or brighter students in her class, so she felt that it was a blessing for her. And yet it was, I think, a nightmare also, because they're not only gifted, but they're social butterflies. There are a lot of girls in that grade, so it was kind of a nightmare trying to keep them focused on their work and really get them to progress.

Q: Were your children in school with a diverse population of students?

Photographer: Yes, very much so because there's a very strong mix of racial backgrounds in the community.

Physical Therapist: And they do come from all over. We know it seems like that school is a popular one, so a lot of people want to come.

Q: So they transfer in?

Physical Therapist: Right. A lot of children have more of a Hawaiian background. And there are others with military backgrounds — so a lot of Caucasians. But there are also the other local mixtures as well. It's a very good school for ethnic diversity.

Q: And is it generally middle class, or does it have a range as well?

Physical Therapist: I would say there's a range because they offer one of those free lunch programs. And I think they have students that qualify. It's a pretty big range.

Q: Are they making friends with kids outside their group, so to speak?

Physical Therapist: Yes, I think so. The other nice thing that this school offers is Japanese classes after school, but it's through the DOE. And again, we're just so pleased with that because we both took Japanese language when we were growing up. Normally, you have to pay for this Japanese teaching, but we're fortunate in that one of the students who goes to the school has parents who lived in Japan. They have taken over the instruction for this Japanese class. They have done a tremendous job, and I think the enrollment has grown. I think the principal said they have over a hundred children in their program. It was probably less than fifty before.

Physical Therapist: I was thinking that I really couldn't compare it to a private school because — I don't know — but I guess because we're so pleased with our school and the teachers and the parents and everyone, we wouldn't even consider a change.

Q: Do you have any sense that your children will continue in [public] middle school and high school?

Physical Therapist: Probably so. I think some of the public schools are better than others. So it's the ones that maybe don't have a very good reputation that have tainted the opinion of public schools for a lot of people.

Photographer: I think our public school system is good. Then, of course, there's some improvement that could be made, but the teachers are doing the best with what they have — and we do have some very good teachers. We're fortunate to have a lot of those in our school. And it's not so much the teaching part, but the caring part, the recognition of the child as an individual, the challenge that the teacher presents to each child. I think that's very critical in any kind of teaching situation: to really want to develop the child, not so much to show off, but really to enhance the child's learning and to enhance the child's desire to learn. I think that's very critical.

A military officer who decided to send her two children to public schools talked about the initial difficulty with her youngest child because the cultural mix in the classroom made her child feel like an outsider. The cultural mix also included children who speak Hawaiian Creole English (commonly called "pidgin" in Hawai'i). This problem was resolved when a second class was added and the mix was more balanced. From that point on, she describes her experiences with the elementary school as being positive for both children. The second child's middle school experience will be described in the next section.

Military Officer: My six-year-old goes to our neighborhood elementary school, and my eleven-year-old goes to the neighborhood middle school. He just started the sixth grade. It was hard at first. My daughter started kindergarten here, and she had a very hard time, because she was really the only Caucasian in the classroom, and the kids wouldn't play with her. She'd come home miserable. They had too many children for the teachers, so they hired another kindergarten teacher, and luckily, my daughter was placed into this new classroom, and there was a better mixture. She had a much better time.

Q: And, initially was it because the other kids were distant with her? Was that the difficulty?

Military Officer: I think so. It took my children a while, and they're used to making friends really quickly. They were probably disillusioned by our European community experience because it was very close-knit, and we had to live on the base. They saw the same kids not only in school, but also after school, in the sports programs, and at church, and at the movies. It was a very small community. So, it was easy to make friends there. And I think here it was just a little bit different. A little bit of a culture shock, but they adjusted.

Q: So now, are they comfortable moving across various ethnic groups?

Military Officer: Yes.

Q: Okay. And did you worry about the children learning pidgin?

Military Officer: Oh, I'm not worried about it. I don't speak it at home. You know, my children have a pretty good vocabulary, and if they revert to that a little bit, that's okay.

Q: You feel that they have been challenged in school so far?

Military Officer: Yes, I do. Actually, our public elementary school has a great program. I think it's a great program. In the first and second grades, they keep the same teachers. My daughter is in second grade now, and she has the same teacher she had last year. She's very used to the routine, and she went right into second grade — no problem. Because it is year-round school, she really didn't forget much. I like that too. And her teacher is very strict — very strict — but has the students' best interest at heart. If we have a problem, we'll go in and sit down and talk about it. She's very accommodating about my daughter's needs, and it's a good relationship. And having her last year, we know how she approaches things, and she knows how we approach things, and it works well. If we had a teacher we didn't like, we probably wouldn't like the program so much, but I think trying to keep the children in a familiar environment helps them a lot.

Q: And you find that this teacher is receptive to your suggestions, and is willing to be flexible?

Military Officer: Absolutely.

Q: And academically, is your daughter challenged?

Military Officer: Yes. Her teacher is pretty tough, actually.

A legislator mentioned that his wife was a little unsure about their initial decision to send their first child to public school, but after a positive experience in the public elementary school, there were no further concerns about choosing public schools for their two other children. They found that the teachers range from very good to exceptional, the textbooks are up-to-date, and the test scores are high. This father also acknowledged that, while the state school bureaucracy is not as responsive at the school site as it could be, the teachers and the principal at the school do not use this lack of responsiveness to detract them from providing a good education for their students.

Legislator: [My children are] eleven, nine, and six, and they're all at public elementary school. When my first daughter came along, and we enrolled her in a public elementary school, my wife wanted to reconsider up until the day of school opening. But once my oldest daughter started, my wife said the school has exceeded her expectations for public and private school. And the school is a blue-ribbon school [a national honor]. The teachers are very committed. They have a very experienced staff. They do very, very well on all their academic testing and all of that kind of thing. So I think that was part of the conversation, and that was part of the reason for choosing this school, I guess. And like I said, after [my oldest daughter], there was no question about the next two kids.

Q: Your children are being academically challenged, and they're happy?

Legislator: I think for the most part. Like anything else, we do see a difference in the quality of teachers, and some years we feel like our children are luckier than other years because they get exceptional teachers. But by and large, we've been very fortunate in that all of their teachers were very good.

Q: And when there's an issue, do you go to school and talk to the teachers? How active are you?

Legislator: I am probably somewhat more active than others. When there is an issue, I will send e-mails or notes to the teachers to ask them about it. There are always issues with grading policies, with report cards, and why the grade is such-and-such. So we do ask a lot of questions. I do ask about progress a lot, and I do ask about assessment. They do assess children pretty much every year. So we are fortunate that we can see progress against national norms, other than just within the school, and I do find that useful.

And I'm pretty active in terms of school reform, and in terms of schools focusing on student demonstration of capabilities rather than just purely book-and-pencil kind of assessments.

Q: I've been hearing that there seems to be a difference between the success of the parents and the child in a particular school, and the frustration of the bureaucracy of the DOE — the delay in getting resources, conflicting lines of authority, and so forth. Is that a conflict for you as well?

Legislator: Well, you can definitely see that the bureaucracy isn't as responsive to the school-level people as it might be. I think what has been reassuring for us is that the teachers and school administrators don't think of that as a reason to not be able to move forward academically. I do hear all of the horror stories about students having fifty-year-old textbooks, but my daughter comes home with sixty pounds of current textbooks, and new textbooks in math and science and reading all the time. So to me, it's just a symptom of poor school administration, or unsuccessful fundraising, or — I'm not exactly certain what it is. But I do know that the textbooks my children are learning from are very current, and that's never been an issue. In fact, I think the issue is that they carry around too many books, and they're doing too many things, and the backpack gets heavy.

I do know that there are people who use bureaucracy as an excuse for their children not learning. And our experience at this elementary school is that it has never been an excuse about why children can or cannot learn. The school and the school administrator and the teachers have been very, very responsive. They're just focused on student learning and student achieving, rather than on all the reasons why it can't happen.

An attorney talked about transferring his children from private elementary school to public elementary school.

Attorney: My younger two went to private school, actually, when they were very little. My son went until fourth grade, and my daughter went until sixth grade. Then we moved to [a new community and] decided that it would too hard to continue them in that little school from the standpoint of distance. It's a very small private school. I thought they had very good values, and I think my kids learned a lot. It was a tiny school, though. The entire student body was [approximately] eighty kids. So we said, "Well, it might be a good time to transition them into public school."

So when we moved, my son went to public elementary school and my daughter went to public middle school. And even during his first year, we could see the real big difference. They had all of the projects. The equipment the school had was very up-to-date. And there were projects that I didn't think that the private school kids were doing.

Q: So you were satisfied with the experience your kids were having?

Attorney: Yes, I was. I was very impressed.

Q: And academically it was . . . ?

Attorney: Academically I thought it was okay. Yes. My kids do very well academically. When they take standardized tests, they do very well.

Q: And were the children happy there?

Attorney: Yes. In fact, we were very surprised at how well they transitioned from a really small, private school setting into a larger, public school setting. And the kids came from the same socioeconomic background that my kids came from, so I think that made the transition very easy.

Q: So there are a lot of professionals' children who go to the public school?

Attorney: Well, the neighborhood elementary school where my son attends —I think if you look at the people who live there, a lot of them are white-collar workers.

Q: So if the schools in that neighborhood hire good teachers and the facilities are also up-to-date, then the parents [who are professionals] will send their children to public school?

Attorney: I believe so.

In the next several interviews, all the parents discussed the importance of parental and community involvement in the elementary schools their children attended. They focused on how the parents involved themselves, or how the school principals involved the parents, or how the community at large was involved in supporting the neighborhood school.

At the time of the interview, this professor's child was in one of the public high schools, but this father took some time to reflect on his son's experiences in a public elementary school located within a very supportive community. He also speaks to the idea that the goals of the school met those of his and his wife: namely, a curriculum that focused on the core subjects, established high standards, and produced high test scores.

Professor: Our experience at his elementary [school] was generally very good. It's an interesting little school because it has so many district exemptions because so many university faculty and professional people working at the university try to transfer their kids so that they're right near by.

And the school has a tremendous amount of support because it is the sort of central gathering place and meeting place for an incredibly sort of coherent community. The other thing was they were running—before A+ [a state-sponsored after-school program] —their own after-school program because you had this weird demographic of these kids whose parents were all working professionals. So they actually had their own organized [after-school program]. On parent night or something like that, there would be three, four hundred people there. And they have an annual fair and fundraising activities. When we were going through, there was one family that made a big deal of keeping people organized.

Q: So the parent group was very active?

Professor: Yes.

Q: Is this a sense of the school being central to the immediate community?

Professor: I think that's part of it. But the other part is the nature of that particular community. The parents, as a matter of course, are intensely interested in what's going on as far as the education of their kids. . . . They want to be able to see the entire room filled with computers and know their students — my son was learning how to touch-type at the age of five. They weren't fooling around.

Q: So you were happy with the teachers as well?

Professor: Yes. There was one that wasn't very good, but, in general, they were very good. They tended to be very strong in teaching the fundamentals and teaching to the texts and making sure they had the material covered. They placed a great deal [of emphasis] on SATs and that kind of thing, but they were always first or second in the state. And they were aiming toward that. The art stuff wasn't as strong as I would have liked to have seen it, but in the last couple of years, they started really working on their music program. So, and frankly, given that's it's 8:00 to 2:30 basically, that's what we were looking for. Was he doing his science? Was he doing his math? Was he doing the English? Was he getting some kind of history and culture stuff? Did it seem like it was being moved through in some coherent way? Were they being consistent about the grading and that kind of thing? And that I was seeing all the way through.

In the next interview, this father discussed his philosophy about what is necessary to promote children's academic success in schools. He believes it requires teachers who effectively motivate children to have high expectations (which are also held by the school) and requires parents who also set high expectations for their children. He also shared his knowledge of a principal at a neighboring island's public elementary school who was able to motivate teachers and involve parents.

Q: In your active role with the public schools at the state level, you said you've seen evidence of high standards in some classrooms and in some schools because of the educational leadership?

Nonprofit Executive: That's correct. The other thing that needs to be pointed out is, without question, the importance of the level of parental involvement. The standard set by parents for their children plays a crucial role. An example of that may be that each year, even for some of the worst public schools, children graduate and go on to schools as prestigious as Harvard and Yale and Stanford and Princeton.

Within those schools, there's invariably two variables that create that child's success: one would be the ability of an individual teacher to motivate that child to do more than they thought that they could, and, two, high standards set by both the school and the parents, whether it's two parents or a single parent. If children are expected to really do their best, and are allowed to be creative, they're much more likely to succeed at a high level.

Q: And what schools do you think have evidence of having been successful in meeting those kinds of goals?

Nonprofit Executive: Well, on the [neighboring island], the principal there was able to really motivate teachers to work together, and the school was able to track children horizontally rather than longitudinally, allowing an instructor to really have a full knowledge of a child's talents and skills and behaviors. They did this by setting up small working groups within a very large school — at one time, the largest elementary school in the state of Hawai'i.

I knew the principal personally. And he was the first principal that I ever saw who really sought out parent input, and valued their input, and used it to his advantage. And he also looked for parents to bring to the school and to the classroom what they wanted to bring, not necessarily what school administration or teachers wanted to bring. For example, if a child's parent was a hula dancer, that was fine if that parent came and chose to teach hula. I often was the example of [someone skilled in] auto mechanics, or tying a fishing net. Or I might speak to people about valued parent involvement.

Finally, the last parent to talk about parental involvement provided personal examples at his children's school. He made the connection between observed cause and effect, discovering that the school held high standards for his children partially as a result of parental involvement.

Q: Did you feel that, by and large, the teachers held high standards?

DOE Administrator: I think there was a mixture. They held high standards for my children. And I think part of it is because we kept in touch. And I know as a teacher, if a parent is coming to me and asking me questions or inquiring or something like that, I know I always paid a little bit more attention as a teacher and as a principal. I know I always did. And I didn't do this in a hostile way, or in a way that I was looking over their shoulder, but from a parents' point of view,

I was always very much interested in what my children were doing. And so if I saw something innovative or something my kids really enjoyed, I talked to the teachers about that or I'd question. My daughter was a very serious student. She's so serious. And then my wife and I actually worried about her because we thought, as she got older, she'd put too much pressure on herself. But it was her second-grade teacher who recognized this and confirmed it in the initial parent-teacher conference. She said, "You know, [daughter] has got to lighten up. And I'm going to help her lighten up." This teacher would kid her and joke with her. And to this very day, she and my daughter are good friends. Second grade, you know. Whenever my daughter comes back, she goes to visit her.

Issues

Six parents expressed dissatisfaction with some part of their children's public elementary school experiences. They talked about four types of incidents. One parental observation was related to a concern that the "average" child in the public school system is not challenged or provided with assistance when needed. This issue comes up again when parents talk about their children's middle and high school experiences.

Q: And speaking of your experiences with the public schools, were you satisfied with those?

Marketing Executive: I sensed, from my limited exposure, an inability in the public school system to take care of the students who are average, academically. There is nothing wrong with average, but it seems that the teachers seem to focus their attention on the really good kids, which is a joy, and the kids who aren't good at all, which is a chore, but a challenge. Kids in the middle don't present either of those.

In an earlier interview, one military family discussed finding an excellent public elementary school for their children. However, in the following example, the children of another military father experienced a temporary school placement that he felt became negative in two ways. First, he felt that his children were viewed as "outsiders" by some of their teachers. Second, he found out that his older son's experience on the first day of school in a new city was in an overcrowded classroom with an overburdened teacher.

Q: Was that public school a good experience or a bad experience?

Military Officer: I would say that it was a little bit bad, yeah. I work in education. I really hate to speak about this, but this is for your study. I am a Caucasian, a haole [Hawaiian word originally for all non-Hawaiians and foreigners, but now generally for anyone of European descent], so therefore, when we first got here, we were perceived as outsiders. "Oh, you're military, you'll just be passing through real rapidly." So, my children were treated a little differently when we first got here, until they realized my kids were really good kids. (*Laughs.*)

Q: And were they treated differently by the teachers, or . . . ?

Military Officer: Actually, the teachers, yes. The peers? Not by the peers at all. The kids were not a problem whatsoever. No, it was the teachers. But the school system has a tremendous number of very senior teachers, too. They also have a lot of young teachers who I would say . . . were good young teachers. If they didn't have the experience to be a good teacher, they at least had the enthusiasm. They really enjoyed what they were doing. They wanted to be in the classroom. They wanted to be there. So that was very encouraging. On the contrary, the older teachers didn't really want to be there.

You want to hear another example? I'll try to make it short. When we first got here, we stayed at a military hotel, as a transition type of living until you find out which part of the island that you're going to live. And once you get there, you find housing and you find a school in the area. So, a lot of military, when they first get here, their children go to — if they're elementary, they go to the elementary school downtown. So we did, for the first two weeks. And for my youngest son, it wasn't a big deal.

For my oldest son, who was in the fourth grade at that time, it was a big transition because he was coming from the private schools on the mainland into a public school. He went into a class that was glad to have him for only one reason: because they were way over the number of students that they could have. They were looking for another student because that would allow them to bring on one more teacher. And, as I brought my son to class to meet the teacher, the teacher was so very overwhelmed with the size of the class that there was no control of the class. She was screaming at, I think we counted, four different people. And I remember my son sitting down and just dropping his head down on his desk. And I can imagine what he was thinking: "Where am I? What's going on here?" And the teacher didn't have time to say hello to him. Didn't even have time to acknowledge me as I dropped him off. I thought she was going to have a heart attack right there.

Next, a public school teacher whose three children went all the way through the public schools, from elementary through high school, talked about the impact a principal can have on school culture.

Public School Teacher: My daughter had a different principal when we first started at the school, and she had built up the school's reputation as being really good, really interested in academics. After she left, you could just see the morale go down. So I'm so glad to be out of there because I'm so unhappy with the principal. The atmosphere went from where we were close to my daughter's teacher — and we were very involved, and you always felt like you were very welcome on campus at anytime. Then with the new principal — at first it was okay, but slowly, you could just see the teachers weren't happy. We didn't feel as welcome in the school. It got to the point when my daughter, who started there in kindergarten, was like, "I don't want to be there."

I didn't know any of the teachers, and nobody made you feel like you were really welcome. I think a lot of it had to do with whom she hired, and who stayed. Even though she did hire some excellent teachers, they chose not to stay. And of course, they said, "Oh, I'd like to move to a larger home," but, every once in a while you'd hear, you know, a bit of gossip that that wasn't exactly why they were leaving. It's too bad.

Finally, one other parent mentioned that he was upset because one of his daughters was placed in special education classes when she was in elementary school. He talked about the placement serving as "a self-fulfilling" prophecy for his daughter. She made no improvement until she went to middle school, where she was no longer placed in special education and did fine academically.

The next section presents interviews in which parents discussed positive as well as negative experiences in public middle schools.

Public Middle School

The children of the study participants attended fourteen public middle schools in Hawai'i. The same idea of the Good Public School discussed in the previous section applies here as well. Again, this idea was described by parents as academically challenging curriculum, good teachers, and strong leadership at the schools. But parents also discussed additional categories for the middle schools. A new concept related to school organization was introduced: the middle school team approach. This approach typically consists of a team of teachers working closely with a group of middle school students to provide them with the type of close student-teacher relationships so common in elementary schools. This organizational structure also usually includes clustering these teams within the same geographical area on campus so that all sixth graders, for example, take classes in the same part of campus. Not all public middle schools have this team approach.

The parents' values, which were related to "real world" diversity and which were discussed in an earlier chapter, also were reflected in these next interviews as parents talked about their children's middle school diversity experiences as an opportunity to develop life lessons for getting along with others different from themselves. They also discussed increased opportunities to participate in leadership positions in extracurricular activities in school government, band, and sports. In fact, one surprising finding is how often the band and the band teacher are mentioned specifically as being a positive contribution to their children's education. I placed both of these topics under the category Opportunities Provided by Public Education.

This first excerpt is from an interview with a military officer who described her son's experiences in middle school, focusing on the school team approach, the curriculum, the advisers, and the parent-school liaison.

Military Officer: My eleven-year-old goes to our neighborhood middle school. He just started the sixth grade. I don't think that we publicize it enough at all that there are some outstanding schools in Hawai'i, and we found one of them. I'm very happy with the school system. And the sergeant that works for me, his daughter goes to — I can't think of the name, but it's just down the hill here — but it's a high school. He's just so pleased. His daughter is doing really well, and the school is ranked fairly high in the country for the standardized test scores.

People are amazed when I tell them some of the curriculum that my son is doing in the sixth grade. I think it's awesome. . . . He had the choice to do biotechnology, and he chose to do radio technology instead. They're really starting to incorporate industrial technology into the schools, which is what my bachelor's degree is in. That makes me happy because it finally gets me into the school system. There's a lot to be done here — but not just here, [also] across the country — to get technology into the schools. But we have great programs, and we just need to get out and look at the curriculums.

And he's on multi-tracking, which is a little difficult, but he has a queue of six teachers who are assigned to his track. We went to the open house, and we got to sit down with those teachers and go through their curriculum, and what they plan on doing. We got to see the classrooms, and they go pretty easy on the kids when they have to change classes. They don't have to go all over the campus. They stick with these core teachers.

Every day, he sees an adviser. His first class every day is with an adviser, and if the adviser thinks that there is a problem, she goes to either the teacher or parent. If it gets to the point where the adviser thinks that he's doing well and he's adjusting well, then he doesn't necessarily need to see her every day. She'll make that recommendation. But I think it's an outstanding program.

Q: So every child sees an adviser?

Military Officer: Yes. And then they have one particular teacher within their track that they go to. We'd call him a homeroom teacher, I guess. But I forget what they call them. But they have an adviser. And then he has this other teacher. So they look at both sides — his emotional well-being and how he's fitting in and his education. So it's a good program.

Q: And how involved at the school are you and your husband?

Military Officer: My son just started in July. He just started school, and we've been up there a couple of times. The school liaison has walked us around, and if we have any questions or problems, we just e-mail her.

Q: So the school liaison is the individual who contacts parents?

Military Officer: Right. She's there if you want to discuss anything, and if you want her to point you in the right direction, or if you have a situation. She's also the one who sets up programs for the teachers who need something for the classroom. She'll have books in the office so you can go and look at what the teacher needs, and you can go out and buy it and give it to him. And she just tries to help the teachers and help the families.

Q: Is she a parent?

Military Officer: I believe she is a parent. You know, I'm not really sure. And I don't know if she gets paid for it. I think it is a voluntary thing. But it's good. It's a good situation.

This next parent also talked about an academically challenging curriculum and good resources. The middle-school team approach, discussed above, has been implemented within this public middle school as well

Bank Executive: [Public school experiences have] been great. My older daughter is an excellent student — very quick mind. She usually gets between a 3.8 and a 4.0 and she doesn't need to be motivated. It's important for her to be the best. So I don't need to motivate her, but my younger one — I could see her being very much like me — so with her, I have to go in and what I call "wake up the teachers" [to indicate] that I'm paying attention. And so this year, I've had two conferences with the teachers.

Q: And were you satisfied with their responses?

Bank Executive: Absolutely. I was very impressed with the response. In the second meeting, I asked to meet with two of the teachers. The whole team showed up.

Q: So it's a middle-school team approach?

Bank Executive: Right. There's three hundred in a class. And so then they break them up into about a hundred each, and then they break that up so that the hundred is in five different classes. There's about twenty-five, maybe twenty, in a class, and it works very, very well.

Q: The class size is not large?

Bank Executive: No.

Q: All the teachers get to know all the students?

Bank Executive: Yes.

Q: And do you feel they are academically challenged?

Bank Executive: They're challenged. They are. I see the work that the girls do.

Q: And did you participate in the school in other ways? Were you active or was it mostly just making sure you knew the teachers and teachers knew you were involved?

Bank Executive: Well, I'm only involved at the level of—whenever the kids have a science fair or some kind of an open house, or something's going on at the school that the parents are invited to [attend], I go. And the teachers have even said to me, "Why are you here? Your child's fine. Everything's fine. They're doing great." I said, "I'm here because I want to know that from you. I want to talk to you, I want to meet you."

Q: Do they welcome that or not?

Bank Executive: I think some of them do. Some of them are sort of, you know, "I've got problem kids, why are you taking up my time? You know, your child's doing great." But they get to know me, and they realize that I'm going to be there.

Q: What would you change about your children's public school?

Bank Executive: I'm not sure that I would change anything. One of the things that I have observed is that the public school has a lot more resources than the private schools do in terms of activities, like the girls being in the chorus. They've done band. They do intramural sports. So they have all these things to pick from that they can get involved in. And I just felt like the private schools in the area didn't have that, especially at those elementary and intermediate ages.

Q: Will your children go to public high school?

Bank Executive: Yes. My little one now, she's stated very clearly she does not want to go to private school. She wants to stay where she is. And as far as I'm concerned, it's perfectly fine. As long as nothing changes in terms of how she is, you know. If she's motivated, gets great grades, remains very creative and very much involved in athletics.

Q: And what would be the high school that she would go to?

Bank Executive: It's a relatively new public high school. They just had their first graduating class this year.

Q: Oh, I see. How big is it?

Bank Executive: [I] would guess there's several thousand — two thousand, maybe.

Q: Do they do any of this team teaching that they do at middle school?

Bank Executive: You know, I actually have not investigated yet. I know they have a very good science program with their Explorations Academy. And they work with the OTEC, Ocean Thermal Energy Lab, and they actually have a classroom down at the Ocean Thermal Energy Lab.

Q: And when you talked about your own experience in public schools, you said that part of the advantage to public schools was the ease with which you developed friendships with children of other ethnic and socioeconomic backgrounds. Do you feel that that is an advantage repeating itself for your children?

Bank Executive: Absolutely.

The next parent talked about how changing demographics led to a smaller school population in this middle school, thus allowing for smaller classes — a clear asset in his perspective. He also felt that his daughter experienced a challenging academic curriculum.

Q: And so you have . . . one daughter. She's now going into seventh grade.

Professor: Right. She had her last day of sixth grade yesterday.

Q: Oh. Big change.

Professor: Yeah. Actually, she went to middle school this year.

Q: Oh, she did? And what happened?

Professor: Oh, she did very well. She really — she liked it a lot, and she did very well. She was the student of the year.

Q: Why do you think she liked it?

Professor: Well, she liked the grade. She liked her classmates. You know, she has some good friends and she's at an age where that's very important. She liked her teachers. Her teachers were good. And generally, I have very little to complain about, actually, as far as that school goes. I think she did very well at that school. And probably it was better for her that she went there rather than staying for the sixth grade at the elementary school, which is also good.

Q: Was she in the gifted class?

Professor: Yes. That was one of the reasons why we felt comfortable sending her there. It was actually one of the things that we felt was an advantage over the elementary school at this point. There were several things. One thing was that the classes were quite a bit smaller. The class size at the elementary school got bigger in the last couple years because they only have two classes instead of three, and so she was going to be in a class of thirty, thirty-one students. And it is a mixed class — randomly mixed.

At this middle school, she was going to be in classes of about twenty, and there are only three groups. They are tested and the top third is put in one class — not for every subject — just for English, math, and social studies. The others are randomly mixed, right, so that she got both things. But see, that was one of the advantages — where she had different classes with different teachers so that she could get instruction in English and math. That was going to be more interesting and challenging to her because she was going to be in the advanced class, and still not be [completely] segregated from all the other kids.

Q: Did she develop friendships with kids with different backgrounds than she had?

Professor: A little bit, not a whole lot. Her best friend is the kid who went over with her from the elementary school. They became close friends. They were already pretty close friends, and I think they became much closer by going over there together. She became friends with the kids in her class. Certainly, she was exposed to kids who, I think — the variety of ethnic and socioeconomic backgrounds was greater at her middle school than it was at her elementary school.

Q: What is the mix?

Professor: [Within the community,] you get a lot of Pacific Islanders, and then there's a large older Japanese and Chinese American third and fourth generations — you know, people that have been there a long time. That's the dominant group. Most of the kids that she got to know were local. Almost all the friends that she made come from that background. And I don't know about socioeconomic status. I think it's pretty middle class. My impression is that, at least out of her friends, basically they come from that kind of second-, third-generation local [group]. That's most of the friends she made.

At the time of her interview, the mother quoted below (and who also was a professor but at another college) spent some time talking about her son's public intermediate school experiences even though the son had already graduated from public high school in Hawai'i and was attending an elite private college on the mainland. She said she initially had been concerned about his public intermediate school because it had a bad reputation and the facilities were poor. She mentioned the difference at and the positive impact on the school when a new principal arrived. The importance of strong principals and how they can set the tone for the entire school is a recurring theme in this study. She also talked about "the wonderful band teacher," another recurring theme, and the opportunities that band and sports participation provided for developing friendships across ethnic and socioeconomic groups.

Professor: I have one child. And when we moved here — I guess junior high is one of the critical points where people in Hawai'i decide: private school versus public school. I knew that he was going to be going to the neighborhood public intermediate school, which had this reputation as a bad school — not a good school. I was a bit concerned, except that I had learned that a woman who had become the principal there and had taken on changing the school — getting community involvement in terms of cleaning up the place. One of my biggest shocks when I went there — compared to the public elementary school — was that the place looked like a ghettoized school — falling apart. The physical school itself was just in horrendous shape.

It must have been fall of '91? And I think the new principal maybe went there in '92. I'm not sure. I remember being a bit concerned going to one parent meeting where parents were upset about some sort of a racial incident that happened. And that concerned me a bit.

Quite honestly, it was more important to me that my child be happy at school and enjoy the experience than whatever any of the academic criteria were there. He had a wonderful band teacher that year.

Q: Did he end up going to the public intermediate school?

Professor: Yes, he did. And probably one of the best things that happened there was there was a wonderful band teacher who seemed to really pull all the students in. My son was enjoying school, and that was really critical. I'm sure he was in the college prep track.

Q: Do you feel he was academically challenged?

Professor: I think it varied according to class and assignments. I think some things he just automatically did better than other things.

I'm going to shift into philosophy. I have a very different philosophy than most parents in that I'm not a fan of homework, and so I don't feel that homework really serves the purpose that some people think it does. And so for me, having hours of homework in the evening didn't necessarily equate with learning and having a good academic experience. My son is very sociable and adaptable. I guess I created what I looked for. He seems to have friends, not only from that academic track that he was in, but also from all across the school. He's able to fit in and blend in with different groups.

Q: Was he always in classes with the same group, or did he have mixed classes, or mixed activities? How did he meet people outside his track?

Professor: I don't know enough about the classes because I was sort of laissez-faire in terms of the parent-school relationships. I'm going to get involved if there's a specific problem, but I didn't have time to be room mother. My son is athletic, so I think the sports and the band, too, were probably activities where he became exposed to kids from other social groups.

The third professor in this section also addressed the impact of a strong principal. He had four children who graduated from public high schools. He described how a creative public school principal facilitated student learning with innovative strategies and how she set up tasks that allowed students with different talents and backgrounds to work together successfully for the benefit of both. He began by sharing the experience of transferring one son from a large public intermediate school to another, smaller public school where another son attended.

Professor: So we went to this principal and asked if she would consider taking the second son. And she said bring him in and let me talk to him. He said, "I'm willing to try. What do I have to do?" She said, "You have to go to summer school. Would you do that?" He said, "Yes." So she said, "Come back in a week. Meet me on this bench where we're sitting and talking now, and I'll tell you what your summer school assignment will be." And he was there. We made sure he was there.

We found out later she had brought a young woman out to meet him. And the principal introduced her as a young English instructor from the university, who had just come back to Hawai'i and who wanted to get in tune with young people. The principal handed my son a copy of the *Talk Story* anthology, which had just recently been published. And she said, "Your summer school assignment is to teach her how to read this. And at the end of the summer I'll test her, and if she understands it, you can come to our school."

Brilliant move. For the circumstance, this principal was a saint to us for that move. And it really worked. It made a big difference. So he went to that school.

Q: What would you say were the advantages?

Professor: Well, it was also school size, but it was also the diversity of the population. The principal made a brilliant move with another son too. There was a student who was a second-year star, most valuable basketball player in the state. He came from a different socioeconomic background than my son. He had some academic trouble in school, but he was an incredible basketball player. The principal put the two together, and she told them they had to work together and help each other. And that student's job was to teach my son basketball moves. And my son's job was to coach this other student academically. And so, ultimately, they developed quite a bond. They had this deal . . . if the basketball player got a B+ or higher, my son would pay when they double dated with their girlfriends. And if my son scored more than twelve points in a basketball game, [the basketball player] would pay for the double date. (*Laughs.*)

Q: Were you and your wife very active in the school?

Professor: We were very active. We were always active in all the schools. And we felt that was a commitment.

Q: Did you find that the majority of parents were active?

Professor: There were lots of parents active in the school community. But our kids became involved in sports. One of the things about that school, and the story I just told you is related, is that everybody had to participate. No matter how weak you were, the good kids needed you to be as good as you could be, so they helped you instead of ragging on you for being weak. They'd help you get better. And we noticed that kind of spirit, camaraderie.

Q: Why did the good kids need the kids that were not so good?

Professor: If they wanted to win. There weren't very many kids to choose from, so everyone had to play. The size of the school limited it. So in athletic contests, the weaker players would have to be helped, if possible, by the stronger players in order for the stronger players to have a chance to win.

Q: So would you say that, at that school, there was more of a sense of community?

Professor: Definitely, oh, definitely. . . . And there were a lot of parents from a lot of different backgrounds. That was outstanding to us.

Q: Well, what would you say makes the difference? Who helps to create a sense of community?

Professor: I'm sure it was the composition of the student body. That was one of the things that created part of what we responded so positively to. And I think the principal herself, personally, played a very strong role.

Typically, the secondary public schools have student populations that are more diverse than many of the private schools. In fact, several of the private school parents talk about preferring more homogeneous student populations. The next group of interview excerpts connect this notion of diversity explicitly to the category of Opportunities Provided by Public Education, including the opportunity for their children to develop "life lessons."

Besides a good academic education, many parents believe that public schools afford their children the opportunity to engage in life lessons that are beneficial to their development. They believe that their children develop the ability to make reasoned judgments and to find solutions when they are faced with conflict or other dilemmas in environments that hold values different from one's own. Life lessons are considered practice for the "real world," and going to school with diverse groups provides the opportunity to encounter these lessons. And like the real world, these are not easy lessons.

An attorney talked about the life lessons her daughter learned as she figured out the value she placed on friendships.

Attorney: I have a son at public middle school this year and a daughter who's a junior at a public high school.

Q: Are they content with their school experiences?

Attorney: My kids come back and they'll say something about the facilities and the toilet paper, and I'll say, "You know, life is not always going to be where everything's handed to you. Go problem-solve it if it's really bothering you. What do you want to do about it? These problems are out there in the real world. What are you going to do about it? It may not be something you want to take on right now, but you need to know that that's the way it is. And don't run away from it. Either solve it or find your own personal solution to it." But every day there's a challenge, and I value that for my kids so that they'll be stronger people.

Q: And how do they feel about this?

Attorney: They're into the whole public school thing.

Both of my kids have had their challenges at middle school in terms of finding their social group. My daughter had more trouble than my son. And she was hanging around with a group that we all knew was not her group. And my husband and I didn't do anything about it other than to ask her some critical questions like, "What do you value? How do you define friendship?" I went over that over and over again. This was a turning point in my daughter's life.

This was a group that was pretty out there in terms of who we would want her to be hanging out. And they were just being mean to her anyway. They didn't really appreciate her at all, except for her [doing] their homework for them. So finally one day, she said — this must've taken at least a year of doing this — and then she got up one day and said, "I think I'm going to change my social group." And she got up one day, just left and went to somebody else and said, "Would you be my friend?" And ever since then — that was such a good thing for her because I knew she could get up and leave when it wasn't the right situation.

She'll talk about values now sometimes, about values of her friends, so that whole thing, even though it took a long time — and I could've told her, "Get up and leave. Don't go hang around there." But I didn't do that. I just knew that that wouldn't have worked. I asked, instead, "What is it that you want? What is it that you value?" And she got up and left that day. And she never went back to that group. She went to a whole other group, and it opened up a whole other world for her in terms of friendships.

Another attorney talked about life lessons in relation to learning to choose a peer group, and learning to exist with students who make choices different from one's own. Once again, the positive impact of band participation in middle school was mentioned.

Attorney: My son is at a public middle school. Every time I drop him off, he's like, "Oh, so-and-so smokes. These other kids that hang out over there, they swear all the time," or whatever, that kind of stuff. "And so what do you do?" I asked him. "Well, you just stay away from these areas." I think that's a good thing to learn. The school is big enough where you don't have to be in those situations every day. You can avoid them as you're going to class with everybody else. And he has a good bunch of friends who are a part of his Boy Scout troop who go to that school, so they have a pretty tight group.

Q: Is he enjoying school?

Attorney: He enjoys it. He enjoys the band. He took the band course, and we were asking him about two weeks into the school year, "What have you decided to play?" He was talking about the saxophone or trumpet and then he said, "Well, not everybody could afford their mouthpiece, so some of them aren't even playing their instruments yet." He understands that some students can't afford even the basic things they need for school.

Q: So he's getting that experience with the wide spectrum of society?

Attorney: I think so, yes. It's not quite — I guess the word is — sheltered.

When this dentist discussed his daughter's experiences with diversity, he explained that it is important to experience this when she is young because he feels it is much harder to acquire that sense of comfort with diverse groups as an adult.

Q: And what has the middle school experience been with your daughter?

Dentist: Well, it was a different experience. She went in from the public elementary school, and she knew some people. She's actually blossoming very nicely. She's just thriving in the environment in eighth grade. She went in as a seventh grader instead of a sixth grader because her elementary school has such a nice sixth grade, you know. No one wants to leave at sixth grade. And she's actually the eighth-grade class president, and she's doing very well socially, and her grades are all 3.7 to 3.8, I don't know, but very high. And she's very happy.

Q: And so you feel comfortable, obviously, with her academics?

Dentist: Yes, yes.

Q: And what's her peer group like?

Dentist: Very nice young girls — a couple of them from her elementary school, but she's [also] made friends from other schools. They're all a nice group of people, and since she's president — and the group of people that are very active with the student body are in her homeroom, and most of those are her friends — she is friends with other people.

When I was thinking about [this interview], I made it a point to ask her about her experience and what she's thinking and whether she's happy, and she says she's very happy, and I said, "Well, are there any troublemakers?" and "Oh yeah, there's those." And she says, "Some are my friends, but there aren't a lot of them." So she has a diverse group of friends. And that's important because it would be just hard to . . . work with everybody like I do without an understanding of diverse groups. If you grow up in a somewhat sterile environment, you might miss out if you don't have those experiences as a child. You won't understand a lot of things.

Safety

One of the concerns that parents in the community at large (as well as the private school parents in this study) often express when considering school choice is safety. A general perception is that secondary schools in Hawai'i are not safe. And although several parents did talk about their children's awareness that there were students on campus who smoked and used other drugs, surprisingly, given public perception, few parents reported problems related to safety. The next two parents responded to this concern and illustrate the fact that, while the parents in the study view diversity as an opportunity to learn life lessons, they would not knowingly expose their children to safety risks. They also continue to bring up the issue of diversity, mentioning groups from communities that are culturally and socioeconomically different from their own.

Executive Banker: My older daughter is at a public middle school. And interestingly, most of her class is from her public elementary school. And the elementary school staff was struck by how much of her class — two went to private schools, and a couple couldn't keep their district exemptions, but, other than that — that whole class moved to the complex middle school.

Q: Do you think that your daughter is academically challenged?

Executive Banker: Oh yes. The bright kid that's most in danger in the public schools is the one with no "oomph" and the parents don't have any "oomph" either. But if the parents do and if the kids have any desire, the top end of the public schools can compete with anybody.

Q: What about the safety issues?

Executive Banker: Not at this middle school. I can't speak for other schools, but I know they had a bully problem three or four years ago, and the school just dealt with it. They called an assembly. They brought in people [well known in the community], and there was a band teacher and some others that just jumped on this and talked to all the kids about it, and they haven't had that problem since. I'm sure they have people push each other around, and there's probably a rough element off at the edge of school. But I've asked my daughter for both years now, "Do you feel any safety issues?" And she said, "No." There was one case where some kid felt she had ratted on her, and my daughter was sort of flustered for a day, and then she just righted herself back up, and said, "I'm not scared of her." This was not a fight.

I asked my daughter, "What about the druggies?" She said, "Oh, they hang around at the courts — the basketball courts. There's a group of them that hang around. They're the druggies. We know that." "But what about [girl's name]?" "Ah, she's with a group over by building X." They're kind of . . . you know, a little rough edged. It looks like they find their niche of who they're most comfortable with. And they just kind of stay out of each other's space. So if you don't want to be part of the druggies, you don't have to be. And if you don't want to be part of the brainy group, you don't have to be.

Q: Does she have friends across socioeconomic groups?

Executive Banker: Yes. And that's the other thing that, for us, is very important. She's in a hula class that's turned into a *hālau*, and the two *kumus* are from Wai'anae and Nānākuli. And so the class that meets at the Y is mostly town kids, but when they do performances, the other half of the group comes from Wai'anae and Nānākuli. And what they have done for two years is to participate in a big competition in the fall.

Every Sunday afternoon, they meet halfway at Blaisdell Park in Pearl City, and the combined group works together. So those kids are all out of Wai'anae and Nānākuli. This experience is something that allows her to hear what life is. So who knows what she'll finally be. But for example, she really wants to be a teacher. What's ironic is the teachers are telling her, "What a bad idea" [to be a teacher].

But she really likes the idea of working with people. And she'd like to be a public school teacher. And she'd like to be an elementary school teacher. So all of that, to me, reflects that she actually had a good time.

In Hawai'i, public schools provide geographic exemptions (GEs), which allow students to attend schools outside of their districts — a provision that is offered partly in compliance with the No Child Left Behind (NCLB) act but that, even before NCLB, has been offered for other reasons, such as convenience (as when a school is nearer to a parent's place of work). The parents below did some research on several middle schools before they applied for a geographic exemption so their son could attend a middle school they felt comfortable with. They thought the school was "lovely," but the feedback they received from their friends was that the school was rough. "Rough" is not what they experienced.

Professor: [My] younger [child] goes to a public elementary school, and the other one goes to a public middle school.

Q: You mentioned that you're quite happy with your children's experiences so far. Do you want to talk a little bit about that?

Professor: We had this incident, just recently. My older son, who is going to the public middle school, gets fairly good grades, pretty good grades. He was talking about it to his friends who were going to private school, and his friends' retort was, "Well, you're going to public school. It doesn't count." And my son reported this back to my wife, and my wife said, "Well, with that attitude that's why you're not going to private school." (*Laughs.*) I think that it starts immediately. [The attitude] is, "I'm going to private school, you're going to public school. Clearly, whatever I do is better than what you do." That's assumed.

Q: And besides academics, what about the question of safety? That often comes up when people talk about public school at the middle school level.

Professor: You know, my wife [visited] the neighborhood middle school, and she wasn't really happy with what she saw there, and so at that point, she said "He's not going there." And so she looked at two other middle schools, and those two she felt more comfortable with. So we got a GE to this other middle school, and everyone thinks it's so rough. Remember, we're from [a mainland city]. We know about rough schools. And maybe our standards are a little different in terms of what's rough, and what isn't. We think that this middle school is lovely, and we're not worried about it all. But some people say, "Whoa, he's going to [that school]? That's pretty rough." Well, not to us.

Q: You and your wife are active in the schools?

Professor: I think, for a kid in seventh grade, we're a little too intrusive. We're constantly checking.

Issues

Three parents talked about what they viewed as negative experiences. One parent discussed the lack of resources in his son's English class and his concern that the school was not providing after-school programs where students could study and receive assistance if needed. A second parent introduced issues that accompany adolescence as he talked about his son's choice of a peer group. Unlike the earlier example in which the child switched peer groups, thus solving the problem, this parent felt that closer scrutiny from his son's teachers would have been beneficial. Finally, the third parent's complaint involves the teachers of a Gifted and Talented (GT) program.

To begin, the father in this next interview spoke of his concern for students other than his son — students who may have little outside resources to help them with their education. He compared the after-school resources of a private school his son had attended with those of the public intermediate school in which his son is currently enrolled.

Professor: That was the real shift when my son went over into public intermediate school. The one thing that really started coming up was lack of resources. I was talking to my son's English teacher and discovered her dreaming about one day being able to teach the same book to all her students. There was no complete set of any book that her students could read. That's the resources business. But when I looked at the homework he was doing and what he was being required to do, it was demanding. It was consistent. It was well organized. It was well prepared. It was tough.

And as I was struggling over it with him one night, I also realized now what is happening to other students where there are three or four at home. They're in a small apartment somewhere in the neighborhood. There's not a room where they can read or work on this, all right, and the school shuts down at 2:30.

Each of these teachers has a hundred and fifty students all in the same grade level. As a result, if the student can get through that and figure the stuff out and have the support and the resources to do it, they'll be fine.

When the next father talked about the not atypical changes a child goes through during early adolescence, he thought closer oversight by his son's teachers would have been helpful.

Q: And as they move into the middle school, how has that experience been?

Dentist: My son, who is a very bright boy, needs to be pushed academically. He's a sports guy and very social and very good looking, and just a very good kid. We had a geographic exemption into another elementary and then his middle school. I think there were four or five children from his elementary school who went to the middle school. All of the kids from his elementary school did very, very well, right off the bat. Academically, his friends would get 4.0, and first quarter he got 3.0. But then after that, he figured that there wasn't anyone really pushing him to work real hard.

The elementary school is a very closed, sheltered environment, and it's a very nice elementary school. And then you go to the middle school, and you're getting all these other influences. All these other socioeconomic groups are there. So he made it a point to ally himself with a group of kids who no one was going to pick on. And, unfortunately, these kids were less than studious, and a little more trouble-oriented. So he, unfortunately, saw that as the way to be. He didn't get into a lot of trouble, but he didn't perform academically as he had [when he started]. He was gung-ho. He was going to do well, and took up [a musical instrument], and I thought, "Wow, this is great!" And all of a sudden, things started to slide.

But that was that experience, and I can't necessarily blame it on the school. You know, I don't blame it on the school. You know the school was a good middle school. They offered good programs and a very strong math and science program.

Q: Was he not being challenged academically? You were saying something, that he was in a bigger school and probably needed more attention, more guidance?

Dentist: Yes, in a way, I think that that's what he needed. To say if he was challenged or not, yes, I think he was challenged. It was amazing, though. He just wouldn't do the homework. And there wasn't the pressure, like at an elementary school. "Hey, where is this homework?" It was more relaxed, it was like, "Well, hey, if you're not going to do it, you'll get this grade, so be it." I get a sense that he kind of looked around and saw that these guys aren't turning in homework, and nothing's happening.

Q: So from your point of view, would it have been helpful to have had more careful follow-up?

Dentist: I think so, yes.

Q: Did you have that follow-up at the elementary school?

Dentist: Yes. Maybe it's just the change from the young child going into adolescence and not responding to authority quite the same way. And you're feeling, as an adolescent, you're spreading your wings a little bit, and "I don't care what you say!" and I think there's a lot of that.

The last reported negative experience was with a teacher in the middle school's GT program. Again, an involved parent followed up with the administrator.

Computer Programmer: Can I give you one example? In seventh grade, the kids got into the Gifted and Talented class, and one of my daughters asked me, after seventh grade, "Can we get out of GT?" And I said, "What?" Oriental, local, you always think the teacher's right. "Well, Mom, seven or eight of us are not coming back out of our class of fifteen."

They wanted to mainstream. After I talked to my daughters, I talked to parents, and I talked to the teacher who would be teaching English in the mainstream class. I liked her curriculum, and I liked the way she talked, and what she seemed to offer her students, so we left the GT class.

And I called the principal, and I said, "Do you realize out of fifteen students, you have seven dropping? Doesn't that tell you that something's wrong? You got to take a look." But I had to let him know that they were in trouble.

In the final section of this chapter, public school parents talked about their children's experiences in public high schools.

Public High School

For the fourteen public high schools attended by the parents' children, an academically challenging curriculum, good teachers, and strong administrative leadership remained the basic characteristics of the parents' concept of the Good Public School. High schools are more complex in their structure and academic programs than either elementary or middle schools, so parents' comments typically referred to particular programs or activities. In these next interviews, parents expanded on the importance of remaining involved, the opportunities available to their children in public schools, and what happens post-graduation.

In the first interview, a mother talked about the type of parental involvement in which both she and her husband participated. She felt her involvement made a difference: she had a say in a number of school-related issues. She also emphasized the life lessons for her children as they figured out how to get along with diverse groups of students different from them. She acknowledged that that experience wasn't always easy for them, but that "they have come out better people for it."

Professor: I have two teenagers and both attend public high school.

Q: What do you like about these public schools, and what don't you like?

Professor: I think one really important thing in public versus private school is that in public schools, through SCBM [school/community-based management] councils, you have a great opportunity to be involved in the decision-making process at the school level. And this is something I don't think you have the opportunity for in private schools. There are always plenty of opportunities for parents [in private schools] to fund-raise and help with fun fairs and to be on the Parent-Teacher Association [PTA], but you don't have that opportunity to be involved in meaningful, important decision making, which you really do in the public schools, if you take advantage of it. And either my husband or I have been on SCBM councils ever since elementary school — elementary, intermediate, and secondary. And it's a very valuable experience. You really can contribute to what happens in terms of curriculum, in terms of teachers, pedagogy, hiring of principals. And that's really important. It's too bad more parents can't take advantage of that, or don't take advantage of that.

Q: What percentage of the parents at your children's public schools do get involved?

Professor: That's a real issue too because the idea is that the SCBM council is supposed to be a representative group of parents, and of course it's not. It's only representative of a certain group of parents who would've been involved no matter what. And it gives them an avenue to be more significantly involved. But it still leaves a whole lot of people out of the conversation. And that's certainly an issue, still. But it has opened doors, and I feel like, in terms of my kids' education, it has been really valuable, and I've had a lot of input.

Q: What would you say are advantages for your children to have had these public school experiences in Hawai'i?

Professor: I think there are a lot. They have learned really important life lessons that I think are very valuable. I think in private schools you're much more sheltered — you're around a certain group of kids from certain social classes, and certain ethnicities dominate. My kids have been in just as mixed a situation as you could ever imagine. They're a minority. There's 13 percent Caucasians at this public high school. So they've learned a whole lot about people — differences, diversity, and discrimination. They've experienced it, and I think that's good. They've learned firsthand how wrong it is and how hurtful it is to judge people by the color of their skin or their appearance or their ethnicity. They've also learned through some difficult situations that they can handle these things. They would not have had those experiences in a private school. And I think they've come out better people for it.

They have a very diverse group of friends in terms of ethnicity, socioeconomic status, and sexual orientation. They have many gay friends. They talk to their friends who are in private schools and they say, "Oh, we don't have any gay kids at our school." And of course they do, but they're closeted. They've learned to look at people for the kind of people they are, and not by any labels or name tags or color of their skin. And I think that's been really one of the greatest benefits. And like I said, it hasn't been easy. And as a kid, this is the time you should be learning how to handle those situations and develop those strengths for your adult life, when you have people around that can support you in those situations.

Q: Have they been challenged academically?

Professor: Well, this is another issue. The school system tracks and groups kids — the public school system does. And my kids have always been in

Gifted and Talented classes. If I were a parent who had kids that were on the lower end of things, I'd probably be really fighting to change that system, but because they've been in GT classes, they have had excellent teachers — I feel every bit as good as they would ever get in a private school.

They've had challenging and good curriculum, high expectations, and they've done very well academically. So I feel a little bit torn about the fact that, philosophically, I don't necessarily agree with tracking, but again, it's another situation that when it's your own kids, you want the best situation for them. They've had a very good experience. [And] 90 percent of their classes have been on the high end.

Another thing that I've liked about the public schools, with my own particular kids, is they've been able to kind of be big fish in a little pond, as opposed to the opposite. So many kids are in the private [high] schools, my children really stand out and have gotten a lot of recognition and a lot of positive attention for their academics, which has been great for their self-esteem and for their self-concepts. So that's been really nice. They wouldn't have gotten that in the private school. They'd just be one of the crowd.

Q: Are you talking about the elite private schools, or all private schools?

Professor: That's what I'm talking about. If I had sent my kids to a private school it would've been to one of those two [elite private schools].

I think one other advantage for my kids, and for a lot of kids, has been — and I don't know this for a fact — but I think there's somewhat less pressure on the kids in the public schools. Maybe there's a little bit too much pressure on the kids in the private schools, so that they don't have time for a lot of extracurricular activities and other things they'd like to be involved with. I've heard this from a lot of private school parents, that there's just so much. My kids have a lot of homework, but they still have time to be involved in dance and theater and music. And that has really made them much more well-rounded people. It really added a lot of pleasure to their schooling experiences.

Q: And one daughter is seventeen? So she will be applying to college. And where will she apply, do you think?

Professor: Well, that's a big question. We're going to go look at colleges this summer, but she's thinking of Stanford. She's thinking of U.C. Santa Cruz. And there are about six small, private liberal arts colleges that we're looking at.

Q: If a parent's goal is to make sure the public high school experience of their children includes challenging academics so that they will have options for college, you feel that those options will be available?

Professor: Absolutely. That's a real myth that the kids in public schools don't get well prepared for college. And I think that's something else that could be better publicized. They can start taking the SAT [Scholastic Aptitude Test], and you can see how your kids are doing and if they're well prepared. And they clearly are, so her options are very good.

The parent in the next interview also spoke about the benefits of a diverse student population and the "big fish" concept, in which his son could take advantage of the opportunities available to him. The father is also an involved parent, and he did his research on the public high schools. He knows that his son's high school has a good reputation in that it offers an Advanced Placement (AP) program, the students have above-average standardized test scores, and teachers hold high expectations for their students. He believes that parental involvement is probably responsible for the high expectations. In fact, he said that he would not send his son to a school that did not have high parental involvement.

Data Consultant: [My son goes to a] public high school. He plays basketball. He has friends from sports. He's also a very academic-oriented person, and so he has his academic friends. Chinese, Japanese, also some, you know, white kids. So he has friends from all over the place.

Q: Do these friends also represent the various socioeconomic groups?

Data Consultant: Right. Some are very, very rich, if you like. Big houses. He was invited to sleep over. And also some who are eligible for a free lunch program in the school, and who don't even have basic things. This is why I'm thinking this is such a good experience for him. And you wouldn't find such a rich environment in a private school. And I want him to experience that.

Q: And what has been his experience when he runs up against problems in this heterogeneous environment? Has he had to confront fights or has he had conflicts?

Data Consultant: This, again, is another [reason] that I found that the public school is so good for everybody. Everybody should have that kind of experience because it's not a peaceful world out there. There are conflicts where people are polite and then those who are not so polite — all kinds of people. So he had problems, but he learned how to handle them. He learned how to be school smart and also street smart — when to say "no," when not to say "no," when to stand up for himself, when to give up.

He is also the class president. He's been trained as a mediator in the peer mediation program at the school. So that has also given him the opportunity to not only handle his own conflicts, but to help others. So that's good.

Q: Did he also come home and talk to you and his mother about problems he faces?

Data Consultant: Yes. A lot.

Q: And what kinds of things were you telling him to help him cope?

Data Consultant: First of all, there's always some discussion about going to private school or public school between my wife and me because most of my peers are trying to send their children to private schools. And my wife looks at that as something that we should do to measure up. Okay? She says, "Well, they're doing that. We should also do that." So I've been arguing with her not to do that, and we discussed this openly in front of our child. And we just talked about the opportunities in the public schools. We talked about what's missing from private schools, and we talked about the money. Although money is not a problem for us, we talked about it. So my wife always wanted to send him to a private school.

Our child is there [in the room with us], and he is listening and he would also contribute to the discussion. Our son says, "If the child wants to learn, there are plenty of opportunities in the public school." Probably the fewer the peers who want to participate, [it] gives you more opportunities. So this is what he understands. So if there's something to sign up for, he always is the first one to sign up. He said, "See, all these opportunities — you know, computer classes, and all those kinds of things. If I want to learn, I will take all the opportunities. Even if you put me in the private school, if I don't want to learn, I just don't learn." So we talk, and he's really kind of up-to-date about what we think. We often learn a lot from him.

Q: Are you feeling satisfied with the academic challenges he's had?

Data Consultant: Yes, I am. Well, this public high school is one of the academically advanced schools in the state. It has all kinds of programs, and their SAT scores are way above the average. It's above the national average in both math and reading. And they have what is called Advanced Placement courses. They have a special course for computer science. And they also have a lot of things that check the students' academic standing. I like that school.

Before I put him into that school, I really did my homework. I did do this research. Although they are all public schools, they're different kinds.

Q: Do you feel that the expectations are high, so that the teachers have high expectations for the students?

Data Consultant: Yes. That's probably from the pressure of the parents.

The parent involvement shows me how much the community wants to be involved, while in other communities, the lower parent involvement shows me those parents don't care. Either they don't care, or don't know what to do, or they'd rather the schools do it, which to me is not complete. The complete experience is the school plus community plus family. So if the parent involvement in the schools is low, then I wouldn't send my son to those kinds of schools.

Q: How are you involved?

Data Consultant: I attend conferences with the teachers and participate in the schools' activities. I also offered to help them with their data, so I had several meetings with their vice principal and their decision-making cadre. I help the school from that perspective. I casually met with the principal to talk with him.

Next, a mother who had one daughter in public high school and one daughter in private high school talked about her public-school daughter's opportunity to play on her school's volleyball team as another example of being a "big fish in a smaller pond."

Computer Programmer: And there was something else that I noticed [in the public high school]. Our children are short, but they enjoy the athletic camaraderie. They both played volleyball. Our daughter who attended private school could barely make it to the junior varsity, and the JV had two teams. Our public-school daughter could make the senior varsity volleyball team because there are not as many kids trying out. Of course, she was one of the last ones on the bench, but she was a part of it, you know. In fact, what happened is, when they each did have competition, we had a tendency to go to the public school because we felt they needed the help more.

Q: So parental support was noticeable?

Computer Programmer: We would bring post-game food. And I don't feel comfortable feeding just my child, so we started bringing Costco's — thank goodness. We would bring hot dogs for everyone. And pretty soon they had a JV team, and then we said, "Oh well, we'll feed the JV team." And pretty soon, the girls started feeding the boyfriends. And I said, "Don't you dare feed your boyfriends. I don't do this for your boyfriends!" (*Laughs.*)

The parents in the next interview initially had their children in private schools, but then, after much thought, decided to transfer their children to the public schools. The father felt that the high school they chose was in a middle-class neighborhood and had a school culture with high expectations for the students. He found that the teachers, while varied, were dedicated. And the administrative staff earned his respect.

Vice President: [My son is] a junior in one of the public high schools.

Q: And how is the high school experience for him?

Vice President: He is on the math team. He's taking three Advanced Placement courses this semester. He participates in, I guess, all the school activities. My daughter was the same way. Well, my daughter was actually very active socially, but she did a lot of things with the school also.

Q: So you were happy with the high school experience?

Vice President: I would say that there's no such thing as being totally happy, even with private school, but I think it is more positive than negative. I felt that the people at the high school — not all the teachers are the best — but I think they're pretty well dedicated, and I had a lot of respect for the administrative staff there. I had a daughter that was in special education, too, and I felt that they supported us pretty well.

Working as a public school teacher, this next mother sent her two children all the way through public education. Her children were in the honors program, which, she believed, had better teachers. And overall, while some teachers were better than others, and while she did have some philosophical differences with some of them, she is grateful for their commitment and dedication to providing a good learning environment for her children. She also acknowledged that her children had opportunities to participate in some exemplary extracurricular programs, namely theater and the leadership core program.

Public School Teacher: I have two children. My son graduated [from a public high school] last year. He will be a sophomore in college this coming fall. My daughter will be a junior in high school.

Q: Were you satisfied with their school experiences?

Public School Teacher: My kids were in the Gifted and Talented/honors track. I noticed those kids had better teachers in English, math, and science. They had this one really good math teacher. In the science department, some teachers were better than others.

I was grateful for what my children had received. I had philosophical differences and pedagogical differences with their teachers. I did. And at the same time I was appreciative.

I knew a lot of their teachers because of professional affiliations, and many of them have become very good friends since. I know what I saw in these people who were really dedicated. I might not have preferred a certain strategy or approach to some of the curriculum, but I just feel really grateful about what I saw as commitment and dedication and a sincere desire to provide a good learning environment for my child.

I also felt that my kids were beneficiaries of some exemplary programs. They did have excellent, excellent experiences because of the school leadership and because of the theater programs.

I kind of feel greedy. I really do because I certainly know that that [theater program] is a public education program, and my kids received what I feel was something that would be placed at the top of the nation's programs in terms of quality.

And again, one of the really good, wonderful programs that they were able to take part in is this leadership core. There's a leadership camp that the public school complex schools run. It begins in elementary school with leadership campers, grades four to six. At the end of sixth grade, students are elected from this group to move on to the middle school. They stay together for six years. The current group is missing some of the leaders who went to private schools.

In the next two excerpts, parents also talked about the extracurricular opportunities available at their children's public high schools. The first parent is a legislator whose child has always been very active in band, an activity through which he, as a parent, can also remain involved in his daughter's school.

Legislator: Both children are in the band program. My older daughter is the field commander, one step below the drum major. They were in the Macy's parade in New York City and the Rose Bowl parade in Pasadena.

Q: How did they get interested in band?

Legislator: We got them interested at their intermediate public school, where they had one of the best band instructors in the state. Our older daughter played the violin and then clarinet and was a member of the youth symphony. The younger one plays clarinet.

I really believe that band helped one of our younger daughters. I like to believe that music helped her academically.

Q: How?

Legislator: Discipline. Music teaches discipline. It forces concentration and the discipline transferred into other areas.

Q: How active are you?

Legislator: I'm very involved in the band program. We have to be. Parents are a key to the success of the band program. Without the parents we couldn't be the tops in the state. We must have parent participation for fund-raising, volunteering at football games, chaperoning overseas trips, etc. It's critical.

The second parent, a university administrator, spoke about her children's opportunities to have diverse groups of friends through the sports programs at their public school. She felt that her younger daughter, who is in the National Honor Society, is sufficiently challenged academically. The older daughter graduated from public high school and is currently in college planning a career in mechanical industrial engineering.

University Administrator: [One daughter] is going to be starting her sophomore year in college, and one is a going to be a junior in high school.

Q: Do you feel that your children have been well served by their public education experience?

University Administrator: My daughter and my son, too, now. But my daughter from the beginning was always active in athletics. So she blended well with all levels of students. And that's what I thought was nice. She was in the honor society but she ran around with the football guys, the basketball guys, the volleyball girls, the soccer girls. It was nice to see when she had parties and when she got to together with people, there was a whole mixture of people that she got together with.

Q: Did you find they were academically challenged?

University Administrator: It was a sufficient challenge. For my daughter, I think she has to work hard for what she gets. But she became assertive enough to ask for help when she needed it, and to go and do extra credit things when she needed it.

Q: Where is the older daughter?

University Administrator: She's doing very well. She wants to go into mechanical industrial engineering. And she is getting the grades, and she is doing what she needs to do.

A father talked about the opportunity his daughter had in her public high school to meet classmates in her social studies class who are not in her college-tracked math and English classes. This father values her experience with diversity as a life lesson that teaches her to develop strategies for getting along with classmates she wouldn't ordinarily get to know. He also shared the difficulty of staying involved at the high school level, as adolescents don't typically want their parents around. He described what he and his wife did to stay engaged.

Q: And you said having [your son and daughter] be with diverse groups of students is an asset?

DOE Administrator: Yes, because it's knowing how to get along with a diverse group of people, right? At my daughter's high school, when my daughter was a sophomore or junior, they changed their social studies classes into heterogeneous groupings. And her comment was, "This is the most interesting class that I have." And I said, "Why?" And she said, "Because I'm with people that I'm not normally with in the higher math classes or English classes. I got to know people I don't normally get to know."

One time we went to Baskin-Robbins, and she said "hi" to the girl across the counter. And they were talking, and I'd never seen this girl before so I said, "Oh, who is she?" "She's in my social studies class."

Q: Did she feel that she was as challenged intellectually in that class?

DOE Administrator: I don't know, but I know that she won the social studies content award. She did well in social studies. It seemed as though that was an area she excelled in. So I guess she must have done well.

Q: You were saying you and your wife were very active, very hands on. Was that typical of the parents?

DOE Administrator: For the parents that were around us, it was kind of typical, I guess. There is a point when teenagers don't want their parents to be around. I remember, very specifically, telling the children why we want to be involved. It started out with things like sports. We'd say, "At the end of the game or after everybody's finished eating, look around you. If somebody's sitting around and doesn't have a way home or something like that, always offer. And then we'll always take them home. I don't care where they live. We'll just take them home. But always offer." The kids would say, "Why don't you come? My parents can take you home." And then we'd stop and buy ice cream or something like that. It was a way of getting to know the kids and their friends.

As they get older, in high school, it was very natural — my daughter, for instance, who was very involved in student council, would volunteer us: "Oh, my parents can do that." And so she'd just offer and then we'd come through.

And this was the same way when they went to parties and kids needed a way home. We'd say, "Look around. Just offer." We can always take them home, no matter what. And it proved to be a real opening for our kids and us in terms of them not being ashamed of us being there. I think they were less hesitant for my wife to be there than me because if I were there — I'm an educator, and so now I'm interacting with their teachers, their class advisers, and the principal of the school. But I was always there to help them. But that's how it worked. But we did that consciously.

Q: So do you think that because you were so engaged, you really got to know their school experiences as well? Do you think other professionals just don't know much about public schools, and therefore they feel the safest thing to do is send their children to private schools?

DOE Administrator: That's a unique and interesting point. I never really thought about that. But in many ways, because I know what the schools are like, I'm always aware. For instance, I know the importance of something small like thanking especially good teachers for the work that they do. As a former teacher and as a former principal, I know that a note, at the end of the year or at the end of the quarter, or after something significant that the teacher has done for my children, a note is always appreciated. So we always did that. And in a particular case where a teacher was very good, I wrote letters to the teacher and cc'd the principal.

On the other hand, because I'm an administrator, when my children were in school, sometimes it's difficult because you know what the teacher's life is like in the classroom. If something is not going right, especially academically, how do you sit down at a parent-teacher conference and really try to explore or help the teacher look at different ways in which they can shift their instructional strategies so that the child might get more from it?

Q: Did you feel that, by and large, the teachers held high standards?

DOE Administrator: I think there was a mixture. But I think in many cases they held high standards for my children. And I think part of it is because we kept in touch. And I know as a teacher, if a parent is coming to me and asking me questions or inquiring, I know I always paid a little bit more attention as a teacher and as a principal. I know I always did. And I didn't do this in a . . . hostile way, or in a way that I was looking over my shoulder, but from a parent's point of view. I was always very much interested in what my children were doing. And so if I saw something innovative or something my kids really enjoyed, I talked to the teachers about that. If I saw something that I thought was not on the right track, then I'd question.

Issues

The most frequently mentioned concern at the high school level is the inadequate number of counselors and the services they provide in preparing students for entry into college, as well as overseeing students who need to be counseled into taking more challenging courses. This latter finding is connected to the concern with students who are viewed as "average"; who are not in AP, GT, or honors classes; or who are not always academically challenged.

The following parents' children typically had positive experiences in the public high schools, but the parents wanted to talk about the insufficient number of counselors as an important omission in the public high schools. These parents believe the problem can be resolved by having the public schools emulate the elite private schools that seem to make having an adequate number of counselors a priority.

One father talked about the need to employ more college counselors to help their children through the college application process.

Professor: He's heading into his junior year, and I'm sure he'll do very well. This is actually, in some ways, the toughest point, and this is the point where the prep schools really become prep schools. The kids he knows in private schools are already getting heavy-duty training in how to get ready to apply for universities, moving scores of them into rooms, making sure they take the Scholastic Assessment Test [SAT] three times.

We found out, for example, that regarding the national merit scholarships, there's no public school program for taking the kids who do really well on the PSAT [Preliminary Scholastic Assessment Test] and working with them before they take the next one, whereas that's actually built into the private school programs. They march all of their sophomores in, and they find the ones who [score] around 190 as sophomores, and then they target them and move them on.

Q: So, again, the public school parents have to be very alert and involved and work to obtain different services?
Professor: Yes.

Another father, whose four sons went all the way through the public school system, expressed frustration with having to go to see a college counselor at a private school because that counselor had in-depth knowledge of mainland colleges and universities.

Q: So you were saying they were challenged academically [at their public high school], and you mentioned that two of them went to see a private school college counselor. Why didn't they go to the counselors at their public high school?

DOE Administrator: They did. They did. But those counselors didn't know the colleges as well as the private school counselor. The private school counselor was the kind of a counselor who went to the colleges, stayed there for several days, and in some cases weeks. He knew the colleges' strengths and the weaknesses. He even could tell you whether their lunch is good. That's how much he knows.

Q: Do you think it would be helpful for the public schools to invest more in their counselors for just this reason?

DOE Administrator: Yes. I think we should have excellent college counselors.

Q: I've heard this from several sources. I remember last February when there was a speaker from Stanford University here in Hawai'i talking about his children who go to public schools in California. He said that they don't have enough counselors. And his argument was that one of the things good private schools do is they have a number of counselors who pay close attention to the students and give them the kind of assistance that typically public schools with a 1:250 student ratio each are not able to give. His recommendation was that one of the top priorities he would recommend for improving public education was actually to increase the number of counselors. And that's the first time I had heard that. And since then, I've heard it on a number of occasions.

DOE Administrator: Yes. I think they should have counselors because a lot of these students don't know what the college expects when you, for example, turn in your application. You know, what the quality of the application should be. Like in my case, I was looking at my son's application, and I was telling him, "I don't think they're going to accept that."

These next two parents repeated the concern about the scarcity of college counselors, leaving much of the work up to the parents.

Professor: My son basically had a very successful experience coming out of the public schools system here. There are a couple of things where I would critique and criticize the public schools in that I think they could do a better job. If you talk to anyone whose child is going to elite private schools, they will tell you that those schools are really on top of the whole college process, whereas in the public school, particularly at the high school level, I never heard from my child's counselor. Maybe that was because there wasn't a problem, but I feel like I had to do the work in terms of researching how to get him into college, or how you would apply.

A second professor agreed that public high schools need to provide better college preparation assistance.

Professor: [I think the public schools should] really gear the college-bound kids for college. Give them the preparation, the information about the SAT classes, and encourage them to get the kind of preparation they need for that. That assistance isn't quite there. You have to kind of seek out the information, and you have to really be on top of it yourself.

But additional counselors are needed at the high schools — and not only to assist students with the college application process. Parents say counselors are also needed to follow up with students who may need extra help, as teenagers are liable to need counseling for any number of reasons. The parents recognize that the high student-counselor ratio makes it difficult for the public school counselor to give attention to individual students. Again, they believe that this issue needs to be made a priority.

University Administrator: For example, I'm hearing that one of my cousin's children at a private school is having a hard time focusing. You know, it's a teenage time. So he's not doing as well. But he must be intelligent enough to get into the school, so I know that's not it. But what the school does automatically is to assign him to a tutor. And they'll provide the tutoring services for him and set up the schedule for the tutor and make sure he's doing okay in the class.

But as long as public school parents take an active role in going over the courses that their children sign up for the next year, they'll be fine. I know we have to sign the card for the courses the year before.

Like my son, he wanted to take weightlifting as his elective. I don't particularly consider that worth the time you're going to spend in a year's course. You can take art. You can take something that has less homework maybe, but you can do weightlifting on your own time. (*Laughs.*)

And I don't know if other parents make those kinds of considerations when they're sitting down with their child and planning out their school year. So I think if you take the time and think about what they'll need for their future, then you can do just as good a job.

Q: One suggestion that's been coming up is the notion that the private schools have very good counselors in that they provide a lot of information and services for their children who want to go on to higher education. What you were also saying is that public schools have more students who may be the first one in their family to go to college, and they need that kind of assistance?

University Administrator: Yes. They need help because the parents oftentimes want their children to go to college, but they have no clue as to how to get them there. And being a senior in high school might be too late because you might not have adequately prepared yourself for the courses either. I can see that, and my experience with the counselors at the public high school have been mixed.

One counselor . . . is supposed to be one of the better college counselors on the island. She was quoted in the paper the other day, talking about what mainland-bound students will need and things like that. She's very busy, and she's good. She knows her stuff. There are some times, though, that I felt maybe she was just overloaded, and she could not provide the individual attention that would've helped us. But in general, she provided helpful hints and information on things to stay away from, which was also good because you get bombarded with stuff from schools.

I've talked to some of the counselors. They [each] have three hundred students that they have to take care of.

A related issue is that of lower expectations for students viewed as "average." The following parent talked about the experience with his daughter, who today, while successful, was not challenged to do her best in high school. He believes that students will respond to teachers' and counselors' expectations of them. He has observed that high expectations are held for those students in the GT or AP classes. His argument is that the "end goal" of public education ought to be high expectations for all students.

Nonprofit Executive: My daughter graduated from public high school. She certainly was allowed to choose courses that were less than challenging. She took a lot of electives that allowed her to not have to work very hard in order to pass them — although some of those electives had great value in her life.

She is doing very well for herself, but I don't believe that she was educated to the level that she could have been. And I think that when we talk about education, that that should be an end goal.

She did have a counselor for a short time who pushed her a little hard and told her, "You know, you can do a little better than that. You're able to achieve more than that, and we need to set you up in a slightly higher-level class." But students very quickly will fall into the patterns that the teachers expect of them, and if you don't expect high levels, then they will fall into those patterns. And as I said, I'm very happy with both my children. They're honest, they're bright, and they're self-sufficient. (*Laughs.*)

It would be unfair not to mention that there are students who are as well prepared here in the public high school; however, most of them have fallen into a different category, and they have been classified as Gifted and Talented. And because they're classified that way, the motivational factor, both on the part of parents and teachers, raises the bar to a higher level that the children are expected to meet. Perhaps the best thing you can do for your child before he leaves elementary school is get them classified as advanced placement and Gifted and Talented, whether or not that really holds true or not, but because the expectations will be so much higher.

Q: So there are high expectations for that subcategory of students?

Nonprofit Executive: Yes, absolutely. My concern is, as I said before, that I might sound that I'm negative toward public schools, but I'm not. What I am is very positive about public schools, but I know that there's a long way to go for them to be able to meet the kind of levels that they need to for most children.

Once again, if you have parents who are actively involved in their children's lives, those children tend to be more successful in school. And that, coupled with teachers who really care about really making a difference, small work groups of teachers who can really track a child's progress through a number of years, and great administrative leadership, now you can have children who can accomplish anything. And that's the end goal.

Having high expectations for all students requires strong educational leadership at a school site. Parents shared a belief in the important role of the school principal and how he or she creates a positive (or negative) school culture. Related to this issue is that of whom the principal hires to teach. Parents in this section talked about their occasional experiences with mediocre leadership and "the bad teacher."

During an interview with a couple, a mother talked about the impersonal nature of the communication with the high school principal versus their experiences with their children's elementary school principals. And both parents spoke about the role of the principal in establishing a school climate. They believe that the leadership at the high school was more effective when their oldest son attended the school, and that the current leadership has created a more lax atmosphere.

Q: Was the secondary school welcoming if you wanted to get more information regarding what was going on with your child?

Public School Teacher: I wouldn't say that. Well, I'm sure they were welcoming, but there were procedures. For example, "Call this number, and the teacher will call you back." It was sort of impersonal, and you didn't necessarily always get a call back when you wanted information.

You know, in elementary school, it's really clear. You have the parent-teacher conferences, and it's all set up so that both child and parent understand when we're going to meet and when we're going to talk. It doesn't happen at the secondary level.

CEO: I felt much closer to the teachers and the faculty in the elementary school.

Q: What role do you think size of the school plays? Was your elementary school smaller? Did the schools get larger as you went up to secondary schools?

CEO: There may have been an impact, but I think that it goes back to the fact that our children only had one teacher [per grade] in elementary school, as opposed to five or six when they go to middle school.

Public School Teacher: I wouldn't say that that's a bad thing. I think it's really the administration that needs to pull all that together because—if you compare, for instance, the high school's administration when our oldest child was there versus the administration when our youngest attended, you could see that things are a lot more lax, and expectations are not defined as clearly.

Q: So the key role of the principal is establishing the climate in the culture of this school?

Public School Teacher: Yes, regardless of size. The role of the principal is key. . . . The public high school got smaller from the time that our oldest was there to the time our youngest was there, so you would think that it would be easier, huh?

CEO: I think it was the leadership. The principal was very outstanding at the time my oldest son attended.

The next two parents talked about running into some poor teachers. The first talked about parents needing to be aware so they can find solutions. And this parent introduced the topic of unions when he mentioned that "teachers are protected in the public schools." (The role of the unions, both positive and negative, will be discussed in a later chapter.)

Q: What are your children's experiences?

Attorney: I think it's a mixed bag. There are certain departments in some of these schools in which there are a lot of bad teachers. They know the subject, but they're just bad teachers. And more than bad teachers, they're unfair. I think kids know fair from unfair, and unfair is not good. So our message as parents has got to be to support the teachers, unless the teaching is really bad. And we have talked to the principal on certain occasions about this. Groups of parents have gone in to talk to the principal.

You know, at private schools, if the parents are all complaining, then the teacher's gone. But the teachers are protected in the public schools. So if you're unlucky to get some of these teachers, then you have to have other methods. For example, some of the parents are getting together and hiring tutors for the Advanced Placement chemistry class because the regular AP, an excellent teacher, had to leave. The replacement teacher is just not very well qualified. So you have to be more proactive.

The second parent believes that the vice principal was responsible for hiring some poor teachers in one of the high school's departments, thereby highlighting the crucial role that principals play in developing school cultures.

Q: So do you feel that they were academically challenged all the way through high school?

Public School Teacher: No. They had some superior teachers, too. They really did. But it was mixed. The public high school had some poor teachers in one of the departments. It was a reflection of hiring. One of the vice principals was responsible for hiring in one department.

What Happens Post-Graduation?

In the final section, several parents talked about post-graduation. In earlier discussions, parents were self-reflective about their own peers, observing that they see no differences between those who graduated from private school and those from public school. As is true in the following sample of excerpts, parents indicated that there were no significant differences for their children.

Public School Teacher: She was a bit worried because she knew that [at her mainland college] all incoming freshmen from Hawai'i were from private schools. She was one of four from public schools. She just figured that everybody going to this university was going to be coming from a private school, but she found out that the mainland kids don't go to private school. They go to public school. . . . I think she had to put forth a little more effort, but she did well.

Computer Programmer: [This parent had children who went to both public and private schools.] It was not apparent to me that there was a major difference between the public and private schools. You can get good things out of public school. You just have to work a lot harder for it.

Where did the public high school graduates go to college? The parents I interviewed have children presently attending or who have graduated from the following colleges and universities:

California State University
Claremont College
Columbia University
Harvard University
Indiana University
Lewis and Clark College
Oregon State University
Purdue University
Stanford University
University of California at
    Berkeley
University of Chicago
University of Colorado
University of Hawai'i at Mānoa

University of Puget Sound
University of Texas at Austin
Washington State University
Washington University in St. Louis
Willamette University
Yale University
Case Western Reserve University
    School of Law
New York University School of Law
University of Hawai'i William S.
    Richardson School of Law
University of Hawai'i John A. Burns
    School of Medicine

In sum, whether at the elementary, middle, or high school level, the public school experiences of the children of these professionals were positive. Typically, the parents believe that their children were academically challenged, safe, and engaged in a variety of extracurricular activities, often in leadership positions.

Why report children's experiences in public schools? Hawai'i has the second-highest percentage (18 percent) in the nation of students attending private schools (Essoyan 2008, A4). Within this context, the parents in this study are "going against the grain" compared to many in their peer groups. What kinds of reactions did they receive from family, neighbors, and colleagues about their decision to send their children to public schools? That is the topic of the next chapter.

"Going Against the Grain"

Attorney: Actually, there're not too many people who have sent their kids to public school who are in my situation. So I'm alone in this, especially in here, in this office. But I kind of take pride in that. You know, I'm holding the banner for something.

In previous chapters, parents explained why they chose to send their children to public schools and have described their children's experiences. Their reality is in marked contrast to the belief in the community at large that Hawai'i's public schools are failing, and conversely, that the private schools are succeeding. I was interested in discovering how others reacted to the parents' decisions to send their children to public schools. In this chapter, the parents talk about the type of feedback they received. Typically, the decision to send their children to public schools found little support from peers, thus placing these parents in the position of "going against the grain" in their peer groups. Most of the feedback was in the form of daily conversations with family, neighbors, and professional colleagues.

In most cases these parents were very comfortable with their decisions, often based on a combination of factors, including a philosophical belief in public education and personal research conducted on the schools. However, there were cases in which these parents, all professionals, encountered peer pressure that resulted from nonconformity to the community norm by sending their children to public schools. This pressure increased when children attended public secondary schools. The professional community more readily accepted the idea that a number of public elementary schools have "good reputations" and thus generally were more likely to accept parents' decisions to send children to these public schools. But secondary schools, as noted earlier, are viewed by the community at large and, more specifically, the professional class as unsafe and low achieving. However, this study suggests that such beliefs typically were not substantiated by firsthand experience.

Adding to the difficulty of making such an "against-the-grain" decision is the impact of public school teachers who send their own children to private schools. For the children of the parents in this study, it was typical to have at least one public school teacher who sent his or her own children to private schools. Further, it was not unusual for a child's public school teacher to recommend that the parents in this study do the same. The reaction to these experiences was, by and large, negative: public school parents' feelings ranged from sadness to anger.

This issue of public school teachers sending their children to private schools was not on my original list of interview questions, but the topic was raised quickly and fairly regularly in the early interviews, so I decided to include it. I also chose to add interviews with public school educators who sent their children to private schools to find out their reasons for doing so.

Feedback from Peers and Family Members

Here, parents talked about whether or not their professional peers, family members, and friends accepted their decisions to send their children to public schools. Approximately twice as many were against these decisions as were in support of them. The following excerpt is from an interview with a couple who sent their children to public schools from elementary through high school. The children graduated and went on to attend mainland universities.

Both private and public school parents want "the best for their children," but the definition of what is "best" differs somewhat. The husband said that his colleagues chose private schools because they view it as "giving your child a better chance to succeed later on in life. . . . The child will be better prepared." Private schools also have higher status, generally. Conversely, this couple emphasized that the "best" education results from a combination of what happens in the home and in the school. Their decision to send their four children to public schools allowed this mother to stay home with them rather than have to continue working outside the home to contribute to private school tuitions.

This couple also discussed their belief in the importance of encouraging their children to be self-motivating and to be problem solvers. Both their personal values and the "real world" opportunities provided by attending public schools would help their children develop these traits. But the husband also talked about peer pressure from his professional colleagues who believe that a senior executive should be sending his children to one of the elite private schools.

Q: Was the decision to send your children to public schools supported by your colleagues at work, your family, and friends?

Public School Teacher: Well, not for my husband. (*Laughs.*)

CEO: Yes, not for me. I had a lot of pressure. I'd been an executive for a long time, and all my peer groups' children had gone to private schools. And they'd always ask me, "You're getting away with murder. How come you don't send your kids to private schools? Look at us." And I said, "Well, that's your decision. I made a decision. My wife and I have made our own decision to keep our kids in public school."

Q: Did they ever talk to you about why they made their decision?

CEO: Well, some of them went to private schools. Half of it is driven from someone coming from a private school, and the other half is driven by status. You know, they expect a senior executive to have [his/her] kids go to private school. It's kind of an expectation.

Public School Teacher: I think there's another strong influence. It's the belief that if you send your child to a private school, you're giving your child a better chance to succeed later on in life — that the child will be better prepared and will have an advantage later on.

Q: If you were in a conversation with a person who was sharing that belief, what do you say back to that person?

Public School Teacher: I don't think that I've been in any direct conversation.

CEO: I have. I can't argue with it. If that's what they believe they're paying for, then they should believe that their child should be getting a better education. I just think that the public schools can offer up just as much. And my response to them was that education really starts in the home. And that's why my wife and I made a conscious decision that she would stay at home. You know? And I shared that with them. We're making the sacrifice by having my wife not going to work and staying home because we firmly believe that education is the home and school together — rather than just buying a private school education and saying that that's what it's going to do.

A lot of my friends, in the end, have come back to me and said, "You know, you probably were right" because some of their kids haven't done well. So a private school education doesn't necessarily mean success.

And I was going to add that we always emphasized that it was up to the child to seek the knowledge. No matter what's available in your environment, if you're not going to seek it out and use it appropriately, then it doesn't really matter what's there. So we felt that they needed to build skills so that they can make a determination about what their needs were, or how they were interacting. If things were going well, good, and if not, then, how do you solve your problem? So that's another thing that we emphasized.

Q: So you had to be secure in your belief system if all your colleagues are sending their children to private schools?

CEO: I wouldn't say that that is the bottom line, but I would say it's a force. It's peer pressure. I got peer pressure put on me. You know, "Why are you sending your kids to public school? You should be sending your kids to private school, like we all are." So it's peer pressure. Kind of like them giving you the feeling that you should send your children to private school. They're going to do automatically better. I don't think that's right.

In this next excerpt, the parent talked about his colleagues' muted reaction to his decision to send his child to public schools, especially beyond elementary, leaving him feeling that they thought he was "nuts" or "cheap."

Professor: I know a lot of people from Hawai'i who have moved either to California or New York City, and we would generally meet some of these people at parties, or faculty stuff [on the mainland]. We'd ask about the schools in Hawai'i. And so we had heard of [a public elementary school]. People said, "If you're going to send your kid to public school, send them to [this public elementary school]."

We'd been sending our kids to the public schools [on the mainland], but the general assumption was that when we got here, if we weren't going to send them to [the public elementary school], then we were going to send them to private school. Certainly when my child graduated from public elementary school, it was almost an unstated assumption that he would be going to a private school. I think the fact that he's not is surprising.

Q: And what kind of feedback do you get from your colleagues?

Professor: I think they think we're nuts. (*Laughs.*) And I think that the overwhelming, unstated assumption that people make about the reason that we're sending him to a public middle school is that we're cheap. And I think that's the only basis by which anyone, on any level, understands why we're doing this.

Q: So, when you're engaged in this conversation with your colleagues, what actually do they say?

Professor: They don't say anything. It's sort of interesting. I mean, they say, "Oh, that's interesting. Do you like it?" And we say, "Yes, we think it's great. And we're very happy." And that's the end of the conversation.

The feedback this next attorney received focused on the "courage" or "guts" she had to have in order to make the decision to send her children to public schools from elementary through high school. She said her colleagues associate "the best education" with private schools only.

Q: Was this decision to send your two children to public schools supported by your friends, your colleagues at work, your neighbors? Did they think this was a good idea?

Attorney: No. (*Laughs.*) I mean, I get these weird comments like, "Wow, you have a lot of courage," or, you know, "That takes a lot of guts," or—it's just really strange. And it was the easiest decision for me. I told my husband that of all the things I've been involved in, with public education, that's the one I think I'll probably get most credit for—that I had the guts to send my kids into public education, and that was the easiest one for us. It's like, "Wow, how do you do that?"

Q: How did they come to have that kind of perception? To send your children to public school takes a lot of guts?

Attorney: I think they just think that the quality of education they're going to get there is not up to par. Therefore, if you're a professional—and aren't you striving for your child to become a professional? And wouldn't you want them to have the best education for them to achieve that?

Q: So they believe that if your goal is to have your child become a professional, you cannot go through this public school system?

Attorney: Right.

This next father, who himself went to private school, talked about the decision he and his wife made to send their children, who are bright and highly motivated, to public schools because of their belief that they would do well in the public schools. He also believes that a public school education is better preparation for "the real world," a common belief among the parents in this study, as noted earlier. Nonetheless, several of his professional colleagues tried to talk him out of his decision. They "believe that private school is the only way to go." But he is a private school graduate, and he doesn't see significant differences between private and public schools. He also mentions that private schools have more status.

Q: Were there people at work that would talk to you about your decision and try to convince you to send them to private schools?

Vice President: Absolutely. There are several people that I work with who send their children to private schools, and they always, always used to ask about why we weren't sending our kids to private schools. My belief is that our children are bright kids. They're highly motivated, and I believe that they will do well in public schools. I think that the entire experience is probably going to be more realistic in a public school rather than a private school, as far as what life is like.

Q: When you explained this idea, did they understand what you were saying?

Vice President: They understood what I was saying, but they weren't buying it. And I think part of the reason is people have to justify why they're spending ten thousand dollars a year per child to go to a private school. If you're that committed to a project—say you have several kids and you're spending twenty, thirty thousand a year, it's kind of hard to say, "Oh, private school and public school are similar." You really have to believe that private school is the only way to go.

You know what's really funny is that a lot of the people that were sending kids to private schools in my office come from a public school background. I don't know if it was somehow drilled into them that private schools are always better than public schools, but being in a private school, coming from a private school and a private university [myself], I think, yeah, there are some differences, but I don't think they're significant enough to make that much of a difference. I think part of it is status.

An executive banker shared his knowledge with the community-held perception that private schools are the schools of choice in Hawai'i, especially among the professional class, even if individuals have not actually conducted any research on individual public schools. They view private schools as providing the best education for their children.

This parent also noticed that when his colleagues praise his daughter's competencies, they always attribute them to good parenting only and not to a good education in the public schools.

Executive Banker: Oh, I think there's a strong sense downtown [in the business community] that private schools are the best place for a kid to be: [private schools] have the best facilities and the best libraries; kids from that school go on to college and network; and therefore, if I'm trying to do right by my kid, that's where I ought to send them.

Q: Does anybody support your decision to send your child to public schools?

Executive Banker: No, none of the colleagues who have sent their children to private schools. [In our child's play group, ours is] the only one of the six families with the kids in public school. All the rest are in private. They have also known that that was a very conscious decision with us. We're very committed [to their attending] public schools all the way.

Q: Have they done any kind of research on the public schools?

Executive Banker: No. I think they automatically assume that a good parent in Hawai'i wants their kids in private schools.

Q: So with your peer group, would you say that the parents don't know what's going on really in the public schools?

Executive Banker: I think there are a lot of perceptions. What I'm most struck by is people tell me, "Gee, your child is a great kid." And they really enjoy being around her, and she's grown up so much, and she just seems so much in command of herself. They always ask why. I mean it never occurs to them that maybe it's public school, and maybe that's hula, and maybe it's some other things. That it isn't just an accident or it isn't just, "Okay, we like [her parents], and they must be good parents and therefore, in spite of where she's in school, she's a good kid." You know, I think if they thought that some kid who went to private school looks or acts smart or whatever, they would try to say, "Well, that must because they're at private school."

This physician's professional colleagues and friends raised their eyebrows "a little bit," but they didn't question the decision to send his child to public school. He talked also about the firsthand research he and his spouse conducted on both public and private school options. But a social gathering with friends made obvious the unstated assumption that professionals in Hawai'i send their children to private schools.

Q: So have you received much support from your friends and professional colleagues for your decision?

Physician: Maybe their eyebrows are raised a little bit, yeah, but they don't question it. That's just our personalities, and they wouldn't do that. But I don't think most of them even did the research that we did. I don't think that most of them went and looked at the school like we did and walked around and met with teachers and watched them teach. We went and looked at private schools. We looked in the classroom. We were trying to decide what to do at that point because we weren't that happy with the little private school where the children were. It was really small.

We went to [a private school]. We observed the teachers and the classrooms, and we went to the public schools and observed the teachers and the classrooms, and we felt that the public school looked at least as good as what we saw at the private. Our friends — do they support that decision? I don't know. Their reaction is not negative or anything — maybe a little bit of a raised eyebrow.

Q: You said they did not go and do the research?

Physician: I don't think so.

Q: So would you say they were making their decisions based on a shared belief among your peer group and also reinforced by the media?

Physician: Right. An example . . . we had a gathering of some friends and family not too long ago and there must have been six or eight friends there with their children. And one of the fellas looked around the table and was making a toast saying, "Here's to the two hundred thousand dollars per year of education sitting around this table." You know, "of private school education" sitting around this table. Forgetting about us. And so I chimed in and said, "And ten dollars for public school." And he later apologized to me. He said, "Oh, I'm really sorry, I didn't mean to . . ." you know. What he did is he looked around and he realized everybody's going to private school at this table. He forgot about our family, and he felt bad about what he said, you know. And I said, "Don't worry about it." But that's just kind of a little anecdote.

Q: What about your medical colleagues?

Physician: I am, to my knowledge, virtually the only physician parent at this public high school, and there are a lot of physicians who live in my area.

A number of public school parents talked about conversations that take place with other parents when children are in the same play group. During these conversations, parents talk about which schools they are going to send their children. In this parent's case, all the other members of the play group decided to send their children to private schools. Later, when this same group got together for a reunion, they critiqued this parent's (who also happens to be a public school teacher) decision to continue to keep her oldest daughter in public school for her secondary education.

Q: And is this a decision that your friends and neighbors and colleagues at work support?

Public School Teacher: No. When my oldest daughter was in a play group, about two to three [years old], there were other parents in this play group, and everybody in that play group sent their kids to private school except for me. And after the play group we lost touch because people moved, but we got together just when my oldest was going into high school. They just told me that she was just going to be wasting her time there, and that I wasn't really giving her a challenge, even though they really didn't know her at that point.

The next parents interviewed are military officers. The military presence in Hawai'i is large, and there is a fair amount of concern among military personnel about Hawai'i's public schools. The community-held belief that "public schools are failing and private schools are succeeding" has traveled through the "military grapevine." In the following excerpt, an officer talked about his peers' reactions to his decision to send his children to public schools, as well as about some of the sources that reinforce this perception of public schools.

Q: And so when you put your children in public schools, did you get any support from your peers by doing that?

Military Officer: No, it was very strongly questioned and [they were] surprised. The majority of my peers, as senior officers, had their children in private schools. I don't know that for sure. I would say that. And it's a safe bet.

Q: Did they go and visit public schools?

Military Officer: No. I don't really think they did.

Q: So, they were basing their decision on what they were told by their colleagues?

Military Officer: They were basing their decisions on what they were told by their colleagues, and what the community told them. So the community tells them several things — by turning on the TV, by picking up the newspaper. And what the newspaper and TV say over and over again is that Hawai'i schools are in a crisis, whether it's the repair and maintenance of the schools, the inadequate pay for teachers, the teacher shortage, the curriculum, the school system not being able to manage its own affairs — do they know where money is going?

The second military officer received some support for her decision to send her children to public schools. Because of her willingness to be an advocate for public school and to talk about her choice, another officer talked to her about her experiences and also decided to send his children to public school. He was happy with his decision.

Q: When you made the decision to send your children to the public schools, did your fellow officers support this decision?

Military Officer: Some did. My peers were supportive of it. The senior officers were like, "You don't want to do that." My kids are in elementary school, and I can't imagine that it would be so horrific that we wouldn't be able to notice a problem and be able to interject, and they said, "Well, it is worse when you get into the higher grades." So some of my peers were supportive, but my senior officers were not so supportive.

Q: So they send their children to private school?

Military Officer: Yes. Across the board, the senior officers send their children to private school.

Q: Are there any senior officer families who have their children in public schools?

Military Officer: That I know of, no. So that's probably part of the problem right there. The senior folks are sending out a message. I think they just look at me like I'm nuts. (*Laughs.*) Oh, no, I take that back. Just the other day, I had an officer come up to me and say, "You know, I heard that you're really happy with your kid's schools, and I want to put mine in a public school system." And he wanted to know what school they go to. And so I told him. So he did ask me, and I thought, "Oh, good. I'm glad to hear that." And I think he's actually going to move out to that community. And there's a public school system that he was talking about yesterday — an elementary school that his kids are going to be going to. And he's very happy.

The last parent in this section is a state legislator who found that he had to defend his decision to send his children to public schools.

Legislator: I do find myself, in social situations, having to justify why I chose to send my children to public school, especially to people who choose to send their children to private school. I don't look for validation from colleagues or people, so it's less important to me than it would be to other people. I do take responsibilities for my own decisions, whatever they are. I was determined to make the best decision. I truly believe that there are elementary schools, for sure, that are clearly better than most of the private schools here. And there are intermediate and high schools that do as good a job as private schools.

While the majority of parents received negative feedback regarding their decision to send their children to public schools, this was not true in all cases. In the next two excerpts, parents whose children were in elementary schools—especially those with "high test scores" or a "good reputation"—did not receive any negative comments.

Q: Do you think that you were going against the grain by choosing public education for your daughter?
Professor: No, certainly not through elementary school.
Q: Then going to a public elementary school is not considered "going against the grain"? That's perfectly acceptable?
Professor: Well, only with [a certain public elementary school], for some reason. You know, that school, then, had very high test scores, and it had a reputation. It wasn't just . . .
Q: . . . not any elementary public school?
Professor: Right.

It is interesting that in this next excerpt, a dentist's patients assumed that he would have sent his children to private school rather than public school.

Q: And was this decision to send your children to public schools supported by your colleagues?
Dentist: There weren't any negative responses because of where they were going. I think it was because the reputation of [the public school] is very strong. When they publish the test scores, they're always on top.

Well, I get this sense, when you're socializing, it's "Where do your children go to school?" And there's always this—I don't know if it's pressure that I have of my own, or I just sense that people have this pressure to have their kids going to private school. If the kid isn't going to one of them, and I say they're going to [the public school], they go, "Oh, well, that's a good school. I wish I could save my money and have my son or daughter go there."

And as a dentist, you talk to patients, and they ask you where your children are going to school, and you tell them public school. Some might say, "Well, I thought they'd be going to private school, Doc." You know, that kind of thing.

A public school administrator talked about the assumption that his son developed at his public elementary school. He thought he would be going to private school for his secondary education because most of his sixth-grade classmates were transferring to private schools. This father had to explain that as a public school educator, he has a commitment to public education, and he would therefore be continuing their education in the public schools. Within his family, the decision to send his children to public school was accepted as a "private family decision."

DOE Administrator: A couple of funny stories — when my son was in the sixth grade at his public school, he came home one day and he says, "What private school am I going to?" And I said, "Well, what do you mean? Why are you asking this question?" He said, "Because most of my friends now are going to go to private schools."

And so I looked at my wife, and I said, "We have to sit down and talk about this." So we had to actually sit down and talk to the kids about my commitment as a public school educator, and why they're not going to go to private schools. And with that one explanation, they were satisfied, and they said, "Okay," and that was it. And we never heard anything more. . . . I think they bought my rationale, and they understood it.

Q: So your children's friends go off to private school after sixth grade? Did any of your colleagues or friends or family disagree with your decision to send them to secondary public school?

DOE Administrator: No. It was a family decision and both my wife and I supported it. My wife is a proud graduate of a public high school. It's just a family thing that we decided. And the other thing we said — [it would allow them] to go to the mainland for college.

What Do Private School Parents Have To Say?

Two of the five participants in the study who were identified by peers as "private school parents" actually sent their children to public elementary schools. Both parents talked about why sending their children to public elementary school was accepted by their peers, but that would not have been the case with public middle schools.

The first private school parent said attending public elementary and high schools would be "okay," but not the public middle schools because "everybody says" all public middle schools have negative reputations.

Q: Was the decision to send your son to public elementary school supported by your families and friends, and colleagues at work? And then, was the decision to send him to private secondary school also supported by family, friends, and colleagues?

Private School Parent: Yes, and yes.

Q: Were they just saying whatever works—whatever is best for you?

Private School Parent: Yes, and you know the reputation of middle school is—everybody says, if they can just miss that and go to high school, then it would be okay, but . . .

Q: So the reputation about middle school is negative—all public middle schools?

Private School Parent: Yes, all.

The second private school parent's colleagues also supported her family's decision to have her children in public elementary school. Again, both public elementary and high schools were viewed as acceptable choices, but public middle schools were perceived negatively.

Private School Parent: A lot of people understood and supported the decision for my son going on to [private school] after public elementary school. A lot of my friends have their children at this public school. It's a good school. It really is a good school. And I tell everybody that it's a great school. If you get your child into that school, it's wonderful.

It was really like family down there, and I really felt like I was leaving my family. I think a lot of my colleagues understand the choices of private schools. And even friends I know say, "I wish I could afford private school," especially when you're looking at intermediate.

Q: So the problem comes not so much with the concern for elementary because you can find a good elementary school, but the problems and the worries come from intermediate public school?

Private School Parent: Yes.

Q: Do people talk about the high schools the same way they talk about the intermediate schools?

Private School Parent: Not necessarily. I have a friend whose son just graduated from [public] high school this year. I think any kid, in any environment, if they're focused, can excel. And he just won scholar-athlete of the year, and he's getting a full ride to [college]. But, you know, he's got a great family—very, very supportive. They also have a religious background that is important to them, and he's got great friends, and he's in sports, and he's really focused. I think that if your child doesn't have this kind of support system, he can be easily more lost in a public school.

In sum, the majority of professionals in this study who chose to send their children to public schools were not supported by their professional peers. The exception to this typical response was when the children attended one of the public elementary schools with a "good reputation." These responses raise the question about the underlying degree of negativity toward public education in Hawai'i, especially by the professional class, who hold a lot of power in any community.

An alternative community-held belief would be the view that both public and private schools are viable alternatives, especially since there is a consensus that elementary public schools can provide standards as high as those of private elementary schools. And while this consensus doesn't presently exist for public secondary schools, evidence does exist of programs at individual middle and high schools that can provide an academically challenging and well-rounded education.

Unfortunately, another factor contributing to the environment in which parents need to "go against the grain" to choose public schools is the impact of public school educators and Hawai'i Board of Education (BOE) members sending their own children to private schools — a topic addressed in the following section.

When Public School Educators Send Their Children to Private Schools

Public School Teacher: I remember very distinctly, years ago, it was one of our institute days . . . And I remember whoever was the speaker kind of really charging the teachers sitting there with that call to have their own kids in public school. And out loud, in front of this big assembly, the speaker was saying, "How many of you are sending your kids to private school?" And it was that blatant. And I'll never forget that because I was sitting with my friends, and we were all public school teachers. And I realized that on either side of me were parents of private school kids.

Q: Did they have any reaction to that?

Public School Teacher: They knew what they were doing and why they were going to do it. But I remember feeling, you know, I knew why the speaker was telling us that.

As I mentioned earlier, this topic was not in my original set of interview questions, but parents wanted to talk about it. And it's not unusual to read about this subject in letters to the editor and in newspaper columns, such as the following question from a parent to June Watanabe of the "Kokua Line" help column.

> Can you tell me what the ratio is for public school teachers' children attending private schools? This has always been my concern. I had planned to send my daughter to public school but noticed my public school teacher friends all had their children in private schools. I then decided against public schools because if the employees have no confidence in their own system, there must be something wrong. (J. Watanabe 2001, paragraph 1)

In the May 2001 *Honolulu Magazine* article titled "The Death of Public School," the author stated that 45 percent of government-school teachers send their children to private schools (Napier 2001). This is a controversial statistic because there is no current local survey to support or refute that number. However, the practice of public school educators in Hawai'i sending their children to private schools is common.

So I decided to add a question on the experiences of parents whose children's teachers send their own children to private schools. I was curious about the impact of the teachers' decisions on these parents. I typically quoted the *Honolulu Magazine* statistic and the newspapers letters to the editor addressing this topic.

When legislators, public school teachers, public school principals, and BOE members send their own children to private schools, parents view it as undermining confidence in the public school system. The public school educators are perceived by the parents as not believing that this public school system can provide "the best" education for their own children. It is difficult for educators to be viewed as advocates for public schools when they send their children elsewhere.

Parents in the study also talked about reacting with sadness, doubt, and anger when they learn their children's teachers send their own children to private schools. In a number of instances, parents reported that teachers suggested that the parents take their children out of public school and send them to private schools. One typical response from the parents was to use analogies to other professions. Several parents talked about how odd it would seem if other professionals indicated a similar lack of confidence in an organization for which they worked (e.g., a lawyer employed by one firm recommending that his or her clients take their business to another law firm).

There are over thirteen thousand public school teachers in Hawai'i, and, as in most large organizations, their level of competence of ranges from exceptional to poor. Parents in this study speculate about connections between educators who view teaching "as a job" to pay for household expenses, including private school tuition, and those who are uninspiring, uninvolved, or unwilling to make the effort to work at solving problems at a particular school. It is beyond the scope of this study to state with any certainty whether there are any such connections between public school teachers sending their children to private schools and professional effort "on the job." Indeed, there are many instances of just the opposite. Nonetheless, this practice creates such speculation among a number of parents in this study.

Related to this speculation is the idea that public school educators who send their children to private schools identify with those private schools rather than with the public schools in which they work, thus setting up a conflict as to where to focus one's extracurricular energies.

Legislators were also mentioned. These parents point out that, no matter how well intended, legislators whose children are in private schools may be less likely to understand complex issues related to public schools, as they would not have had recent firsthand experience with such issues. A similar case can be made for BOE members. In 2005, for example, only two BOE members had children in public schools (DePledge 2005, B1).

It is important to note that no one in the study suggested that public school educators — whether teachers, principals, DOE administrators, or BOE members — have no right to make the choice to send their children to private schools. Rather, what they discussed was the collective, negative impact of these individual decisions; it reinforces the community-held belief that "public schools are failing and private schools are succeeding. Send your children to private schools." This impact contributes to the development and reinforcement of the social climate in which professionals have "to go against the grain" of their peer groups if they decide to send their children to public schools.

Lack of Faith

We'll begin with parents who talked about their belief that when public school educators send their children to private schools, it undermines the community's confidence in the public schools. It sends the message that these educators don't have faith in the public schools' ability to do a good job educating their own children.

This first parent talked about attending an open house program at her child's public high school where the teacher, upon introducing himself, told the parents that he sent his daughter to private school. The reaction to his words, she said, was a physical one as parents' facial expressions changed. The message she received was that it was okay for them to send their children to public schools, but not for him.

Q: You said that as a public educator that you wanted to be a model, and as a public educator you need to have faith in the public education system. There's a perception that a fairly high percentage of public school teachers send their children to private schools.

University Administrator: I know. I recall when we went to an open house at [a public high school], and the teacher there said, "We welcome your son or daughter to [the public high school]. It's a really good school," and he went on to say that he really believes that your son or daughter will get educated in a public school here, and this and that. And then he says, "Well, I'm going to tell you a little bit about myself." He was a graduate of [another public high school], and then he says he sends his daughter to private school. And I was like, "What?" And so everybody there—their faces kind of changed. So I know it affects parents. It's like, "It's okay for you, but it's not okay for me." I don't know—that just stuck with me.

This sentiment is reflected in additional statements of concern over public school educators' choices of private schools for their own children. I read the following two letters to the editor to the next parent, who is a legislator.

If there were a requirement that all elected officials send their children to public schools instead of private schools, I believe public education in Hawaiʻi would be a top priority. Because their children's education would be directly affected, the lawmakers would be more inclined to appropriate the funds. (Otake 2001)

I propose that every elected official be required to enroll his or her children in public schools. . . . Perhaps then our decision makers will have a vested interest in making meaningful improvements to public education. (Gon 2001)

I asked the legislator-parent to talk about these letters. He said he estimated that about 50 percent of the legislators do send their children to private schools. (That actually is a fairly accurate estimate; the 2003 KITV4 News Researchers' Survey results stated that 53 percent of legislators send their children to private school.) But, he said, regardless of that fact, public education remains a top priority for legislators. He then responded to my question about public school teachers who send their children to private schools. He has asked teachers why they make that decision, telling them it seems to indicate that they don't trust the public schools. Their response: it's true — they don't.

Legislator: Public education is a top priority for legislators, whether people believe that or not. When the economy was down, that was the only department budget maintained, compared to sixteen other departments.

Many of the legislators don't have children, or their children are grown. There are a few legislators who have young children and, off the top of my head, I would say about 50 percent send their children to public schools. The others do send their children to private schools. Several have sent their children to public schools, and they were disillusioned like many others, and then went to private schools. Most of them could not afford it.

Q: What is the impact of DOE teachers who send their children to private schools?

Legislator: I ask [principals and teachers] constantly. "Why would you send them to private schools? That tells me you don't trust the public schools." The teachers responded, "Yes." The principals responded, "Yes." They don't trust the public schools, which is terrible.

I shared the 2001 *Honolulu Magazine* statistic with the father in the next interview and asked him about the impact. He said it would be like his working for one company as a contractor, then hiring another contractor (from another company) to build his house. It raises questions about whether one has too little faith in one's own institution. He also questions the accuracy of the statistic. For him, the bottom line is that the message conveyed is this: public school teachers who make such choices don't have faith in the very system in which they work.

Q: So, what do you think is the impact on the system of public schools if you have a very high percentage of public school teachers sending their children to private schools?

Nonprofit Executive: I think the impact is what you just read me. And that is, that if you run an institution, whether it be a school or not, and you are unwilling to have your own children serviced by that [institution], it would be like me hiring a contractor to build my house while I was working for another contractor. It says that I don't have enough faith in the company that

I work for to build my own home. I mean, it's a very interesting analogy, but the reality says that the public school teachers don't have faith in the system in which they work.

I'm not sure that that number is completely accurate — 45 percent, did you say? Yeah, that sounds awfully high to me. But whether it's accurate or not, the fact that some public school teachers choose not to send their children to public schools says to me, and probably to the public at large, that they do not have faith that the system in which they are working is doing an adequate job.

The following attorney made a similar analogy. He indicated that he had never participated in discussions about this topic nor heard this topic raised in the community at large, but he thought such a community conversation would be beneficial. He also believes it is unprofessional for public school teachers to advise parents to send their children to private schools.

Attorney: I think if one of my lawyers was telling our clients that they really would do better at another law firm, I don't think that lawyer should be in our firm. That lawyer should go work for that other law firm. Now, we allow a teacher in the public education system to advise parents to pull their students out of the public education system and send them to the competition.

I think the union would have a big part to play in it because — I mean, I support public teachers, and I think that they ought to be paid more, but it's a chicken or egg situation because very frequently, they don't act professional. Advising kids to go elsewhere, to me, is not a very professional thing to do.

After having been stationed in a number of geographical areas, this next parent, a military officer, came to realize that any state has both good and bad schools. And in his perspective, public school teachers who send their children to private schools convey the message that they don't value their own institution. He also speculates about the impact this lack of faith has on the way they teach and the way they perceive their students.

Military Officer: It says a lot to me that public school teachers would rather have their children in a private school system than in the system in which they're working. They don't value their own institution enough to invest their children. . . . If it's not good enough for their kids, then, I don't know, I would just think that it really could affect the way that they teach, and the way that they perceive the students in their school.

I hope that the perception changes soon because there are some really good schools out there. And there are some really bad ones; but you know what — if you go to [another state], I can pick out some really bad schools there. And I've heard a lot of talk about military folks who want the Department of Defense [DoD] to come in and set up schools, and I think that that would be a very big mistake.

Just "a Job"

In this section, parents talked about their perception that public school teachers who send their children to private schools view teaching as a mere "job" rather than a profession. They speculated about how this might have a negative impact on the teachers' perceptions of public school students, their commitment to solving the schools' problems, and their willingness to support extracurricular activities at the public schools.

The first parent thought it was "sad" that public school teachers don't seem to believe in the system enough to enroll their own children.

Q: Do you have an opinion about the issue about public school teachers sending their children to private schools?

Vice President: Yes. I believe that it is really sad to see people like public school teachers who don't believe in the work that they do enough to send their kids to that system. It's like saying, "I'm part of the system, but I don't believe our system is good enough to let my kids come here." And that's really a shame. It kind of shows how the public school teachers view the public school system. They themselves don't believe the public school system is fit for teaching.

Q: What kind of impact do you think that has?

Vice President: Well, I think it relates back to the way the teachers do their jobs. You have some very good teachers. You have some teachers that are not very good. And the teachers who are not very good view teaching as a job. Teaching is not a job. It's a profession. It's a career. It's kind of like a religion. A good teacher believes that what they're doing is very, very important. And it's not an eight-to-five job. It's a career. But you have a lot of people that go to schools and believe that teaching is basically an eight-to-five job. I think the kids are the biggest losers.

Thinking back to his college days, when he worked as a tutor at a public school, another father remembered hearing public school teachers refer to their work as a job that provides the money "to pay for private school."

Attorney: I've known of at least three [of my kids'] teachers who send their kids to private school.

Q: Do you think that's a problem?

Attorney: (*Sighs.*) I would think so because what kind of message are you sending if you send your kids to private school while you work at a public school? I was tutoring in the public schools when I was in college, and I would hear a lot of that [conversation] from the intermediate school teachers.

Q: That they were using this as a job?

Attorney: As a job, yes. You know, typically it would be — okay, the husband has one job and the wife is a teacher. The husband makes enough to pay the mortgage, and then the wife's salary would be enough to pay for private school.

The next parent, a public school teacher who sent her children to public schools, addressed this issue in her interview. She believes that a professional would view teachers as responsible for collaborating to make any needed improvements in their classroom rather than merely complaining about problems.

Public School Teacher: There's no way they would send their kids [to public school]. Even though they themselves are public school teachers. I think it's that belief that "I'm doing the best for my child: I'm sending him to a private school."

I can tell you what happened at one public school because one of my son's teachers has one child, and she sent that child to private [school]. I feel my son is bright, and I wanted him to be challenged. When he was turning in work that I didn't think was up to snuff, I would say to her, "You know, I can tell him that I'm not happy with it, but when he turns around and tells me you're happy with it, then, I don't win, and neither does he. You're not making him perform up to what he could do." And I've talked to her twice and said, "You're not challenging him, and I want you to." But she never did. My personal feeling was that she knew he was never going to be going to a private school, and for her, it was just a job. It was just someplace to go — and since her attitude was, "You're not going to private school — here, you can do mediocre work, and I don't have to work hard at making you grow."

Most of the public school teachers I know send their kids to private schools, so I don't have this conversation with them. (*Laughs.*)

Q: So nobody talks about it?

Public School Teacher: [No.] And, you know, teachers don't tend to squeal or say anything about the bad teachers. So when teachers aren't doing their job or pulling enough weight, or trying to motivate the students or trying new things, nothing gets done. And we had one teacher that left because of that — because she wanted to try new things and get her grade level going in a kind of different direction. She met too much resistance from all of them, even though the parents there loved her and the kids loved her because her class was just so wonderful.

I guess the only thing that I can think of is that if I'm teaching at a school, and I see the other teachers treating it as just a job — you know, "I'll come in and do my work, and then I'm going home"— then yes, I don't think I'd want my child to go to that school if that's the kind of teacher that they're going to have.

Q: Would a teacher's attitude be influenced by the fact that his (or her) child may not be in a public school?

Public School Teacher: So kind of like, "Which comes first?" (*Laughs.*) I don't know. I'm assuming that most teachers start teaching before they have children, and so they're seeing what's going on at their school and perhaps where it's lacking, and so then they will choose to send their children elsewhere.

But to me, that's a real reflection on me. If that were me, and I was teaching with these teachers and I thought they were "ugh!" then that would also be a reflection on me. "How come we're not doing better? We have to work together to make our school the best it can be." And I had this conversation with this teacher that I work with. She didn't send her kids to public school, and I said, "That's a reflection on you! If you think public school teachers are bad. " She didn't quite know what to say. Out of the teachers at our school, I don't think she's a very good teacher. She doesn't seem to enjoy her job.

One father connected this type of decision by some public school teachers with their unwillingness to participate in the public school's extracurricular activities. It raises the dilemma of "divided loyalty," given the time constraints faced by most families.

Consulting Firm Executive: I would say I find this really interesting that a lot of teachers aren't willing to go the extra mile in terms of helping out at the school in extracurricular activities. They don't show up to the sporting teams and all this.

Q: Do you think that there's a connection between the percentage of teachers who send their children to private schools, and the —

Consulting Firm Executive: The demise of public schools? Absolutely. (*Laughs.*)

Q: — lack of participation in the civic life of the public schools?

Consulting Firm Executive: Oh, absolutely. Let's just use, as an example, a particular private school — if you don't participate in the fund-raising activities of your private school, you're out of there, or your kid's out of there. It's part of the contract.

Q: It's part of the school culture?

Consulting Firm Executive: Exactly. But what does it do, though, to the public school teacher who sends his or her kid to the private school? Essentially, then, all the time that they could be really enhancing their own profession as a public school teacher gets siphoned off to do fund-raising for the private school, where they're sending their kids. So they're working at cross-purposes.

"Take Your Children out of Public Schools"

Parents talked about their children's teachers who not only sent their own children to private schools, but also recommended that the parents do the same. There are valid reasons for any public education teacher to recommend an alternative school for a child. However, these parents said the message they got from their children's teachers is that bright children should be in private school.

This father was stunned to hear of children's teachers or principals recommending that parents move their children out of public school. He felt that such an opinion damages the public's faith in the school system.

Attorney: One person [I know] who's an attorney — the teacher comes up to him and says, "You really should send your kids to private school." That just takes you aback when their own teachers are saying that. Or the principal is saying that your child is so bright, you should send him to private school. It's like, "Hello?" But that happens a lot. I think it really does undermine people's confidence in the system.

The following parent describes how her daughter's teacher assumed she would be enrolled in private school after completing public elementary school.

University Administrator: Her sixth grade teacher said, as [my daughter] was exiting out of elementary school, "Oh, you know, you didn't ask me for a letter of recommendation." So I said, "Oh, I didn't know that they needed a letter of recommendation for public middle school." And she said, "Oh, no. This is for private school." And I said, "Oh, no, you know, we're going to send our daughter to [a public middle school]." And she says, "You are?" You know: "Really, you don't — a student like your daughter, you should send her to private school." And so I said, "No, I think she'll do fine at [a public middle school] and [a public high school]." She said, "Oh, I guess so." And she kind of left it like that. . . .

And even going to public elementary school, people asked if we were going to test her to go to private school, or at least just take the test. They told us, "Take the test." And I said no because we had no intention of sending her there.

The next father also observed a lack of confidence in the public school system in the actions of public school teachers and administrators.

Technology Consultant: It's also sad that, in public schools, the teachers or other administrators of public schools send their children to private schools. They don't have the confidence in their own jobs. So that's sad.

Q: Have any teachers or principals ever tried to counsel you to test your son and send him to private schools?

Technology Consultant: No. No. They asked me the question, though. They said, "How come you don't send your kid, your son, to private school?"

When the next father moved to Hawai'i, he conducted research on the public schools. After making a decision about which high school he wanted his child to attend, he visited the principal. She told him "the best" for his son would be private school.

Q: Did you find principals or teachers trying to convince you to send your children to private schools?

Consulting Firm Executive: Oh yes, absolutely. And they're matter-of-fact. When I went [to visit the school] — and I always went and introduced myself to the principal — she says, "I think you should consider private schools." I said, "The reason why I'm here at [this public high school] is because this is the best public school by far [of] what I've looked at, and I'm a little chagrined that you would say that I should send my . . ." She said, "Well, don't you want the best for your kid?" I said, "This is the best for my kid." I gave her the reasons. She replied, "Well, I'm glad you feel that way." And I said, "Well, I'm sad that you feel the way you do."

Another father recounts how a principal whose children attended a private school asked him and his wife when they were going to have their children tested for admittance to the same private school. Instead of promoting and providing information on opportunities in the schools within his public school complex, this principal conveyed this message: "Look, public education isn't good enough for my own kids. Why do you think it's good enough for yours?"

Q: Well, you mentioned earlier something about the issue about public school teachers and principals sending their children to private schools. What impact do you think that that has?

Attorney: I think it has a great impact. Our elementary school principal, by grade two, was asking us when are we testing our children for private school because her kids went to private school, and that we really ought to send our kids to the same private school. And this is a principal in the public education system, who ought to be saying, "You know, your next level is this middle school, and they have great things, and you really ought to go visit this school. And these are the courses that you might be interested in, and then the next level is the high school."

But there isn't this cross-selling. There isn't this complex marketing. Beyond that, there's a personal kind of plea that says, "Look, public education isn't good enough for my own kids. Why do you think it's good enough for yours?" And there are very few parents, I think, who are equipped to say, "I don't believe you, and I'm going to prove you wrong." Or, "By the way, I'm going to start speaking out to undo the bad you're doing by telling all the parents that you're wrong."

And so I've been [speaking out] since [my kids were in] elementary school. And there's a hard-core group of parents, some of whom have come back to me and said, "You know what? We sent our kid to [public schools], and we're so much happier now. They're doing so much better. This is great."

This isn't always true for everyone. I'm not saying private schools are bad. But I just don't think that people should feel that they have to send their children to private schools in order for them to do well.

The next parent believes that public school educators need to be advocates for the public school system, not private school. When one of his children's teachers recommended private school, his response was to become an advocate for the public schools. This parent used the analogy of a doctor who recommends a different doctor. He also described his belief that public school educators who observe problems in their school should work toward successful solutions.

Q: Were there ever public school teachers who advised you to send your kids to private school?

Nonprofit Executive: Yes, actually, there was one teacher who said that, which actually kind of bothered me. I have a hard time with teachers who tell me to do that, and who also send their children to private school. It's like, "Why?" To me, they should be doing the best they can for the public school system, and advocating for the public school system — that they don't really surprises me.

It makes you question what's going on, you know? It's just like when she said that to me, it was everything I thought about the public education system in the state of Hawaiʻi. She just loaded onto it, just like that. Just those few words she said to me. And that's probably around the time that I got really active because I knew that it didn't have to be that way. I actually heard from a lot of teachers — that they send their children to private school. I'd love to be able to do some kind of survey and find out what the actual numbers are.

I think it's almost like if you go to a doctor, and he's an intern, and he says you should really go see this holistic doctor, or vice versa. I just don't get it. A teacher should be there doing her absolute best and if she sees that there is something wrong with the system, then she needs to help correct it.

I would like to see what other teachers think about it. . . . Why do they even tell the parents that they should send their students to private schools? Why do they feel that way? Why do the ones who do send their children to private schools — why do they? Why don't they send them to public schools? I think a conversation on that topic would be very good.

At first, the next parent couldn't think of a time when his children's teachers recommended private school, but then remembered that it did happen with his son. He explains that the teacher said his son was "so much further along than the typical first grader" that she thought the parents should investigate private schools.

Q: Have your children's public school teachers ever discouraged you from sending your children to public schools, or conversely, encouraged you to think about private schools?

Media Executive: It has never really come up. There's not been anything either way — well, except this year, which is actually the first time that one of our teachers, in our parent-teacher conference, really encouraged us to pursue private school with one of our children. This is the first time. My oldest daughter is in the sixth grade now. So for the seven years that we've been at this public school, this is the first time. . . . But with my youngest son, during our parent-teacher conference, she suggested that we look into it.

Q: Did she give you a reason why?

Media Executive: She didn't really say, other than she did believe that my son was exceptional. When I looked at his report card — they grade very hard at his elementary school. This elementary school gives very few grades at the high end.

When you meet with the teachers in the parent-teacher conferences, they're trying to identify strengths and weaknesses of the child. And in my son's case, his report card came back all "E"s, which is equivalent to all straight "A"s in the first quarter. So I did ask her, "How is it that he can do this? Because I've never seen it at this school. It is not typical." And she said she couldn't justify giving him anything less than an "A" because his work was so much further along than the typical first grader.

Q: So was she saying that the public schools couldn't handle exceptional children?

Media Executive: She didn't say that explicitly, but, you know, I guess you could read that inference into her recommendation.

This belief by some public school educators that public schools cannot provide "a challenging education to bright students" was also encountered by the following professor at his son's elementary school.

Professor: Well, most teachers assume, at this public elementary school, that we were going to send our son to private school after they leave elementary school. That was the assumption. We had a number of teachers who actually sent their kids to public schools for the same reasons we did. And in fact, some of the reasons our son went to public middle school was that one of the teachers sent her kid to the same public school. But the overwhelming assumption at the elementary school is that . . . if you are a university faculty parent, you're going to send your kid to private school. It's so taken for granted that it's not even discussed. And people are surprised when you say, "Oh no, I'm not going to do that."

It is difficult not to come to the conclusion that, at least in these cases, if children are bright, some public school teachers will recommend to their parents that they transfer their children to private schools, especially if they are about to enter middle or high school. It leaves the parents with the impression that these teachers do not believe that, as professionals, they can provide a challenging education to bright students.

While more parents encountered teachers who recommended private school, three (a dentist, a public school teacher, and a legislator) did not, and they responded to this question differently. Each said that they were never approached by their children's public school teachers with such a suggestion.

Q: And did you ever have the teachers discourage you from keeping your children in public schools, or on the other hand, encourage you to send them to private school?

Dentist: Our elementary school is a good one. I can remember talking to a teacher who was the first- or second-grade teacher in a parent-teacher conference, and she made her child go to private school. But she said in this conference that this public elementary school was so good because [it was] almost like a private school. [The kids] were all very similar socioeconomically and culturally. There wasn't a real big diversity. . . . Since they were so close, the class could move along very quickly. They were very together at a pace similar to a private school pace. So she was telling me how good the public school was when her child was going to private school, which is interesting. (*Laughs.*)

Q: Did any of the teachers encourage you to send your children to — or take them out of public schools and send them to private schools?

Public School Teacher: Our children's teachers? No, no.

Legislator: No, never. Teachers are proud of their own respective schools, despite the conditions.

Legislators

Besides being concerned about public school educators who send their own children to private schools, public school parents in this study also felt that legislators cannot be as effective in resolving public education issues if they, too, send their children to private schools. In 2003, among the lawmakers in Hawaiʻi, 53 percent sent their children to private schools (Hickey and Mendelsohn 2003). In the following three interview excerpts, parents talked specifically about how important it is for legislators to send their own children to public schools so that they have firsthand experience with issues for which they are expected to make both financial and policy decisions. In the same way that other parents used analogies to articulate the problem with public school educators sending their children to private schools, so, too, did the first parent, as related to his medical profession, to discuss legislators who send their children to private schools.

Q: In the letters to the editor, there are letters saying that legislators should send their children to public schools. Do you feel that that is an issue or concern?

Physician: I do, I do. I'll give you an analogy from my own field, the medical field. There are a lot of problems with health care in this country, and with the way Medicare is administered. And the people who make the laws related to how Medicare is administered are the senators and the representatives at the federal level — many of whom are over sixty-five, but they do not have to rely on Medicare as their sole source of their health care because they have the federal plan. So they don't really know what's going on from the doctor's perspective or the patient's perspective. And yet they're making these laws, and they don't have the information. They think they have the information. They get a lot of information from lobbyists and that sort of thing, but they don't really have any personal experience.

It's the same thing at the local level of education. The legislators are the ones making the laws, passing the budgets, and that sort of thing for education, but if they all have their kids in private school, then there are a couple of problems with that. There's a lack of information through personal experience, and I think there's a lack of interest. It doesn't affect them.

A public school teacher also expressed the belief that legislators need personal experiences with public schools in order to write appropriate laws.

Public School Teacher: I see it in the paper, too, the cry for legislators to have their kids in public school so they have a perspective in terms of the laws that they're organizing — the way that they finance bills and all that.

The now-familiar theme that parents choose private schools because they believe such an education is better than a public one, and that it enables their children to be successful, is one that this attorney hears from his peers in the legislature.

Attorney: I don't know if anyone did a study on the legislature. How many of the legislators send their kids to private school, you know? What I've heard from a lot of my peers is that, "We'll never be rich. We'll never have this estate to give to them or anything else. The only thing that we can give them is a good education. So that's why we're going to send them to private school."

Q: So you think that decision is made because the private school route is viewed as the route for a good education?

Attorney: For success.

Why Public School Educators Make This Decision: "Only the Best"

"Wanting the best" is a theme that runs throughout the interviews. Both public and private school parents use this phrase, but they have different definitions of what is "best." The following parent shared the conversation he had with administrators and teachers who send their children to private schools. These educators responded that they do this because they "only want the best for our kids." Conversely, by implication, they cannot believe that public education can also provide a version of "the best" education.

Consulting Firm Executive: I've had this conversation in open forums with a DOE administrator. We'd be on these panels together, right? And I'd turn to him and I'd say, "I've got a problem with the way you handle teacher education." And he says, "What are you talking about?" "You should be teaching your teachers to have enough pride in their own public school system to send their kids there." And he looked at me and had nothing to say. (*Laughs.*)

Nobody said anything. I said, "Hey, you didn't answer my question. Why is that?" Then he comes back and says, "Well, everybody should have a choice to do what they feel is best for their children." And I said, "Well, in that case, then maybe what we ought to do is [have] people who believe in public schools insist that anybody who's teaching my kid has to have enough confidence in the public school system to send their own kids there."

I'm very pro-teacher. I think the teachers ought to be paid more. I think the kids should respect the teachers more. We're going to do stuff in school/community-based management (SCBM) in order to do that, and the teachers involved with the SCBM level all back that up.

[Referring to his conversations with public school educators:] But one thing that really irritates me about teachers in Hawai'i is —"You don't have enough confidence to send your kids to public schools. You ought to be ashamed of yourself." I tell them that flat out. And the principal says, "I agree with what you have to say, but somehow or another, we've been — we believe in the public school system. We came through it ourselves, but we only want the best for our kids." And I said, "But are you really giving the best to your kids?"

Of the six public school educators I interviewed, two sent their children to private schools. The following excerpts come from their interviews; these two educators were gracious enough to sit with me and discuss why they thought public school teachers, including themselves, send their children to private schools. Their reasons are very similar to those given by other private school parents: (1) a private school culture defined as having high academic expectations, (2) more homogeneous student populations, (3) fewer discipline issues, and (4) more resources. One of the two parents also mentioned that religion played, initially, a part in choosing a private school.

The first teacher-parent began her interview by sharing what she would say to other parents about why public school educators send their children to private schools. She said that highly motivated students do fine in public schools, but she would recommend private schools for those who are not motivated because, for example, private schools have the resources to provide smaller classes. However, she also believes that anyone who has the resources to send their children to private schools should do so because parents should provide their children with "the best" that is available.

This parent also discussed how public schools vary. In her view, public schools in middle- and upper middle-class communities are almost like private schools and are therefore acceptable; however, she also believes that schools in communities with high poverty rates likely have lower expectations, and most students probably don't expect to attend college. Conversely, the socioeconomically homogeneous community found in private schools is likely, she said, to have "high expectations, high achievement, you're going to college." This parent also felt that additional resources would not solve all the problems in public schools because, she believes, they are bigger than just resources; it lies in the "culture of the school." In sum, the diversity of some public school populations is viewed as a disadvantage.

Q: When the parents learn that their children's teachers send their own children to private schools, it makes many of them upset. They believe that that decision demonstrates a lack of confidence in the public schools, and yet, the public school educators are the professionals responsible for making needed changes to make improvements. What would you say to those parents?

Private School Parent: Well, I'd tell them if your child or your children are highly motivated, and if they're smart, then they could succeed in public schools because they will do just fine. They take the right classes. They're self-motivated. They'll be in AP [Advanced Placement classes] and everything else, okay? Students who have that potential but they are not like that — sometimes I say they actually need the private schools more because the private schools sometimes may guide them. They have the resources or maybe the classes are smaller.

Yes, people can say, "Well, you're a public school teacher and everything else and yet you send your children to private school." I say, "If everybody had the resources to send their children where they could, they should because you should give your children the best you can." I mean, you know? And so I guess that's what it is. We [public schools] don't have the resources.

And then I think, if you were in a community where, you know, like [a certain public elementary school is], or live in middle-, upper middle-class [communities] — it's almost like going to a private school. I'd say, "That's fine."

With high poverty and everything else — it's more the environment sometimes. We have to deal more with students who may not want to be here, and with parents who don't value education. Private schools could kick you out, or they could do whatever they really wanted to.

Q: Is part of the problem [for public schools] resources? You said earlier that public schools have bigger classes. If there were more resources, the DOE could hire more teachers and you could have smaller classes.

Private School Parent: But I think it's the culture of the school. Because I guess if you go to a private school, everybody thinks pretty much the same because of the family background and everything else. The culture of the school — it is like — high expectations, high achievement, you're going to college. It's talked about a lot, right?

I mean, that kind of thing is highly valued. If you go to public school, maybe half of your students or three-fourths of your students — they don't talk college. Or maybe they don't want to study. You have kids talking about "Why do I have to come to school?"

Q: So the public school diversity — the very diverse school population contributes to the problem?

Private School Parent: Yes . . . well . . . there's such a discrepancy between socioeconomic status among the schools, and that has one of the greatest influences on student achievement and school culture.

Q: A lot of what I hear [in the community] is talk about "the school system"

—"the public school system"—as if all 284 schools are identical. But what you're suggesting is that a school may vary according to geography, socio-economic status [SES], and school culture?

Private School Parent: Right. You know the *Honolulu Magazine* [survey] where they name the best public school?

Q: Right.

Private School Parent: If you go to those schools, there is a lot of parent involvement. When you have fund-raisers, the parents will fund-raise. So that all plays into, you know, the whole thing about school. So if you ask those parents, they're all going to say, "Our school's not broken. We have terrific teachers. The kids are terrific. Look at them. They're doing really well."

For the type of students that we have at [a certain public elementary school], we have a large number of second-language learners, and we have a big Special Education department. But we still meet or exceed the state proficiency benchmark for all of the students. We still exceed that because the teachers really work hard.

So I think you can't say "all of the schools." I think you have to look school by school, and taking into consideration what kind of students that you have, and where they're coming from, and what the school has done. They may not be in the same achievement range as [an upper middle-class public elementary school] or whatever, but for the kind of school, if you were to compare them with similar school[s], they may exceed [the proficiency benchmarks].

Q: So if you have high standards, regardless of what SES, you can fulfill the proficiencies?

Private School Parent: Well, you just keep on trying to.

Later in the interview, when I returned to the topic of why her public school colleagues might send their children to private schools, this parent restated her belief that public elementary schools in middle- and upper middle-class areas are acceptable. A lot of her colleagues send their children to public elementary schools, but she questioned the educational experience of the public middle schools, while stating that public high schools are "pretty solid." Interestingly, she does speak well of the middle school with which she had personal experience.

When I asked why the public high schools have a better reputation than the public middle schools, she talked about problems involving the transition from the one-teacher/one-classroom setting to the several-teachers/several-classrooms that middle-school students must make, combined with the vagaries of early adolescence. But by high school, she said, the former middle-school students have sorted themselves into groups, including groups who are "responsive, respectful, have some goals."

During the next interview, a second private school parent/public school educator also spoke about the differences between the public middle schools and public high schools. Nonetheless, she, too, spoke highly of the middle school in which she had personal experience.

Q: Do the majority of your friends and colleagues send their children to private schools?

Private School Parent: Let's see — I wouldn't say a lot of them, but I know a good number of them who sent their children to private schools.

Q: What do you think the reasons are that public school teachers send their children to private schools?

Private School Parent: A lot of them send their children to public schools maybe in elementary. But then, there's a big — 'cause even for myself, I see there are not that many middle schools where I would send our child. I think that we feel that public school elementary (of course, depending where you live) is no problem. High school is more solid. It's that middle-school thing.

Q: Are there any middle schools that you would not place in that category?

Private School Parent: That is a good middle school? [Names a public middle school.] I used to be a vice principal there. It has a lot of middle-class students, and they have a lot of GT [Gifted and Talented students]. And it has, you know, geographic exception students, too, right?

When talking about how the public middle schools would have to change in order to reassure parents, this teacher-parent talks about the middle-school concept that she experienced at her child's private school, where the middle-school students are grouped by grade and physically stay together in one building She goes on to say that she doesn't believe the public school system can fully implement a middle-school philosophy.

Q: How would the middle schools have to change in order to reassure the public?

Private School Parent: I don't know. It's real hard 'cause I think at an elementary school we try to keep on top of our students, right? And we try to nurture them and try and guide them. We know our students because usually we've had them from K to five grades. When they go to middle school, it's only sixth, seventh, and eighth. Maybe it's because there are more students, you know. They don't have just one teacher, or just a few teachers. They get lost in the crowd, you know?

Q: But then the reputation gets better at high school again?

Private School Parent: Mm-hmm. (*Nods.*)

Q: Why do you think there's that difference between that middle and that high school?

Private School Parent: Well, I think the students, when they go to high school, they're either in the group that is responsive, respectful, and have some goals. Then, of course, you have the other group that you could say probably is going to drop out, or you're just trying to encourage them just to stay in school.

In the middle school, I guess everybody's trying to find his way. You know, they don't have a solid foundation yet.

Q: So at your child's private middle school, what's the difference? Is it because the [student] population is more homogeneous?

Private School Parent: Probably the population is narrower. Now they've adopted more of the middle-school concept. They didn't have that when my youngest daughter was there. But you know what? They keep the fifth and sixth graders in a certain wing . . . so they're all kind of together. Their classes are in this cluster, whereas, if you go to most middle schools, it doesn't matter . . . sixth, seventh, eighth, they just cross buildings and stuff. I mean, I think they try to do that [middle-school concept at the public schools], but I don't think it's as strong as I think it is at the private school.

And now that my child's private school has that whole middle-school concept that they adopted, you know, new buildings and everything else, they can really fully implement the middle-school vision.

This parent then responded more specifically to questions about why she and her husband opted for private school. While she discussed school culture as the most important variable influencing her choice, she mentioned that her husband was most influenced by "the resources" of the private schools.

She also stated that private schools vary. Because they differ, her husband said he would have chosen a public school with a "good reputation" if their children had not been accepted into one of the elite private schools.

When I returned to the question about why public school teachers send their children to private schools, she added that discipline is a concern. Only if "consistent discipline, and management, and high expectations" existed would such public school teachers send their children to public schools. This explanation prompted me to wonder why those characteristics are not the responsibility of the teachers and principals in those schools.

Private School Parent: What my husband always says? "It's the resources." I don't know if I answered your question about why I sent my kids to private school?

Q: Well, what I heard you say is that, initially, a school with some religious perspective was important.

Private School Parent: Right — for me.

Q: You said that your husband talked about resources —

Private School Parent: Mm-hmm. [Yes.]

Q: — and also, the fact that the population of students [at the elite private school] are highly motivated. Would you say that those are the top three reasons?

Private School Parent: Yes, because it's school culture. I guess if your child is in a school culture that expects — well, it's the expectation that you'll go to [college]. I mean, there's almost no question about it. So then your kids will be surrounded by that [culture].

Q: So having the high expectations is really key, regardless if you're talking private or public?

Private School Parent: Well, I think high expectations — like [a private school that she thinks lacks high expectations], you know, and I look at the kind of kids that go there.

Q: The private schools are not all alike either?

Private School Parent: Yes. That's another thing. . . .

Q: So while the typical [community] belief is "the public schools are bad and the private schools are good," there actually is a variety of both private and public schools?

Private School Parent: Yes. So even my husband will say, "If I was going to send them to [another private school, which her husband thinks lacks high expectations] or whatever, I'd rather send them to public school" because our neighborhood public school has a good reputation.

Q: Do the majority of your friends send their children to private school?

Private School Parent: My friend in administration and the group that I meet with sent their children to public schools. My other friends sent their children to private schools.

Q: Are there conversations back and forth about the reasons why one would send to private school and one would send to public school?

Private School Parent: No, except I'm often apologetic about it because as a public school administrator, I should have full faith in our public system. I should have sent my children to public schools, but I didn't.

Q: If someone were to just generally come in and ask, "What are the reasons why public school teachers send their children to private schools?" How would you respond to that?

Private School Parent: You know, over and over again, I hear the fact that discipline is a concern in public schools, that if your children are in classes where the children are not as well managed or not displaying appropriate behavior, that [public school teachers] certainly didn't want to have their children wait their turn to get on with their academics.

Q: What would have to change for those public school educators to make the decision to send their children to public schools?

Private School Parent: Consistent discipline, and management, and high expectations.

Q: And the consistent discipline and management — those are leadership [responsibilities], right? And the high expectations — that needs to come from the teachers themselves? And how could the teachers themselves bring about changes to improve discipline?

Private School Parent: Well, this is something that we are going into in our reading program here. We are bringing in external consultants to help these schools. We're also supporting them with coaching, going in and making sure that we coach consistently within that month, going in at least once a month.

And I'm constantly [telling] the teachers to have those high expectations. Know what your target is, and then aim high. So that the teacher does not say, "Oh, he comes from a family that — " or "Oh, you know, he had a late night," or "Oh, what do we expect?" ...

A belief that has gone on too long is that we have too many ESL [English as a Second Language] children.

Q: Where do you think this low expectation for ESL children comes from? ... There seem to be high expectations for the high tracks [according to parents in the study]. But where does this school cultural belief in low expectations for the "average student" or the ESL student [come from]?

Private School Parent: Because it starts out with the teacher assigning homework, and the child doesn't bring back the homework. The teacher thinks, "They won't bring it back, so therefore, I'm going to assign only this much work." So the teacher, then, molds her expectations according to the children's.

Q: So the teacher is reacting rather than setting the standard. How do you change that?

Private School Parent: It takes a lot of talking. It's a philosophical thing because — when I come across teachers who believe that control is outside of their [control] — you know, the socioeconomic condition of the family, the education of the parents, the time they spent in their home doing homework and not having books and everything, not having the resources. That's one philosophy. Another philosophy would believe that your child comes with a lot, and working with that. I believe that you can change and alter behavior, and you can increase learning by making sure that you help each child.

In essence, the reaction these parents received from friends, neighbors, or professional colleagues regarding their decision to send their children to public schools was primarily negative or muted. Adding weight to this decision "to go against the grain" was the parents' discovery that some of their children's teachers were sending their own children to private schools, and sometimes encouraged them to do the same.

In the next chapter, the parents discuss their ideas about how and why the community belief ("Public schools are failing and private schools are succeeding. Send your child to private schools") became so widespread.

5 The "Incessant Conversation"

The Hawai'i parents in this study decidedly believe there is a community-at-large perception that private schools have a higher social status than public schools. Private schools are perceived as safe, with high academic expectations for their students and adequate resources that in turn lead to well-maintained facilities and small classes. On the other hand, public schools are viewed as lower status because they are deemed unsafe, with lower expectations and insufficient resources resulting in inferior facilities and large class sizes.

How did this come to be?

Newcomers

It does not take long for newcomers to hear over and over that if they want their child to receive a quality education in our state, they had better start checking out private schools and saving money for the tuition. (Orr 2004, A9)

Orr sums up the community-held belief that public schools are failing and private schools are succeeding. To discover just how prevalent this belief is in the community, I asked the parents in the study, both newcomers to the state as well as the local residents, "Which school system has higher status — public or private?" The perception that private schools have a higher status is so common that only one parent had difficulty answering. All other parents responded, without hesitation, that private schools have a higher standing. When I asked how newcomers learn about this perception, parents frequently mentioned conversations between newcomers and local residents about school options for their children in Hawai'i. These conversations typically take place with one's professional colleagues, family members, and neighbors, sometimes before newcomers have actually moved to the islands. Newcomers also discussed how information about schools is presented negatively by the media, especially the local newspapers and television stations. They also talked about how those public schools whose physical facilities have not been well maintained give credence to this negative perception.

It became apparent that residents' beliefs are reinforced through a similar process in which local citizens engage in regular conversations with friends, family, and peers about where they are sending their children to school. In addition, local residents use the newspapers as a source of information. These residents, too, are concerned about the facilities at the public schools.

A different topic, introduced by local residents, is the long history of separate school systems in Hawai'i. This history may predispose state citizens to favor private schools. This topic will also be examined further.

But first, we begin with a closer look at the conversations parents participated in as they considered where to send their children to school.

"The Conversation"

Conversation appears to be the primary means of conveying to newcomers and to each other that, in Hawai'i, public schools are failing and private schools are succeeding. Such conversations are frequent and similar.

In the first group of interviews below, as the parents talked about engaging in conversations about school choice, they also discussed their own research on Hawai'i's public schools as a means to help them decide whether they would accept community-held beliefs.

When the following parent (a professor) and her family moved from the contiguous states (locally referred to as the "mainland") to Hawai'i, she said she learned about the public school system by "word of mouth." She talked with neighbors and colleagues, discovering that many professionals were sending their children to private schools. This surprised her because her friends and relatives on the mainland sent their children to public schools. During our interview, she indicated that she didn't think the private school parents with whom she spoke had conducted their own research on individual public schools as part of their decision-making process. In her conversations with other parents, she discovered a caveat in the community-held belief: public elementary schools were acceptable to a number of professionals, but not secondary public schools.

Q: In what ways do newcomers to the state learn about the schools in Hawai'i?

Professor: It's word of mouth. You hear it from your neighbors. You hear it from your colleagues. You hear it from other parents at the schools where your children attend. It's such a common topic of conversation. And it seems like, within the professions, so many parents tend to send their kids to private schools. I also know a lot of parents who wouldn't be considered professionals, but sacrifice tremendously to get their kids into private school too. So it just runs across the gamut, socioeconomically.

When we first moved here, I hadn't really even considered private schools because it really is more of a Hawai'i phenomenon, this predisposition to send your kids to private schools, where I think on the mainland it's more that the private schools tend to be more religious schools. It's only the more elite classes that would send their kids to private schools on the mainland. I never had friends who did that, or relatives. So it was a real surprise to me here when I found out the really disproportionate number of parents who sent their kids to private school compared to the mainland — especially nonreligious private schools. So when we first moved here, it was natural that they would go to public schools.

There was one [public school] that was supposed to be pretty good, right near where we moved when we came here. So we just immediately enrolled our children there. And I had never even considered sending them to private. It was only after we'd been here a long while and I started hearing about all the parents who — I think a lot more parents send their kids to public elementary school, and then around middle school is when typically they send them to private. You're just involved in all the discussions about where your child is going to go after sixth grade. "Are you going have them tested?" And so forth and so forth. So it really didn't become an issue until more like fourth grade, I guess.

Q: In what other ways did you learn that there was another belief system besides having a conversation?

Professor: I became interested in that topic as an issue and, like I said, was thinking actually about doing my dissertation on it, but I didn't. I looked at it and investigated it on my own, professionally. I started doing some research on it, and talking to other professors here who were going through the same dilemma and about which way they would go with their own kids.

An interesting aspect of that I think is, professionally, we know all the arguments and all the issues that surround those decisions. And we have a feeling of professional integrity that we definitely shouldn't send our kids to private schools. Yet, when it comes to your own kids, a lot of people change their mind about that.

Q: What is it about the public schools that creates this dilemma?

Professor: Well, I think that it's a complex issue. I think it depends on your own children first and foremost, what kind of kids they are, what kind of students they are, what kind of peer groups they have, what kind of needs they have. So if you have a child that has particular needs—for example, if they need a small class setting, which you're not going to find in public schools, then that would sway you towards the private school. If they have behavior problems, if they have emotional problems, if they're not motivated, then I think you might think it's going be more difficult to get what they need in the public school system.

And with our particular two daughters, they've just always been very good students, and very good kids. We've been lucky. And they haven't had any special needs that would make us say, "I just don't think they're going to get their needs met or accommodated in the public school system." And I think it mainly relates to small class size and more individual attention in private schools.

Q: And that is not viewed as being an option in the public schools?

Professor: Well, certainly not a small class size, except in the lower grades.

You know, another reason for private schools is, I think, because of this perception that the kids in public schools are less able, less motivated, and that there are lowered expectations. I don't think that's factual. I think that's more of a perception that people have, but it has resulted in kind of a "ghettoization" of the public schools. This huge number of parents who could really contribute greatly to the public schools has exited, and these are the parents who are involved parents in education. And so many of them have left, that it has had a bit of a negative impact on the public schools.

There is the perception, and there is the reality. A lot of the really bright kids have left, but there's this notion that there's a brain drain, and who is left would be like the lowest levels of kids. That isn't true, but it certainly has had a negative impact, I think.

Q: So it is a circular argument. There is the perception, therefore, as a parent you withdraw your children, and therefore they make it more —

Professor: — of a reality then—yes. It contributes to the reality of it.

Q: But the perception, you were saying, is clearly out there about the public schools?

Professor: Oh, absolutely.

Q: Have these parents who are in your peer group, and who have a perception of the public schools as having lower expectations, visited individual schools?

Professor: Visited public schools? No.

Even before she moved to Hawai'i, a military officer heard the "conversation" from parents who home-school their children, parents who had no firsthand experience with Hawai'i's public schools. She said these parents "went off of everyone else's opinion." Unwilling to accept this opinion outright, this officer and her spouse conducted their own research on Hawai'i's public schools.

Q: How do people in the military learn about public schools? You just mentioned that some individuals talked to you when they heard that you were going to Hawai'i. What did they say?

Military Officer: "Oh God, the school system is horrific! You have to find a private school." They chose to home-school, but they also chose to home-school their kids in Europe, and Europe has one of the best Department of Defense [DoD] school systems. So I think that it was their personal preference. I think that no matter where they went, they were probably going to home-school their kids. But they didn't put their kids in the public school system, and the wife just happened to be a teacher, and she just felt that, "Ohmigawd, my children will never go to those schools."

Apparently, they just went off of everyone else's opinion, but how many of those people have their kids in schools? I don't know. You know, maybe they had them in a particular bad school, which can be anywhere. My husband and I knew, coming from our experiences from all over the world, that there's good and bad everywhere. You just got to take the time to research it.

Q: Now, is that a typical response when people heard that you were coming to Hawai'i?

Military Officer: Yes, very much so.

Q: Yet you had a good experience here. So, how is it that, even though there are military personnel who have had good experiences, the typical message is that Hawai'i's schools are so bad?

Military Officer: My own personal opinion? That we're so focused on looking at the problems and trying to resolve the problems that we forget to let people know about the successes.

Q: How else do military personnel find out about schools in Hawai'i?

Military Officer: We receive a welcome-aboard package from the command, and it had a list of all the private schools, and list of the public schools, and so probably that way. And there is a Web page you can go to, and you put in a location where you're looking to move, and learn more about the area.

We found most of ours off the Web. We just went out and searched — not necessarily through the channels that the military told us to go and look, but we went and tried to find just as much information as we could.

Q: So, it's by and large by word of mouth?

Military Officer: Absolutely. I'm just amazed. You hear it around here all the time — word of mouth. It's very powerful. These folks have some really strong opinions, and you ask them, "What's driving this? You don't even have kids in school."

Q: And when you say, "these folks," who do you mean?

Military Officer: Well, down at headquarters, both officers and enlisted will say the school systems are terrible. And it's like, "Really? Well, which ones have you looked into?" It's so easy to be negative and pass along negative stuff like that. And I don't know why. Human nature is just that way.

In the next excerpt, a local attorney acknowledges that there is a widely "accepted premise that our schools are inferior." He spoke about what he has experienced when mainland job candidates come to Hawai'i. His colleagues will inform the candidates that they have to send their children to private schools. According to his colleagues, the public schools are bad, and they will "help you get in" the private schools. This father also spoke about the social role professionals and their children play when they are together in private schools.

Q: When you have newcomers coming to Hawai'i, how would you say they get information about the public schools?

Attorney: I think it's just a widely accepted premise that our schools are inferior and they're unsafe. I think it's just widely accepted.

Q: So if somebody moved to Hawai'i, how will they learn about this perception?

Attorney: Well, if a professional came here, they'd check with their colleagues, and most of them are sending their kids to private schools. They'll tell them that "you've got to send your kids to private schools." I don't think there's even an explanation. It's just, "You've got to do this. The schools are bad. You need to do this for your kids." End of story. "We'll help you get in." And then that's how it's presented.

Q: Within the professional class, in particular, that's the shared belief?

Attorney: Yes.

Q: And so it's not so much that they could necessarily document this opinion with firsthand experience?

Attorney: They don't know. . . . There's also a social thing because out of the kids' associations come parent associations. So social lives are built around, you know, your kids who are going to be mingling with these kids. So you'll hear colleagues talking about the carnival.

"Well, what day are you working?" You know.

"Of course I'm not going to be at work next Friday because it's carnival time."

"Oh yeah, yeah. What booth are you working in?"

You know? It's a social thing, too, so it's like a country club. That's okay. That's not my beef.

My beef is just automatically discounting public education, maybe not considering why public education is good. I feel there's a responsibility. When you talk about community, I think each of us has a responsibility. And part of the responsibility is a commitment to our public education, and how do we demonstrate that? That's the bottom line with me. I wouldn't have friends if I judged them by where they sent their kids to school, so I don't make those judgments. But it's a personal thing with me. I feel that that's one of the things we have to do.

Another attorney and father said that all his colleagues send their children to private schools. He, too, talked about job candidates from the mainland who are warned about the public schools.

Attorney: You look in the office I'm in right now. I can't name anybody who sends his kids to public school.

Q: Do you talk to them about this issue in your office?

Attorney: Sure.

Q: And what do they say?

Attorney: Well, I think it's like their friends all send their kids to the same schools. So if they are new professionals coming into Hawai'i, they are warned and told, you know, "Hey, the only good schools around are the private schools. You don't want your kid hanging out in a public school. Look at the buildings. It's dangerous."

Q: So these people, who are new to the islands, haven't had personal experience with the public schools? In other words, it's not that they've investigated the public schools as much as they're the newcomers coming into this professional group, and the people who are here inform them, "This is what we're recommending."

Attorney: Yes.

The following dentist learned about the perception of Hawai'i's public schools before he moved to the state. As a dental student on the mainland, most of his classmates from Hawai'i were private school graduates, and they passed along the common perception about public schools in Hawai'i. In considering his move to Hawai'i, this view created a dilemma for him. He worried about his children if they weren't in private schools. Would there be a stigma?

He also mentioned that, as a newcomer, it doesn't take long to find out where everyone "should" be going to school. But he and his wife decided to "go against the grain" and send their child to a public school, and he "just loved the school."

Q: And you mentioned this peer pressure to send your children to private schools exists in the community. Where do you think that comes from?

Dentist: Well, that's a good question. I don't know. When I was in dental school, I met a number of Hawai'i kids. I wasn't from Hawai'i at that time, but I hung around with a group of Hawai'i kids. Most of them came from private schools and I was not aware of that whole private school/public school thing. But you get a quick understanding. It doesn't take long to understand.

And even back then, I felt that there must be this real stigma. Kids must feel badly if they're not going to this private school, you know? I mean, it's out there, and it's considered the best education, and all the smart kids go there, and then you're sitting in your little public school going, "Why am I not there, Dad?" You know? I think that [feeling] might be wrong, but I kind of worried about that even before I came here, thinking, "Gosh, do I want my kid to have that kind of feeling?" "Why is he better than me? Why am I not going to that school?" So I don't know.

After coming here and having a child go to public elementary school, I was so impressed. I was involved with the PTA, greatly involved, and I just loved the school, and I was very happy. So I lost that feeling.

Q: So, you got firsthand experience with feeling pressured?

Dentist: Yes. Anyway, I think that's probably why the pressure is there. I mean, it's kind of, "It's better, so why can't I have it? I want whatever's the best, and if I can't have it, I'm being cheated or shortchanged." Maybe that's part of the reason that the pressure's there.

Q: It's peer/community pressure?

Dentist: I think so. And whether it's bad — you know, you look at the results of the kids coming out of these schools. They're really good. Not all of them necessarily, but I think there's definite performance.

Q: And you were hearing this from your college friends while you were on the mainland?

Dentist: Yes. Of course, they were all coming from private school, so — well, actually, one student I knew was a public school kid, so she wasn't necessarily buying into it. She was a public school graduate, the only one I heard from.

Q: How do other newcomers learn about this?

Dentist: I can only guess. It would probably depend on their social standing, or whomever they hang around with. If they were professionals, it doesn't take long to find out where everybody's going, and where everyone "should" be going.

After she moved to Hawai'i from the mainland, the following professor asked her colleagues for advice on where to live and where to send her child to school. From the provost to her colleagues to the secretary, they endorsed private schools over public. She learned that "there is just this value that a private education is a better education." This feedback caused her to doubt whether she should send her child to public schools. So she conducted research by scrutinizing the physical facilities. She discovered that if you compare an elite private school with one of the public schools that "looks bad," then the private schools look like "castles." However, she was uncomfortable with this "idea of elitism and entitlement," and she decided to send her child to public school.

Q: Did your work colleagues support this notion of sending your child to public schools?

Professor: No. When I moved here, I was searching for advice about where to live and about the schools. Interestingly, what I was told by the acting provost of our college is, "You should try to live in [a wealthier neighborhood] and your child should go to [a private school]. The secretary told me I should try to live in [another location] and put my child in a private school. So across the board, there seemed to be this belief that you've got to go to some sort of a private school.

Q: So when you arrived as a newcomer, you set out with questions, and the advice you got is to send your child to private schools?

Professor: Yes. So philosophically, there's a value difference.

Q: Could you talk about that difference?

Professor: I could. I'm trying to think of how to phrase this. I feel like everyone wants the very best for her child. They want them to be successful. There is just this value here that a private education is a better education.

There's almost this feeling among my colleagues that, if you want your child to academically succeed and to be able to compete and get into a college, they have to go to a private school because the public school is just a playground. They won't learn anything.

Q: Now do they know this firsthand? Do you feel that the people who were sharing this perspective have firsthand experience with the public schools? Or do you think this is part of the community belief system?

Professor: I think it's a mixture of both. Some of them have worked in early childhood education where they have had exposure to public schools maybe on the kindergarten level. So I see it as being part of a perceived belief system. And as a newcomer, I really began to doubt myself, thinking, "Well, what if I'm wrong? What if the schools are really as bad as they say in Hawai'i? What if I'm making the wrong decision, and what if my child is going to be an academic failure or not learn?"

I went to look at the physical facilities. When you compare a place like [a private school] and, let's say, one of the public schools that really looks bad, the private schools look almost like castles. And there's this idea of elitism and entitlement that really breaks against my personal beliefs that wouldn't allow me to pursue whatever it took to get my child into an elite private school. I also would hear, as part of the common belief system, the stories about children stressed beyond their capacity with the amounts of homework and the competitive edge to school. But I didn't want to subject my child to that, and so I just thought, "Okay, I'm not going to do this."

I think that there is not a perception of the public schools creating success. And I think it really boils down to that. When I look at some of my colleagues, I almost feel like I should guilt them into thinking, "You know, here you are, someone who works for the public schools and advocates for public schools, and yet you can't make this choice for your own child. And if you really feel that the schools are that bad, you should be making your effort to make them better." I can't conceive of my colleagues buying into that.

The last interview in this section was with a public school teacher who shared a conversation she had with her good friend about continuing to send their children to public schools now that their children would be entering middle school. Her friend had decided that her son was not going to go to the neighborhood public school because "it's rough, and he'll get in with the wrong crowd, and it won't be safe." When I asked if her friend had done any research on that school, she said, no, it was "hearsay."

Interestingly, it was the same middle school in which this teacher's husband taught and which her two daughters attended. She reported that her daughters did well academically, had nice friends, and were never involved in fights.

It was her opinion that parents choose private school either because of the higher status or because they had a bad experience, as in one case in which several friends had attended this school as children and were unhappy with the experience. Even though the school has since changed, they nevertheless sent their children to private schools. These friends, all public school teachers, talked about "doing the best for my child," saying, "I'm sending him to a private school."

Q: Had they done any research on the school?

Public School Teacher: No, they based [their decision] on hearsay. Another good friend of mine, whose son is the same age as my youngest, when it came time to send our boys to intermediate school, she was like, "He's not going to [a certain public intermediate school]." And I was like, "Why?"

"Because it's a horrible school."

"Well, why? That's where my husband teaches! Why do you think [that]?"

"Well, it's rough, and he'll get in with the wrong crowd, and it won't be safe."

Well, both my girls went through that public school, and they never got into a fight, and they both have nice friends, and they've both done well academically. So, yes, people just kind of say things, you know, that they wouldn't send their kids to public schools. They don't know what really goes on, or know the teachers, or know the curriculum. When my one friend went to the open house, just in case her son didn't get into private school, she said she was very impressed with what she saw.

Q: Why do you think that this situation occurs — that such a large part of the middle class who don't have firsthand knowledge about public schools make the choice to go to private school? What is really driving that decision, do you think?

Public School Teacher: I think it is status. They want to say their kid was smart enough to get into a private school, so that they were like, "chosen." That's my personal opinion.

And then a couple of the other people I've talked to who had attended this public intermediate and high school themselves, and they weren't happy with the school. So they're basing what they think is going on today with what went on when they went to school. And there's no way they would send their kids there, even though they themselves are public school teachers. I think it's that "I'm doing the best for my child. I'm sending him to a private school."

A Private School Parent Acknowledges the Conversation

A private school parent agrees that parents in Hawai'i engage in conversations about school choice "incessantly." It is the conventional wisdom, she said, that private schools are superior to public schools. In response to my question as to whether professionals send their children to private schools because of this belief, she said there is nothing to dispute that perception from personal stories and the media. And, having already been influenced by this belief, these parents form their opinions and decide to send their children to private schools without investigating the public schools. She believes that the professional class prefers private school, and only if their children couldn't get in to a private school would they consider other options.

Private School Parent: I think that people that have kids between the ages of newborn to grade twelve talk incessantly about education in Hawai'i. If you haven't heard it from your neighbor, or your friends, or people at the office, it's in the media to some degree. It's always a source of discussion.

Q: Would you say that a newcomer might not conduct the same kind of research on public schools in Hawai'i as they would on private schools because of this belief system that public schools are inferior and private schools are superior?

Private School Parent: I think that is the "conventional wisdom" that private schools are superior. But even if they wanted to do the research, where would they go? I remember some years ago the newspapers had some ranking, some comparisons of the different high schools — because I remember that certain schools were doing relatively better than others. But where would you go?

Q: Well, I was thinking perhaps visiting the schools, talking with the principals, talking with the teachers, looking at the facilities — that kind of thing.

Private School Parent: That's interesting. Because when you say something like that — certainly we looked at the private schools in that fashion. Maybe because public schools weren't within our competitive set for long [we didn't investigate public schools.]

I think most people approach it from the point of view that "if my child can't get into private school, I'll explore the options." I mean, again, you're talking about the professional — the upper middle class — and it's more of a "private school is my first choice, and then if it's the second choice, public school, I'll deal with it."

Q: And private schools are the first choice because of the community-held belief that the private schools would be typically superior?

Private School Parent: Well, it's from personal experiences, and it's what you read in the media. There's nothing to dispute [that belief].

In addition to engaging in "the conversation" about schools, parents talked about the media as a second component contributing to and reinforcing the community-held belief regarding schooling in Hawai'i.

The Role of the Media

Military Officer: Well, they would hear it from their peers in the military community, and they would hear it through news articles. . . . The "news" likes to talk about the "fires" in the schools — the problems — rather than promote the good. So the word is out there, the word is out there.

Parents, both newcomers and local residents, talked about the media as a source of information that influenced their perception of public schools and, therefore, their decisions as to where to send their children.

Public school parents talked about how the newspapers, in particular, frame front-page stories regarding test scores. Private school parents also talked about test scores and the issues of school safety and school facilities. They, too, believe that newspapers, television, and talk radio structure these stories to create a negative perception, particularly that public schools are unsafe.

Newspapers: Test Scores

Presented below are the interviews with public school parents. A legislator spoke on the manner in which media frame a story on education, indicating that one set of statistics can be used to focus on a negative outcome or could be "flipped" to angle the story positively. He also introduced the connection between good public schools and a community's economy. When companies view a community's public schools negatively, it can affect their willingness to relocate and invest in the community. The perception of the state's public schools held by outside businesses is shaped, he believes, by the media.

Q: And you used the phrase, "The community perceives the public schools to be a certain way and private schools to be a certain way." When newcomers come to Hawaiʻi, how do they learn about that perception?

Legislator: I've seen statistics that indicate a large majority of citizens only get their information through the evening news or newscasts, and clearly the media does drive a lot of that perception. You know, it's always interesting when they talk about, "Well, the statewide average for public schools in Hawaiʻi is below the national average in reading, and it is slightly above in math," or whatever that statistic is. It's interesting because you could flip that a lot of different ways. You could say that — I don't know what the specific number is, but I do believe that 60 percent of the public schools exceed the national average. And no one talks about those kinds of statistics.

You can look at the student achievement in the public schools, and I would say that there are many that match up with student achievement in private schools. If you look at [various public middle and high schools], I'm pretty certain that a significant proportion go on to higher education. Now, it's not going to be the 100 percent or the 99 percent or 98 percent that you'll get at private schools because private schools kick out the ones that are not achieving, for one, but I think it's pretty impressive.

Q: So you think that, to a large extent, it's how the media portrays public education?

Legislator: Yes, I do believe that that has a major impact.

Q: Are there other sources?

Legislator: You know, I don't know anyone else who is advocating for public schools. I talk to a lot of high-tech companies thinking of coming to Hawaiʻi, and public education is a big issue. My pitch to them is that they need to investigate and explore the public schools because I tell them that there are a number of excellent public schools here that do as well as private schools. Just because your child is in a public school, that doesn't condemn them to a second-class status, or a second-class life or education for that matter.

Q: Do they come with that perception?

Legislator: They do come with the perception that the public school system isn't that good.

Q: Where are they getting it?

Legislator: I do think they get it from the media.

These topics are repeated in this next couple's interview. The husband said that job candidates from the mainland were advised by their prospective employer to send their children to private schools. It was this father's experience that candidates heed such advice rather than conduct research on the public schools.

His wife spoke about the influence that the test score rankings printed in the newspapers have on newcomers. Her husband joined in to point out that the ranking is "across the board," but individual schools vary.

He has advised newcomers in his field to try public schools first. Some of them followed his advice.

CEO: We used to bring guys in from the mainland for interviews, and that used to be the first question that they asked: "How are the schools here? And where do you think that we should send our kids?" And basically, if they were talking to the senior guys in most of the companies here, they would probably recommend a private school rather than a public school.

Q: Do they investigate the public and private schools and then make a decision? Or do they make a decision based on what somebody at work says they should do?

CEO: For the most part, they try to base their decision on what's being recommended to them. They don't do that much research.

Public School Teacher: I also think, though, that it's widely publicized how poor our public education system is here, so anyone from the mainland from the [upper] socioeconomic group automatically says, "Well, heck, it's not even a question."

Q: And what do you mean when you say it's widely publicized?

Public School Teacher: Well, all the studies that come out about where are we ranked in the newspapers. Where are we ranked? Always at the bottom. So I think that's enough to have people think that we're teaching them on the beach or something! (*Laughs.*)

CEO: The problem with the ranking is that they're doing it across the board for every area.

What I told some of the guys who came in to the company is that "It just depends on where you live, sometimes. What I would do is to try a couple of schools, and if they don't challenge your kids, then you might want to consider private. Because," I said, "private schools here are not cheap. They're not like the mainland. They're expensive. You might want to consider trying out the public school in your area first."

And some of them did that. They left their kids in public schools. Well, the ones that did that lived in the same district I did. The schools out there and the faculty and the standards are pretty good.

Another father heard about the Hawai'i school system before he moved to Hawai'i. He was a graduate assistant at a mainland university when he met both public and private school graduates from Hawai'i. One private school graduate told him that "the public schools are junk." However, he received a different perspective from a public school graduate. And once he moved to Hawai'i, he engaged in "the conversation" about school choice. He also read what the local newspapers printed about public schools. His interpretation of the newspapers' point of view is that the stories correlated "good schools" with "high test scores." He also noted that legislators and newspaper editors focused on public school problems. In contrast, what he discovered is that the public schools vary, with some schools "troubled" and some schools "very, very healthy, good schools."

Professor: When I came here, I already knew about some of the private schools because I went to graduate school at a mainland university, and I met kids from one of the private schools who were my students when I was a graduate assistant. The first thing I heard about the local school system was from them.

Q: What were they telling you?

Professor: Well, different ones were telling me different things. Yes. There was one who was a very, very rich kid and his attitude was very much that the public schools are junk and, of course, you would only send your child to a private school. But the other guy was a product of the public schools. He'd come through public high school. And his father is a faculty member here, so I got a very different impression from him. So the testimony was mixed, right?

But then once you get here you always hear people talking, and reading what is in the paper. What you read in the paper, I find, is often very, I found, often was of very little value.

Q: In what way?

Professor: There's a strong tendency in the reporting in the papers to identify the schools with high test scores as the good schools. And I distrust that correlation. And there's a kind of a line that you hear over and over again from the legislators or from the editorial page or whatever about how the public schools are really in trouble. There are problems — big problems — with the public schools that we've got to fix. My sense, when I talk to people, is that it varies a great deal from one school to another. It's not a systemic thing. There are some public schools that are obviously very troubled. But there are a lot of public schools that are very, very healthy, good schools.

Test scores that are "front page news" contribute, this next father believes, to the public schools' negative reputation because headlines stick in the public's mind. He also noted that private schools' test scores are not publicized.

A consistent finding in the Gallup polls (Elam, Rose, and Gallup 1991) is that parents, nationwide, view public education as in need of improvement, but they are typically happier with the local public school their children attend. This parent perceived the same situation in Hawai'i.

Q: How do newcomers find out about public schools?

Nonprofit Executive: Well, there are a couple of things. I think that one is the media, without a doubt. The media is bad for education in our state, and I'm not sure it's any different in any other state. I know that people perceive public schools in Hawai'i as being fairly bad, but they always perceived their own child's schools a little bit better than public schools in the state as a whole.

Certainly, how we score on the national standardized tests puts a black mark on public education within the state. Of course, these exams, if taken by private school students, are not publicized. We're compared to districts across the country, sometimes with highly different criteria, and don't fare well, and that's front-page news. That's certainly something that sticks in the public's mind.

Two of the public school parents were involved in marketing and media businesses. The media executive said that he doesn't typically engage in conversations about school choice at his workplace, as most of his colleagues are young and without children. However, he said when he worked for a local newspaper, most of the newspaper staff sent their children to private schools. He felt that good reporters wouldn't be influenced by personal school choice when reporting on public education.

When I brought up the media as a topic and told him that the parents I had been interviewing thought the media contributed to the negative perception of public schools, he responded with, "Yes. I guess that would be the test scores. That's always the story of the year." It is interesting that he, too, noted that private schools are not required to release such information.

Q: So, especially in your business, how do newcomers to Hawai'i find out that there is a community-held belief that private schools are better?

Media Executive: I'm not sure about that, but I know that the perception exists. I'm not sure why.

Q: Do you hear people talking about this issue?

Media Executive: No, I don't hear it as a topic of conversation. There are a lot of young guys here, but there are not a lot of people here with kids. But I worked with the newspaper and, at that time, everybody had kids. And most of them sent their kids to private schools.

Q: And did they talk about why?

Media Executive: No, no.

Q: If most of the newspaper staff send their children to private schools, what kind of impact does that have on how they report and cover public schools?

Media Executive: Again, I'm not sure. It shouldn't have any, if you're a good reporter.

Q: Parents in this study talk about how the media portrays public schools versus private schools.

Media Executive: Yes, I guess it would be the test scores. That's always the story of the year, how well the schools fared against the nation in standardized tests. The private schools are never required to release that kind of information. The state always does it for public schools.

The marketing executive described the dilemma television and print media personnel face when balancing business goals against reporting news and informing the public. They work with limited time and space while also needing to attract an audience. This parent believes the business side promotes the sensational. He said, "You will not see a headline that some of our public schools are very good. . . . Far better to say that we are lower than Mississippi." He also believes that, as readers and listeners, the "public" is responsible for the status of the reporting because we demand sensational stories.

Q: How do newcomers find out about the perception of the public schools?

Marketing Executive: Well, they'll hear it. I mean, it's folklore here. People who have never been here will tell you without any basis of information or knowledge whatsoever.

Q: How would you describe the role of the media in supporting this view?

Marketing Executive: Well, the role of the media is to inform, but in trying to do that, what the media does is all on the side of sensation. You will not see a headline that some of our public schools are very, very good. It's just not the nature of the media to cover that angle — far better to say that we are lower than Mississippi.

Q: Is there any way to change that?

Marketing Executive: No, no.

Q: What about investigative reporting or more in-depth reporting?

Marketing Executive: Well, some of the problem is that we don't read longer stories. In Hawai'i, in particular, the place of preference to get our news is the television news that is confined by the time that the story has on the air. And most packages are about two minutes. The reporter gets two minutes, and they've gone to the right place and gotten the right quotes, but most editors would take fifteen seconds out of that. What comes out of the story is the stuff that's not sensational.

Q: There must be a way to bring about some kind of change.

Marketing Executive: Not in the media. To expect that people who work in the news media to do anything less to sell their product is too much to ask. The other [people] at fault are you and me because we demand sensational stories.

What Private School Parents Say about the Schools and the Media

When public and private school parents discussed issues in the schools, they were concerned about different topics. When public school parents talked about their children's experiences, safety was not a subject of concern. These are very involved parents; they know what is going on in their children's schools. This does not mean that their children did not run into conflict or have problems, only that the parents did not express concerns about their children's safety. The problems were solvable.

The public schools vary. There may be those not included in this study that have unsafe conditions. But it is important to separate fact from the perception that all public schools, especially the secondary public schools, are unsafe.

On the other hand, during interviews with the private school parents, public school safety came up repeatedly as a concern, as did low test scores and facilities. Private school parents discussed safety issues as a contributing factor in deciding against sending their children to public schools.

The following media executive, who has three children in public schools, discussed this perception held by his relatives who send their children to private schools.

Q: When you hear your relatives talk about their decision to send their children to private schools, what are they saying?

Media Executive: Part of it is that they think that you can buy an education. "I send my kid here. They'll be taken care of." And the other part was safety —kind of a safety issue. They'll say, "It is a sheltered environment. They won't get into trouble. In public schools, you know, bad kids are there." That's what I hear from relatives.

Q: Did they do research about the safety issues?

Media Executive: No.

Q: Have you found safety to be a problem for your three children?

Media Executive: No, absolutely not.

Where do private school parents get their information about public school safety? According to them, it comes primarily from engaging in "the conversation" with peers and from the media.

The following private school parent talked about her social group, of which all the parents send their children to private schools because they think their children will get a better education. She indicated that they don't do research on the public schools because they already have an opinion on them, as influenced by word-of-mouth communication (what she called the "coconut wireless") and the media. What they read in the newspapers are reports about low test scores, crime, and drugs in the public schools. She is sure that crime and drugs are problems in the private schools as well, "but it's not publicized as much."

Q: Even though your children are out of school, does the subject still come up with your friends? The discussion of private school versus public school?

Private School Parent: Yes, my friends all talk about private schools.

Q: Have they researched the public schools?

Private School Parent: No. They research the private school (*laughs*) —all the private schools, from the religious to the . . .

Q: Why do you think they don't research the public schools?

Private School Parent: I think they have an opinion already formed.

Q: Where do they get that opinion?

Private School Parent: Word of mouth, newspapers, you know, the [test] scores, the standardized scores being low, and the crime and the drugs. I mean, I'm sure it happens in private schools, but it's not publicized as much.

You could study the "coconut wireless." Once it's gone through [that], you can't remake it. Once a school has a bad reputation, everybody knows about it, and that's it for them.

Q: If a school has had a bad reputation, but today it has good leadership, a good staff, and they were doing interesting work, how would that school change its public perception, given the "coconut wireless"?

Private School Parent: I think it would take a long time for people to start talking about it. Like some schools—the public high schools—have good reputations for specific areas [of study], like [a certain public high school] is known for its mathematics, and [another public high school] is known for their music. And so it just takes a while. And maybe the school would get awards or win math competitions.

Q: And it would be published in the papers, so the newspapers are really important?

Private School Parent: Yes.

Q: Would you say that it's more important than TV?

Private School Parent: Yes. Well, I focus more on newspapers. I'm sure television counts too. But you know, after half an hour, it's gone, whereas the paper, you have it the whole day. Or you can clip out things and show people. "Oh, look at that."

Q: If some school had a safety issue, and that issue has changed for the better over the years, somehow that information has to get out to help the public change its perceptions of that school?

Private School Parent: Like, New York. You know how it's changed. Before, it was a scary city to visit, and later it became the safest. I have friends, women friends, who go there by themselves. They go there because they have a meeting, or they go to the shows, all by themselves, and they feel so safe.

I mean, we could do that here. You kind of hear a little bit of it getting better in some places. I mean the academic part, but you don't hear about the other stuff. All you hear about is crystal meth and hijacking and all these gang fights and this and that.

Q: Right. So is that conversation a fairly common part of the discussion of public schools?

Private School Parent: Mm-hmm. [Yes.] But I know the same kind of stuff goes on in the private school too. You just don't hear about it.

Another private school mother sent her children to public elementary schools before transferring them to private schools for their secondary education. She discussed in an earlier chapter that she was very happy with her children's elementary public school experiences. Besides engaging in "the conversation," her sources for information about public schools included television, newspaper, and, especially, talk radio, whereby she heard and read all the negative stories about public schools. She believes that the public elementary school her children attended is an exception. She said it's not possible to think of the public schools, overall, as praiseworthy when one hears and reads such negative stories about lack of texts, low test scores, and poor facilities.

Private School Parent: It seems like anytime a report comes out on the public school systems, we're ranked fifty out of fifty, which is scary when you're sending your kids to school for an education, and you're thinking that you want the best for your child, and education is number one.

You hear that schools don't have enough books. They don't have enough chairs. Teachers have to buy their own supplies. They don't have fans, and it's hot, and on and on and on. There's a lot, and then you hear that they're cutting the budget, and yet they've got this money for "Sunset on the Beach." Some things just don't make sense. And so yes, I think the negative feedback that we hear does affect the parents — hearing continual negative stuff about the public schools.

Q: And where did you hear the negative stories?

Private School Parent: Some TV, some newspaper. I listen to talk radio a lot. If I'm in the car, I'm not listening to music. I'm listening to talk radio, especially the local news in the morning. They, sometimes, will go really in-depth with what's going on with our educational system. And then you hear of friends of your kids that don't have books, and that kind of thing.

And even with our experiences in public schools, we would buy fans if they needed them in the classroom. I think we were really fortunate because we had a lot of parents supporting the schools, so I think we were a lot better off than a lot of schools.

Q: Why do you think that we hear so much about the negative schools, and we don't hear equally about schools such as [a certain school reputed to be an excellent school]?

Private School Parent: Because I don't think that there are many good public schools. I think that there are more negative than positive. And I think that's why my children's elementary public school won the blue ribbon award. Every single year we won some kind of grand award, merit award, for art or for music, or for something, but those parents are actively putting in applications for those awards. It's a lot of work, winning a blue ribbon award. I think that [my children's public elementary school] — like a few of the other schools that you hear about — is like a diamond in the rough.

And the public schools are just not going to get the constant praise overall when you hear about schools falling apart, and the bathrooms that are not fixed, and the girls who won't use the bathrooms, or whatever.

A third private school mother talked about her husband's concern for the safety of their son if he went to public schools, as he was of mixed race, and they had read articles in the newspaper about "Get Haole" day, a reference to alleged hostility toward Caucasian students. While this parent's mother supported public schools, a discussion with a neighbor who was a counselor at a public school and who said the schools are "rough" also contributed to their decision to send their son to private school.

Q: Right. How did he come to hold that belief that if his son, who was hapa [mixed], would be at risk in a public school?
Private School Parent: It was primarily what was covered in the media at that time, and secondarily, from anecdotal experiences from people he knew who said that there were a lot of big public schools that are very rough. At that time, I think there were some incidences of "Get Haole" days, so that really exacerbated his concerns. I think the main thing was the "Get Haole" day.
Q: Yes, I heard of that, too, when I moved to Hawai'i.
Private School Parent: And there had been some [newspaper] coverage of it. I was aware of it. We read the same articles, obviously, in the newspapers, but I guess my reaction was quite different from his.
Q: Was this decision to send him to private school supported by family and neighbors and colleagues at work?
Private School Parent: My mother didn't think that it was a very good idea. My mother felt that there was nothing wrong with public schools. Now that I think about it, I know that we also had a neighbor, who was a counselor at one of the schools in our area, who had also talked about how rough the schools are, and how little respect there is for teachers, and a little bit about the condition of the schools. I remember our discussing that when we decided to put our child into a private school from kindergarten.

A public school educator who is also a private school parent spoke from an "insider's" perspective on media coverage of both public and private school.

She shared some of her experiences from when she was a teacher at a public middle school.

Q: Do you feel that the media representation, say, of [the public middle school at which she was employed] is balanced over the years?

Private School Parent: No, I don't. When [the public middle school] had their food fights, and the administrators stopped their May Day, we read all about it. Teachers may have lost control over a few of the students, but I think it's really blown up [by the media]. They might portray students who were around there watching the fight as part of the fight, instead of just two people in a fight.

Q: When your kids were in [a certain private school], did you find that there were kids who got into fights or were smoking or using drugs?

Private School Parent: We know from what our children would share with us that if there were a fight, they would go off campus. And there's a place that they would go to off campus to fight. There was one boy who did hit another boy on campus after school, and we all heard about it, of course.

Q: But now, how is it that that doesn't get reported in the paper?

Private School Parent: I don't know. I really don't know.

Q: Is it a case that with a public institution, all of that information has to be made public, and with private institutions you can keep things private?

Private School Parent: What happens is that, when you're in a public school, you call the Honolulu Police Department [HPD], depending on the severity of the problem. We've had situations — like fights — where I would have to call HPD. We had a situation where a boy got a stab wound, and so we called HPD to help us investigate and to also report it. The media has access to that information. I don't believe that at [the private school], they would call the police.

Q: So they would handle it internally?

Private School Parent: Right. And what they would do is have a meeting with the dean, and then do the reprimanding, and follow up on their own within the school.

Q: I see.

Private School Parent: I know this because we were called in to meet (*laughs*) with all the deans in the high school, and my son had to explain [his misbehavior], and he had to follow up with a Saturday's detention.

Q: And then if something is severe, they dismiss the students?

Private School Parent: Right.

Q: Whereas at a public school you must report it.

Private School Parent: I'll give you an example. That student with a stab wound, which we had to report, and the father came down and everything. It was very mysterious. We didn't know how he got that stab wound, and he wouldn't reveal any of it to us. The police came, questioned him, and even the police were perplexed because they couldn't understand how he got the stab wound.

We got called by the media that afternoon, right away, about the stabbing. It turned out — because my partner and I had a really good relationship with the children — we were just sitting down chatting with a student, and then he just came up to us the next day and started saying, "Oh, by the way, you know that guy that got stabbed?"

It was a project they were going to do after school with this Exacto knife to make little model cars. We had a club that made little model cars. And they put the knife in the backpack. And so like kids, they're walking along, and one guy loses his balance, turns around, stops, the guy in back of him bumped him, and got stabbed. And so I'm going, "Oh, well it's good to know," but here the media had picked it up as a stabbing.

Both of the following private school parents also gave examples of misconduct that happened when their children were in private schools. These incidents were dealt with internally, not publicly reported, and not published in the newspapers. They include a case of "bullying," a case of stealing, and an incident when a trashcan was set on fire.

Private School Parent: There was an instance where my daughter was bullied, but, at that point, it was because of a boy/girl relationship. I said, "You handle it." Her brother had to step in to help her once. But I said, "You handle it in the best way possible so that everyone wins because probably they want your attention."

Q: At the high school level, at your children's private school, when kids smoke, do drugs, get into a fight, or bully other students, how does the private school handle those issues differently from public schools?

Private School Parent: I don't know because my kids never did drugs. They never smoked. They weren't in that circle.

Actually, there was an incident that happened, an incident when [my daughter] was in seventh or eighth grade. One of the students stole the Christmas gifts from a lot of other students. So they did an investigation, and they found out who it was. I guess they made that person give back the gifts. To me, that person should have been kicked out of school. That would have been my thing because, "You know what? You don't represent what we want of a [private school] student."

Q: Why do you think they didn't kick the student out?

Private School Parent: I don't know. People knew about it. On the other hand, there were a group of students who had been kicked out. They were in seventh grade, and they set a rubbish can on fire in the bathroom.

Q: Now public schools have to report everything. Do private schools?

Private School Parent: They don't.

Besides the "incessant conversation" and the role of the media, a number of residents talked about the role of Hawai'i's history of schooling and how this history also contributes to the current community-held belief about public versus private schools in Hawai'i.

The Historical Contribution

Parents often stated that the higher status of private schools in Hawai'i is a legacy of the missionary and plantation days. Part of this legacy has left a lingering belief that separate schooling for different groups is normal. Parents talked about different groups receiving different kinds of education in different systems, creating a perception over time that private schools are for the children of the elite (higher status) and public education for the children of the workers (lower status).

This history helps to explain an association with the public schools as lower status. More affluent descendents of public school graduates then become attracted to these elite private schools because they now can provide their children access to these schools. This is also associated with the idea of "doing better" than the previous generations.

This first local resident talked about the lingering belief among citizens whose ancestors worked on the plantations in Hawai'i. During that period there existed a large gap between plantation owners and workers, separated by race and economics.

Q: And how does that legacy play into the role of public education today?

Consulting Firm Executive: This is my theory.... When you talk to people —third and fourth generation now—who are sending their kids to private schools—why are they doing it? They may say, "We want the best for our children." That's part of it. I think a lot of it really has to do with, "We want to show that we're just as good as the white guys that came here from New

England." It's still there. And how do they do it? "Well, we take over the institutions that they set up because they're the ones who ran this place for so long."

You see it in industry. You see it in various different places. Some of the cohesion that binds the community together still is a remnant of that inferiority piece that came out of the plantation — even though they all received a good education in public schools. They all come through the [public school] system. Their IQs are high, but there's a cultural problem that's still here that impacts, particularly, I think, public education versus private education.

A professor talked about how surprised he and his wife were by the negative comments residents make about Hawai'i — that Hawai'i is inefficient and corrupt. Compared to his mainland urban experiences, he thought that Hawai'i is just the opposite. He speculated that this image is tied to historical racial issues and a presumption that everything on the mainland is better.

Q: Why do you think that this perception exists?

Professor: My own feeling is that it's the holdover from colonial days. I think there's a perception by people that things in Hawai'i are not as good as other places. We are always surprised at the negative comments that people make about things here that we don't get. For instance, there is this perception about how inefficient and/or corrupt, or old-boy network Hawai'i government is. I've lived in [a certain mainland city]. I've lived in [a certain mainland state]. Don't tell me about "old-boy" network corruption/inefficiency. The fact that the people here think it's worse is, frankly, to me, bizarre. In fact, it's a lot better here than our [mainland] experiences.

We think the parks and the bathrooms — public bathrooms are unbelievably good and well kept and maintained. Coming from other urban mainland areas, what Honolulu does is unbelievable. People think it's worse. I'm trying to think what else. Libraries — the fact that you can go into the library on O'ahu and get a book from anywhere in the whole library system of Hawai'i just by ordering it is just incredible! We're always sort of surprised at how poorly people look at what goes on here.

Q: How do you think that perception could be modified?

Professor: Well, one of my theories on this — I might as well say what I believe. I think it's partly that there's a racial issue involved. I hear oftentimes, at parties — a lot of the times I'm one of the few people who is not haole. You know, there is a sort of code word for colonial. We are a third-world inefficient place. That's a very common theme — inefficient third world, like a third-world banana republic. I think that it's a code. I think that it's a racial code. I think that it's said in certain circles. I think there's a certain attitude that goes along with it. I think that's part of it. I think that there is among local people — I think that there's this built-in sort of "I guess we're not that good."

And I think from colonial-plantation days — I am always amazed at how people think that any place on the mainland is better than going to the University of Hawai'i [UH]. They're spending thousands and thousands of dollars on a small private college institution when they could send their kid to UH, which I think would actually be educationally superior. The question then becomes, "Why do people do that?" "Well, we want to give them a mainland experience." In a small, rural, isolated liberal arts college in the middle of Oregon, you're not going to get a mainland experience.

This next resident repeated, in essence, what the first two stated: the idea that "everything from the mainland is better" reflects a historical legacy.

Executive Banker: We somehow don't believe enough in ourselves as a people still. We still want the extra to come from the mainland. You know we get someone local to say something [and you hear groans]. We get the same thing said by somebody from the mainland we go, "That's brilliant." I scratch my head and go, "Well, we already heard that one."

And we do this to ourselves all the time. Hawai'i puts itself down. Even our leaders tell us we have no choices, but that we're simply buffeted by the economic winds of other places. We're not in control of our own destiny, blah, blah, blah. This community puts itself down all the time. And Jack Burns said it was just a subtle sense of inferiority, and he angered people. I've angered people when I've said it, but I really believe that. I think it is one of the root devils we wrestle with.

A DOE administrator pointed out that from this historical legacy comes the idea of separate schools for different groups of people.

DOE Administrator: The historical legacy I'm sure has a lot to do with it. And when you think about why these [private] schools were founded in the first place, they were there to segregate, right? I mean, the missionaries' reason for founding [a certain private school] was so that their children wouldn't have to associate with the common folk. And so there's that. I think some of that mentality continues to flourish with regards to thinking that the private schools provide a better education.

An attorney said that half of his attorney friends, who graduated from public schools, send their children to private schools. He connected the reason for doing so to the idea that certain racial or ethnic groups now have access to the elite private schools, and so they choose them rather than public schools. Private school is commonly defined, he believes, as giving one's children the best education — the "best" defined as a safe environment, academically challenging work, and a place in which their children will mingle with "the right people." He also felt that the elite private schools have status.

Q: And, out of the half who are public school graduates, they're still making the decision to send their children to private school?

Attorney: Yes. In Honolulu, I think what happened was that as people got — certain races — more economic power, I think that they felt that, despite their doing well and having come through public education with a good education, they started believing the press.

And when you look at the physical facilities of the private schools here, many colleges would be salivating at having what they have. And then you look at the public facilities of the public schools and you say, "Well, yeah, maybe the public schools could do okay, but I really want to give my kids the best." That is a very common kind of attitude. And the "best" being, one, a safe environment and, two, an environment that their children will be challenged in and three —

Q: Challenged academically?

Attorney: Academically, . . . [and] three, being in an environment in which they will mingle with "the right people." Because I think there is that. I think there's a real status component to this decision.

Next interviewed was a local resident who believes that the situation regarding schooling in Hawai'i is partially the result of a self-fulfilling prophesy. Each generation is trying to "better oneself," and sending one's children to private schools is viewed as evidence that one is successful. He believes that the result of this association of "private" with "better" is that families have forgotten where they came from, and they no longer identify with families who are working through some of the same situations today.

Q: To what extent do you think Hawai'i's own special history has encouraged private schools?

Media Executive: You know, lately — this is my own opinion, and I'm just guessing; I don't pretend to be an expert on the subject — but I think we kind of created a situation. It's almost like a self-fulfilling prophecy about public schools. Public schools are how more and more people became professionals. Kids of the plantation laborers come back [from college] to Hawai'i to be professionals, and they're not laborers anymore. The idea was that you always bettered yourself. This was the lesson passed on from your grandfather to your father, and then to you. Every generation tries to be better. You try to be smarter than your father, richer than your father, you know. Every generation should be better than the next.

I think in Hawai'i that's what we're saying. "Let's send our kids to private school." Education was always a big thing, at least in the Asian society in Hawai'i. Education was always a huge part of the society, and now that you could afford it, yes, you send your kid to private school. And I think that kind of started it.

Q: So one part of it might be that within the Asian culture, going to private school is a reflection of having done better than the previous generation?

Media Executive: In some ways, yes. In doing so, you forget your past, which is the big thing about the last election. I forgot that great line they had about how the Democrats were kind of losing power, and that they had had succeeded so well as Democrats that they had created a generation of Republicans. It was a great line, you know, and that is what kind of happened. You lost sight of what made you and your values at that time. Now that you achieved all these things, you just want to protect your own things. You forget that you need to share, and that you need to remind other people of that lesson. You can't forget where you came from, and that your families had to work out of the same situation that these people are working out of now.

These interviews end with a father suggesting that the legacy of "keeping apart" is "just part of history."

Q: Do you think that the public school system or the private school system has higher status in Hawai'i? Was this always the case, and why?

Attorney: Yeah, I think . . . I think, based on my knowledge of the history. I think this was part of the whole missionary culture that came in, missionaries feeling they couldn't have their kids go to the same [local] schools. It's in that book that I read. So I don't know if that's influencing me, but you can kind of see it. So the missionaries created their own schools, and then there were the English standard schools. So there was always this movement toward creating institutions that were special for certain people. It just sort of permeates our history. I don't think it's a new thing. I think its something that's just been part of history.

The interviewees in this chapter mention several historical situations that warrant further discussion. Connecting "the conversation," the role of the media, and the role of Hawai'i's history of schooling to the current community belief will be the focus of the next chapter. It is an attempt to step back from the reasons individual parents make school choices to examining the community in which the choices are made. It will be, in other words, an attempt to connect the dots.

6 Connecting the Dots
The Master Narrative

Private schools are usually judged by their
successes while public schools are judged
by their failures. (DePledge 2004, A1)

Parents in this study describe a community-held belief that private schools have a higher social status than public schools. There also exists a belief that individual public schools vary, with some elementary schools having "good reputations" and some high schools having excellent programs. This second belief is typically not acknowledged publicly.

On the other hand, all private schools (there are more than 130 in the state of Hawai'i) are viewed as safe, with high academic expectations for their students and adequate resources that lead to well-maintained facilities and small classes. In addition, the private schools are commonly viewed as providing a more direct route to prestigious mainland colleges. Only one parent in this study mentioned that all private schools are not alike.

The reasons for the continuing strength of this community-held belief include (1) the impact of a seemingly ever-present "incessant conversation" about school choice in which parents, especially professionals on the island of O'ahu, talk about where they are going to send their children to school; (2) the impact of more distant conversations or stories about public schools as reported in the media; and (3) the history of schooling in the islands. These findings come from the parents' interview data. In turn, these data serve as the basis for the thesis developed in this chapter.

I'm going to step back from the interviews to examine the ways in which I see these three reasons as interconnected, beginning with a review of the history of school systems in Hawai'i.

What Is the History of Hawai'i's Schools?

In Chapter 5 we heard from parents who believe that the higher status of private schools in Hawai'i is, at least in part, a legacy of the missionary and plantation days, and the result of this legacy is the continuing belief that separate schooling for different groups is normal.

Parents discussed how this legacy created a belief over time that private schools are, as they have been historically, for the children of the elite (higher status) and that public education is for children of the workers (lower status).

We heard from parents, primarily local residents, who speculate that this history has left a lingering attitude among residents that might explain the association of public schools with a lower status. More affluent descendents of public school graduates (along with those who traditionally have attended private schools) become attracted to elite private schools, as they now can provide their children with access to schools with a higher status. Private schooling is also, in part, the definition of "doing better" than the previous generation.

The following section is not a full history of schooling in Hawai'i, as I limited my research to documents related to the issue of separate schools for separate groups.

The "Keeping Apart"

The early founders of public schools . . . believed that universal public schooling was a democratic society's best instrument for shaping and sustaining such a society. The interdependence of schooling and society called for a partnership between schools and community.
(Sikkema 1997, B4)

Historically, the goal of public education in the United States has been to serve as the vehicle for upward mobility and development of the community's sense of "the common good" necessary to sustain a democratic society. Communities nationwide have had varied success in reaching this goal. In Hawai'i, for example, when different groups went to different school systems, it created a history of "keeping apart" and served as a mechanism for social stratification, which, in turn, has had an additional impact on the community: "One of the consequences of this dual educational system is that in Hawai'i the social and political elite has little interest in the public education system" (Tehranian 2001, B1). A dual educational system was present in Hawaiian society before the arrival of the missionaries in 1820. The children of the Hawaiian *ali'i*, chiefs of the royal families, were educated separately from the children of *maka'āinana*, the commoners (Wist 1940; Malo 1996).

The *ali'i* had to be prepared to assume their proper place in society and to maintain a position of power while ensuring the well-being of the people and the land. The commoner was educated to "do the common work and to accept unquestionably their status" (Wist 1940, 9), although traditional education did include, for various social classes, the teaching of traditional medical arts, astronomy, agriculture, and aquaculture, as well as important aspects of oceanography critical for fishing and seafaring responsibilities. After the arrival of the Protestant missionaries in the 1820s, the missionaries initially focused their educational efforts on the *ali'i* only. Under the young *ali'i* Liholiho, Kamehameha III, a "kingdom of learning" was decreed. Missionaries taught literacy skills to the *ali'i* households. The *ali'i* then sent their best and most literate retainers to the rest of the regions and villages to establish schools that were quickly constructed and filled with students of all ages, until entire villages became literate and able to compete in annual literacy competitions. However, as *ali'i* power declined, so did literacy rates; except for those who eventually worked in government or education, most commoners could not use such skills for employment in a culture whose power structure was changing and that was altering their way of life (M. N. Chun 2006).

Eventually, schools were established for each group. Missionary-trained native teachers taught in Hawaiian at the schools for commoners (Wist 1940; Stueber 1982). The select schools, on the other hand, which were founded for the children of the chiefs, half-Hawaiians, and a select few Christian-Hawaiian children of commoners, were well supplied, with a Western curriculum (Stueber 1982; DePledge 2004). The underlying belief for these separate schools was that within a social hierarchy, the *ali'i* needed advanced schooling whereas the commoners did not (Benham and Heck 1998). Missionary children at that time were educated at home, then continued their education on the continent.

Separate schools for separate groups continued throughout the nineteenth century. During the period 1830–1880, the O'ahu Charity School was founded for the education, in English, of the hapa-haole (half-white) children of foreign residents, and the Royal School was established in Honolulu to provide a suitable education, in English, for the children of Hawaiian royalty (Wist 1940; Menton 1992). Later, to create educational opportunities for students of Hawaiian ancestry, the Kamehameha School for Boys was founded in 1887, and the School for Girls opened in 1894 (Kamehameha Schools 2006).

During this period Protestant, Catholic, Anglican, and Mormon missionaries also established separate schools in Hawai'i. One of the most well-known elite private schools, Punahou, was founded by missionaries in 1841 so that they could provide their own children with an education similar to that which they received in New England, and one that would lead to higher education (Wist 1940). Thus these children would no longer have to be educated at home. The mission of Punahou would be to educate those who would hold leadership positions in the community. The missionaries also wanted their children to be kept apart from the Hawaiians, both in language and culture (Dotts and Sikkema 1994).

In 1897, 27 percent of Hawai'i's school-aged children attended private schools. The remainder were educated in a public school system in which the buildings, maintenance, equipment, resources, salaries, and number of teachers and schools were deemed inadequate (Dotts and Sikkema 1994).

From the late nineteenth century through the early twentieth century the culture and ethnic mix of Hawai'i was modified once again as a result of the emerging sugar industry, the overthrow of the monarchy, and the annexation of Hawai'i. In order to provide laborers for the sugar plantations, for example, the business and plantation owners imported workers from Japan, China, the Philippines, Portugal, and elsewhere. The living and working conditions of the workers were structured to "keep apart" each ethnic group in separate housing areas (sometimes called "camps" or "villages"). However, these laborers from diverse backgrounds had to work together, and this resulted in the creation of a pidgin language used to communicate on the job. The next generation, the children of these workers, expanded this pidgin until it eventually developed into a Creole language (formally known as Hawaiian Creole English). Today, this regional language supports a robust local literature and remains part of the identity of many residents (Sakoda and Siegel 2003).

But this Hawaiian Creole English was not Standard American English; it was the language of the children of plantation workers. From the 1920s to the early 1930s, the ethnic mix of public school students was predominantly non-Caucasian. This mix, and the language difference, led to the next stage of separate schooling, which took the form of the select English Standard schools.

The European (haole) population also increased during this period due to industrial and military expansion. Not all members of this incoming group could afford private schools, but they were reluctant to send their children to Hawai'i's public schools with children who spoke Hawaiian Creole English (Tamura 1994). These parents wanted public schools where English was spoken; thus enter the select English Standard public schools.

Children who passed an admissions test and who readily spoke and used

Standard American English were admitted to these select public schools. Most of them were Caucasian. This separate public school system made it much more difficult for local students to learn English, since they had little or no opportunity to converse with Standard American English speakers on a regular basis (Dotts and Sikkema 1994). It also encouraged elitism, as only 2 to 9 percent of public school students could attend these schools (Tamura 1994).

The English Standard schools operated between 1924 and 1949 and were completely phased out by 1960 (Tamura 1994), as all public schools were required to raise standards to those found in the English Standard schools (Benham and Heck 1998).

All of these historical policies were designed to keep different groups of the community apart, making the development of a unified communal spirit more difficult.

Attempts to Bring Democracy to the Public Schools

Throughout the nineteenth and twentieth centuries, however, there were public school educators in Hawai'i who believed in providing a better opportunity for all students — educators who worked for change. Three examples follow.

H. S. Townsend, the superintendent of all Hawai'i public schools from 1896 to 1899, believed in providing access to a better education for all children. As scholars note, his beliefs ran counter to the business elites' view that "educational funds should not be wasted on common laborers" (Benham and Heck 1998, 108). Townsend was pressured to resign, and he was replaced by a superintendent comfortable with carrying out a more traditional program (Dotts and Sikkema 1994).

In 1919 another superintendent (in the same mold as Townsend), Vaughan MacCaughey, was appointed by Governor McCarthy. He, too, supported fostering the intellectual growth of all public school students, who were mostly of diverse, non-Caucasian ethnicities. As scholars have noted, he believed in developing a curriculum that endorsed democratic values, resulting in a common culture for all classes and producing a more knowledgeable citizenry. He was critical of the way the public schools maintained Hawai'i's stratified society instead of encouraging change (Benham and Heck 1998; Stueber 1982; Dotts and Sikkema 1994).

Scholars also note that the business elite were concerned that such views "placed the idea of social advancement into the minds of ethnic laborers" — undoubtedly alarming to them, since the business community needed a source of manual labor for the plantations (Benham and Heck 1998, 151). Consequently, MacCaughey was not reappointed by Governor Farrington.

Finally, there was Superintendent R. Burl Yarberry, appointed in the 1960s by Governor Quinn. Like Townsend and MacCaughey before him, he was committed to the goals of public schools as envisioned by the nation's founders. Yet it seems even many decades after the tenures of Townsend and Mac-Caughey, the business establishment was still unwilling to accept such a "radical" view, as he was also ultimately forced to resign (Dotts and Sikkema 1994).

In spite of this history, however, these progressive educators made an impact by introducing and pushing the concept that public education was not primarily to provide a laboring class, but instead, as one scholar wrote, it "was a democratic society's best instrument for shaping and sustaining such a society" (Sikkema 1997). Yet in my research, the educator whose name came up most frequently was not a superintendent at all. Rather, it was Miles Cary, a high school principal.

Cary was principal of McKinley High School between 1924 and 1948. At the time, McKinley was the oldest, largest, and most prestigious public high school. One educator noted that it was considered a privilege to teach there (T. T. Hirata 1988). Students, mostly Asian Americans, were academically inclined, reflecting family-held values toward education, as noted by Eileen Tamura (1994) in her book on the nisei (second-generation Japanese) of Hawai'i.

Ethical Leadership: "Wanting the Best"

A former student from McKinley High School reflected,

> I think the generation of students who went through McKinley at the time [Miles Cary] was principal all benefited from the sense that he was the one who was very much interested in their welfare and always wanted the best for them. (K. Yamamoto, as cited in Shoho 1997, 10)

There exists, in the literature, a number of references to Miles Cary and the historical time period and context in which he worked. Between World War I and World War II, political and business leaders intended to discourage upward mobility for the children of immigrants (Shoho 1997). Teachers were pressured to convey a positive message to such students about plantation work (Tamura 1994).

Cary recognized the contradiction between encouraging youths to be plantation laborers and preparing them for "full, intelligent, and open-eyes citizenship." Some segments of the community, he said, feared that children of plantation laborers were becoming acculturated, filled with ideas of equality and opportunity, and posing challenges to others in the job market (Tamura 1994, 144). Cary, on the other hand, envisioned the school as an institution that would promote democracy by helping students develop a strong ethical character as they engaged in real community problems, preparing them for adult civic responsibility (Williams 1991).

Gladys Feirer, a teacher at McKinley High School, recalled during an interview that some people did not like Cary because he encouraged students to investigate issues that concerned them. "He told kids," she recalled, "if you want to find out about something, you find out about it. If you think your parents are paying too much [in] taxes, go and find out, see what's going on" (Hyams 1985, 214; Feirer 1983).

"Every time he went to the auditorium," recalled former state legislator Akira Sakima, "he used to walk up and down and give his talk. He was always preaching democracy. Think for yourself" (Tamura 1994, 172).

And he modeled "thinking for oneself" with his willingness to speak out against social injustice. By modeling ethical behavior, Cary succeeded in creating a learning environment where students felt mutually respected and empowered. He believed that it was important "for students to practice and to witness ethical behavior being used daily" in order to understand what it meant and how it was used (Shoho 1997, 4). Cary viewed student ethical behavior as a framework through which these future citizens could practice the concepts of fairness, democracy, and equal opportunity — values necessary to promote a healthy, cohesive community (Tamura 1996).

Cary implemented both curricular and organizational changes so that he could put his philosophical beliefs into practice. For example, English and social studies were combined into a core studies curriculum. Each core class also served as the homeroom and the basic unit of the school's government. Student representatives were elected and working committees formed to work on school issues and problems (Watanabe 1962; Tamura 1996).

The goal of the core studies was both academic and democratic in that it was meant to provide students with an experience that would help them learn to shape the conditions in which they lived by examining school-related, city, territorial (before statehood), national, and international research topics (Tamura 1996).

The daily school newspaper, the *Daily Pinion*, was a second innovation. Working on the newspaper gave students experience with journalism as well as another opportunity to examine critical school issues, and it taught students about broader community issues (K. Yamamoto 1979; Shoho 1997; Tamura 1996).

In sum, Miles Cary, a public school educator, integrated the principles of democracy and civic virtue within an academically challenging public school education. He taught students that "democracy meant equality of opportunity, concern for the common good, independent thinking, and civil rights" (Tamura 1996, 24). Cary and his teaching staff demonstrated what is possible when public school educators believe, deeply, in the possibilities within public education. And he continues to be a symbol of what is possible. In a recent editorial column in the *Honolulu Advertiser,* the editor wrote,

> There is a limited pantheon of individuals who have made an indelible mark on the quality of education in Hawai'i, both public and private.
>
> One such was the legendary Miles Cary, principal of McKinley High School between 1924 and 1948. Cary, a committed believer in "progressive" education, established ideals of democracy and civic obligation in generations of youngsters and future public leaders. ("Rod Mcphee Leaves Vast Educational Legacy" 2005, A16)

What Happened to McKinley High School Graduates?

Dotts and Sikkema (1994, 117) believe that "the result of Cary's program and commitment and work of his teachers was a generation of primarily non-Caucasian students who would have influence on the social structure of Hawai'i." Many McKinley graduates developed the confidence and motivation to move into the middle class, modifying the economic and social structure in Hawai'i. Benham and Heck (1998, 156) also state that the "the importance of McKinley High School, Principal Cary, and its progressive teachers to future economic and political life in Hawai'i cannot be underplayed." It was an example of the role of good public education in promoting class mobility.

Many McKinley graduates became members of the highly decorated 442nd Regimental Combat Team during World War II, and graduates became a "Who's Who of Notables" in Hawai'i's history, ranging from a U.S. senator, state governors, an attorney general, and a chief justice, as well as presidents and CEOs of private businesses (Benham and Heck 1998; Dotts and Sikkema 1994).

Many of these graduates were Americans of Japanese ancestry (AJAs) who, along with others in the community, became involved in putting public education reform at the top of the Democratic Party platform in the 1950s, resulting in public school reform during the 1950s and 1960s. Markrich (2000, B4) writes, "Governor John Burns was so supportive that money for education in 1970 made up 50 percent of the state budget. By 1975, it appeared that the Democratic Revolution was complete and that the public schools had been upgraded beyond what many had ever thought possible." Today, approximately 82 percent (180,000) of the student population attends Hawai'i's public schools. All ethnic groups and all social classes are represented.

However, approximately 18 percent of children in Hawai'i continue to attend private schools, one of the highest rates in the nation, indicating that the concept of "keeping apart" remains a robust belief in Hawai'i. Currently, the public schools are struggling, once again, to assert a status of respect. According to Markrich (2000), it fell apart after Burns died in 1975. There was no longer a Democratic Party leader willing to put public education first, or a group of cohesive activists from an ethnic group (as the AJA Democrats had been) to insist on it.

In addition, parent involvement and government funding have declined. Markrich points out that in 1970, when the state population was 760,000, about 94,000 belonged to the Parent-Teacher Association (PTA). Today, out of a state population of 1.2 million, 38,558 belong to the PTA. Although some of this loss is offset through membership in other parents' groups at individual school sites, it is significant. Further, the public education budget has declined from 50 percent to 23 percent (Koyama 2006).

It's as if each generation has to renew attention to the concept of a strong public school system, without which the community falls back into the historical legacy of "keeping apart."

Development of a Master Narrative: Historical Legacy

Benham and Heck (1998, 35) write that the lingering effects of the early separate institutional structures are "powerful and continue to have a long lasting effect on the educational opportunities for particular groups of children in the state." The imprint of this community's history remains, often, unconscious on the present. Dotts and Sikkema (1994) explain that attitudes, values, and beliefs, which underlie action, are usually rooted in cultural experience and absorbed subconsciously as part of daily living within the family, at work, and through participation in various group activities in the community. These beliefs are deeply embedded. One is not consciously aware of them and may even deny their existence. There is often no conscious awareness of the differences between what people say they believe and what they do.

These authors believe that

the vastly differing feelings and attitudes of Caucasian and non-Caucasians were incorporated unconsciously over the years, to varying degrees, by families, by business and industry, by teachers and school administrators, by the entire community. They became deeply embedded, hidden from awareness. Although the tendency is to deny it, they continue to be reflected in various ways in the day-to-day behavior of students, teachers, administrators, and other adults in the community. (1994, 222)

These historical beliefs appear today in a different form, one that continues the legacy of "keeping apart"—not along ethnic lines, but, rather, socioeconomic (Nakaso 2006).

The Economic "Keeping Apart"

Today in Hawai'i, while students in private schools tend to look like children in public schools, Hawai'i's elite private schools carry the potential to divide Hawai'i's children according to family income. In two of these private schools, 'Iolani and Punahou, approximately 10 percent of 'Iolani families ("Hawai'i Guide to Private Schools 2006" 2005), and 11 percent of Punahou families currently receive financial aid to help pay annual tuitions of about fifteen thousand dollars (Vorsino 2007). Tuitions continue to rise, and most parents need to be able to pay.

If public education isn't (once again) given higher priority, according to state representative David Stegmaier (Nakaso 1999, S1), Hawai'i may be creating a gulf between social classes: "It's leading people to not understand each other, not appreciate each other, not being able to communicate with each other." The answer, Stegmaier continues, lies in ensuring a strong public school system that provides "every student with the kind of education and opportunities to rise to whatever level she might wish to, so there isn't any kind of class barrier" (S1).

Looking through the lens of this history, it is reasonable to conclude that the parents' hypothesis is sustained, and it is not difficult to understand why remnants of the historical legacy exist today. We can place the current "incessant conversation" about public schools within this historical context.

"The Incessant Conversation"

How exactly does "the conversation" about schools in Hawai'i keep the historical legacy alive?

To review, in earlier chapters parents in this study reported how they would engage in conversations with their professional colleagues, family members, and neighbors about school choice. As one private school parent indicated, these conversations are "incessant." For newcomers to the islands, sometimes these conversations take place even before they move to Hawai'i. "The conversation" appears to be a primary means of conveying to newcomers and local residents alike the historical story or narrative in which Hawai'i's public schools are failing and the private schools are succeeding. Conversations about schools are frequent and similar. They often include phrases such as, "Oh god, the school system is horrific! You have to find a private school" or "Hey, the only good schools around are the private schools. You don't want your kid hanging out in a public school. Look at the buildings. It's dangerous." A private school parent acknowledged the belief that "It is the conventional wisdom that private schools are superior to public schools."

Given the climate of this legacy, of those professionals in this study who decided to send their children to public schools, most were "going against the grain" of their peers' belief systems. By and large, their peers did not support their decisions. In most cases, however, these parents were very comfortable with their decisions to send their children to public schools and happy with the results. Many shared a philosophical belief in the advantages of public schools. In addition, many conducted research on individual schools so that they had information with which to make a final decision.

However, some parents still felt peer pressure for dissenting against the professional community's norm. This pressure increases when decisions are being made about secondary schools. The community belief allows for some variation for "good reputation" public elementary schools, but less for public high schools, and none for public middle schools. Nevertheless, all public schools are generally viewed as unsafe places of low achievement. In stark contrast to the opinions within the professional community, parents in this study with children in public secondary schools said their children felt safe and that they were challenged academically. It does not mean that their children never had conflicts in school or that they never had "poor" teachers, but such problems were manageable.

However, adding to the difficulty of making an "against the grain" decision were the conversations these parents had with some of their children's teachers and principals who sent their own children to private schools. It was not unusual for public school teachers and principals to recommend that these parents take their children out of public school and send them to private school, just as they had done.

How is it, though, that conversations can be so powerful that they become part of newcomers' belief systems and reinforce those of many local residents? In the following section I share some of my ideas as to how this happens.

Are conversations, used as a means of communicating a community's beliefs and values, unique to Hawai'i? No. The following mainland scenario has a Hawai'i version.

> For decades Buddy Lev's drugstore served as the hub of intellectual and political life for liberal-minded Annapolitans. During the week, Elinor's dad and others in the community found excuses to stop by and chat, and on Sunday a cadre of doctors, lawyers, professors, store owners, and others would regularly congregate at Buddy Levy's, ostensibly to pick up the *New York Times* at one of the few places it was delivered. The regulars would linger, some at the lunch counter with the paper folded or spread out in front of them but not eating, and others, like Elinor's dad, leaning his elbow on the pharmacy counter, his head close to Buddy's in intense dialogue. Wherever they rested themselves, they carried on extended, animated exchanges about political happenings. These Sunday experiences served as an analog of a church service for townsfolk as they told each other what they knew, what they believed, what they felt, and what they wished to be happening. Although often irreverent and challenging, the stories of the congregants cemented their moral positions about political events and about one another. (Ochs and Capps 2001, 1)

Ochs and Capps' point is that this scene is "emblematic of the social life of narrative" (1). Whenever people get together, they talk about what is happening: what they heard, what they read, what they saw on television or in person, and what they imagined might be happening. The talk often takes the form of a story or narrative. Ochs and Capps argue that the personal narrative is a way to understand life events and place them in some logical order that makes sense across the past and the present. Narrators draw in their conversational partners to help them develop frameworks for understanding events. Sometimes the conversational partners do this by agreeing with the narrator, and sometimes they "poke holes in their story" (2001, 2). This conversational narrative is common the world over.

And as odd as this idea may sound, our personal narratives or the community's collective memories are "half someone else's" (Bakhtin 1981, 298). For example, when newcomers arrive in Hawai'i, they engage in conversations with their colleagues at work and with their neighbors about school choice. They talk with residents who are likely to share their version of Hawai'i's public schools, one influenced by the community's stock of stories about schools in Hawai'i. The newcomer is then likely to internalize some of these stories and make it hers. The stories become part of her memory. In the future, when she talks about school choice, she may include in her conversation what she had heard. In other words, her revised narrative may be "half someone else's." This process can explain how we eventually come to share similar narratives in a community.

As Ochs & Capps explain (2001, 8), these shared conversations or narratives are "the communicative glue that establishes and maintains close relationships in many communities. Commiserating, gossiping, philosophizing, exchanging advice . . . builds common ways of acting, thinking, feeling and otherwise being in the world." Narrative aims to create cohesiveness and coherence, often emphasizing a single point of view by eliminating alternative perspectives, and that is the danger. A community's conversational narrative about "schools" can support "a single overarching storyline [that] . . . maintains a consistent stance of certainty and competence in discerning right and wrong" (22).

This appears to be the case in Hawai'i, in which the inherited single, overarching storyline is that "public schools are failing and the private schools are succeeding. You should send your children to private schools." This is the master narrative for the middle, upper middle, and elite classes, in particular. We can call this narrative "The Public Schools Are Failing. The Private Schools Are Succeeding." This master narrative doesn't allow conflicting beliefs to be considered. That is why the parents in this study who take an alternative perspective, and who make an alternative decision about their children's schooling, are often viewed as "going against the grain."

There is what MacIntyre calls a "stock of stories" (cited in Wertsch 2002, 57) that exists in every community at large. And one community's stock of stories may differ from another community's because the stories are developed within the context of each community. Members of a community learn these stories or master narratives at home, at school, from the media, and from other sources. And as Dotts and Sikkema (1994) have pointed out, we are not always consciously aware of the stories we have learned.

The community's "stock of stories" becomes part of the collective memory that community members share — one that comes from the past and is reinforced or modified in the present. This collective memory is not the sum total of citizens' firsthand experiences, but rather the result of stories about our community life we tell each other (Wertsch 2002). For example, private school parents in the study reported that they and their colleagues do not typically conduct research on public schools because they have already formed an opinion, often based on "word of mouth" or newspaper headlines and stories.

Citizens, according to Wertsch, "are often committed to believing community narratives, sometimes in deeply emotional ways having to do with fundamental issues of identity" (2002, 9). And the narratives are not neutral. They often reflect a single, committed perspective of a particular group's social framework, and this perspective is so powerful it maybe viewed as unquestionable (Wertsch 2002).

A community's collective memory could benefit from some critical analysis (Wertsch 2002). Questions could be raised such as, Why does a community have the stock of stories that it has and not some other stories? Who has a vested interest in creating and promoting certain stories that make up a community's collective memory? How are these stories used by the members of a community?

I argue that the legacy of Hawai'i's history of schooling has resulted in a stock of stories or narratives that make up our present-day collective memory about schools. These are authoritative narratives that reflect the historical separation of groups of individuals, however the groups are defined. And this "separateness" is part of our community as we have imagined it.

Imagined Communities

Anderson (1991, 6) developed this concept of imagined communities. He explains by stating that communities (or nations) are imagined because the members "will never know most of their fellow members, meet them, or even hear of them, yet in the minds of each lives the images of their communion." He further argues that the emergence of communities requires what Wertsch (2002, 6) calls our "cultural tools," such as newspapers, maps, and conversational narratives. Cultural tools that lie behind imagined communities are typically employed in order to create a clearly recognizable collective.

Imagined communities require a shared collective memory that "reflects a committed perspective, and belongs to one group, and not to others" (Wertsch 2002, 66). Consistent with this concept is the notion that an effective way to socialize members of a collective into having a particular view of the past is to provide them with the appropriate textual resources, such as a stock of stories about the past (Wertsch 2002). This is what happens when newcomers come to Hawaiʻi. As they interact with their neighbors, business associates, and new friends, they engage in "the incessant conversation" about schools in Hawaiʻi, and newcomers come to understand that the community-held narrative about public schools ("Public Schools Are Failing") is often considered "unquestionable."

As members of a community we learn who we are from the community's texts or stock of stories. Our narratives piece together a set of separate events into a coherent whole (Wertsch 2002). Our narratives convey what we value. But who in the community chooses what we value? Narratives are not neutral, and they are associated with a version of moral order that casts the narrative as, among other things, "a story of failure or success" (Mink 1978, 140). In Hawaiʻi, the master narrative about schooling casts the public schools as failing and private schools as succeeding. One can see evidence of a moral order connected to this narrative that embeds the concept of sending one's children to private schools as "doing the best for my children" and, therefore, as the morally correct thing to do.

It is not easy to modify entrenched authoritative narratives to allow for different versions. The "words" of community members with high status and political power carry more weight in shaping the community narrative, including conversational narratives. If a narrative is connected to those in the community viewed with authority, it is viewed as authoritative, and peer pressure supports an acceptance of this narrative. Alternative views are not invited. The text is taken as something that does not invite modification or commentary from the speaker, and it is to be used as is (Wertsch 2002). But the professionals in this study give voice to an alternative version of the community narrative, one that does not cast public schools as failing and embeds the concept that sending one's children to public schools is "doing the best for my children" and is also a morally justified decision. These parents provide one source of evidence for justifying the addition of an alternative community narrative or modifying the current master narrative regarding public schools: their children did not fail.

However, this version is not readily accepted, even though the parents in the study are also members of the professional and upper classes who carry weight in the community. The "words" of the historical narrative remain dominant. At this point, the professionals in this study represent a group of citizens who are "going against the grain" of history and the majority of their colleagues.

How might a dominant community narrative be modified? In contrast to authoritative narratives that allow no modification, there is a way that conversational narratives could be used by citizens in a community. Lotman's (1988) idea is that the community's conversational narratives could be used as thinking devices. They would be viewed as opportunities to engage in dialogue with others in the community — dialogue that could result in changing the narrative. In other words, this use of conversation could encourage "keeping an open mind." Our stock of stories could be viewed reflectively and raise questions such as, Should I believe this narrative about public schools? What is the evidence supporting it? What is the evidence contradicting the narrative? Am I willing to consider an alternative version?

But our conversational narratives are not the only source through which we reinforce the historical narrative. In order for an alternative master narrative to be added, or for the current master narrative to be modified, we as citizens have to examine our other sources that exist in the community, especially the narratives developed through the media.

Media Analysis

The local newspapers, magazines, television stations, and radio stations also play a significant role in forming and reinforcing resident and newcomer perceptions of the local public schools. Parents in the study talk about how the newspapers, in particular, frame front-page headline stories regarding test scores, issues of school safety, and public school facilities. Both public and private school parents in this study believe that newspapers, television reports, and talk radio structure these stories to create a negative perception of public schools. This is reflective of the authoritative narrative that the "public schools are failing, private schools are succeeding, and you need to send your children to private schools."

Examples from parents' interviews from chapter 5 are included here as a reminder of the impact of the media in reinforcing this historical master narrative.

Public School Parent 1: You will not see a headline that some of our public schools are very, very good. It's just not the nature of the media to cover that angle — far better to say that we are lower than Mississippi.

Public School Parent 2: And there's a kind of line that you hear over and over again from the legislators or from the editorial page or whatever about how the public schools are really in trouble. My sense, when I talk to people, is that it varies a great deal from one school to another. It's not a systemic thing. There are some public schools that are obviously very troubled. But there are a lot of public schools that are very, very healthy, good schools.

Public School Parent 3: I've seen statistics that indicate a large majority of citizens only get their information through the evening news ... and clearly the media does drive a lot of that [negative] perception. You know, it's always interesting when they talk about, "Well, the statewide average for public schools in Hawai'i is below the national average in reading, and it is slightly above in math," or whatever the statistic is. It's interesting because you could flip [those statistics] a lot of different ways. You could say that — I don't know what the specific number is, but I do believe that 60 percent of the public schools exceed the national average. And no one talks about those kinds of statistics.

Private School Parent 1: [Friends] all talk about sending their children to private schools because they feel that they would get a better education.

Q: Have they researched the public schools?

Private School Parent 1: No. They research the private schools (*laughs*) — all the private schools, from the religious to the —

Q: I see. And why do you think they don't research the public schools?

Private School Parent 1: I think they have an opinion formed already.

Q: Where do they get that opinion?

Private School Parent 1: Word of mouth, newspapers, you know — the [test] scores — the standardized scores being low, and the crime and drugs. I mean, I'm sure it happens in private schools, but it's not publicized as much.

Private School Parent 2: Well, it seems like anytime a report comes out on the public school system, we're ranked 50 out of 50. Which is scary when you're sending your kids to school for and an education, and ... you want the best for your child. . . .

You hear that schools don't have enough books. They don't have enough chairs. Teachers have to buy their own supplies. They don't have fans and it's hot and on and on and on. . . . And, so yes, I think the negative feedback that we hear does affect parents — I mean, hearing continual negative stuff about the public schools.

Q: And where do you hear the negative stories?

Private School Parent 2: Probably the news.

Other examples of citizens internalizing news stories that reinforce this "Public Schools Are Failing" master narrative can be found regularly in the letters to the editor in newspapers, examples similar to the following.

Schools offer option to lousy public ed
The Department of Education wants to "lower the educational proficiency bar" in Hawai'i's public schools. Very soon they will have to start digging a hole so that the lowering bar has a place to go. This is indeed a very "grave" situation.

On the other hand, the Kamehameha Schools is trying to keep the bar high, so that qualified attending Hawaiian-blood students can rightfully and proudly continue to hold their heads high. Heaven help them! (Reiziss 2005)

This example apparently refers to the Hurley and Shapiro headline story in the *Honolulu Advertiser* on August 5, 2005, titled "BOE May Lower Bar to Pass No Child Tests," in which the first sentence of the headline story reports this possibility with, "After another round of disappointing test scores at the middle and high school level, Board of Education members are calling for a re-evaluation of the state's academic standards" (A1).

But the beginning of the second paragraph reports that "Hawai'i's academic standards are among the highest in the nation and until now the school system has defended its high expectations, even as more and more schools faced sanctions under the federal No Child Left Behind Act" (A1). This statement that Hawai'i's academic standards are high is repeated on the inside page, where the reporters continue, indicating that there are those who "suggest that Hawai'i's standards, which are among the highest in the nation, be lowered to match other states" (A2).

On the inside page in a related article, "Students' Test Scores Mixed in Fourth Year," by Creamer and Shapiro (2005), it was reported that the superintendent "was pleased with the scores in the third and fifth grades. 'They show a steady growth trend that validates what we're doing in the classroom. It shows what we're doing is working and solid'" (A2). Further, the article goes on to report that the test results show that all grade levels except the eighth grade have improved in reading since 2002. In addition, every grade level had improved in math. The concern is that the improvement rate found in the higher grades is lower than in the elementary grades.

Despite the good news, a citizen's response to this article appears to fit into the community's master narrative that "Public Schools Are Failing."

Notice that the writer uses the same words—"lower" and "bar"—that are in the headline, "BOE May Lower Bar to Pass No Child Test." He also makes a comparison to a private school, indicating that this private school is choosing high standards—again, following the other part of the master narrative that "Private Schools Are Succeeding."

I return to Anderson's (1991) idea of the imagined community because he makes the argument that the novel and the newspaper provide a medium for developing an imagined community. Further, he argues that the newspaper can be viewed as an extreme form of a book—a serial "book" distributed broadly and daily throughout the community. Every morning when we get up and open our doors to pick up the newspaper, or sit down at our computers to read the online version, or purchase and read a copy at the local coffee shop, or read the headlines while waiting for the bus, we know that thousands of our fellow citizens are doing the same thing. Reading the same stories and creating shared narratives allow us to develop a coherent sense of what we imagine the community in which we live to be. And the daily headlines are the titles of these serial stories about our community.

These are authoritative narratives. As Helen Chapin writes in *Shaping History: The Role of Newspapers in Hawai‘i* (1996, 1), "newspapers have not just recorded events since their inception in 1834, they have been active agents in shaping Hawaiian history." In writing about the different types of newspapers, Chapin defines the establishment papers, which she says "exemplify the controlling interests of town or city, region or country, and need not represent the majority of people. Rather, establishment papers, such as large city dailies and community suburban papers, are part of a power structure that formulates the policies and practices to which everyone is expected to adhere" (2–3).

Local Print Media Analysis

The news media has aggressively followed the DOE's struggle with low test scores and aging infrastructure while some of the department's successes have been obscured. (DePledge 2004, A1)

I needed more information about the print media and its role in reinforcing (or not) this master narrative about schooling in Hawai‘i. I decided to focus on the two local newspapers that the parents referred to most frequently, but I also included articles published about public schools in the local *Honolulu*

Magazine because their public school stories generated comments within the community.

Public Schools

I began with *Honolulu Magazine* because it is a popular magazine with a targeted audience that, according to its Web site, "reaches Hawai'i's best educated and most affluent residents, as well as its most sophisticated visitors" ("About Us" 2006, para. 2). And when I started my inquiry, I would hear friends and colleagues refer to *Honolulu Magazine*'s cover story, "The Death of Public School" (Napier 2001). The title alone is probably the clearest recent printed example of Hawai'i's historical authoritative narrative about schooling, the master narrative that says "Public Schools Are Failing. Private Schools Are Succeeding. Send Your Children to Private Schools." There is little question that the article's point of view reflects the first part of the community's narrative; besides the title, the first paragraph reads, "The Hawai'i state Department of Education doesn't know it yet, but it is dead. By any measure, Hawai'i's schools are a failure" (56). The author's point of view is clear.

Honolulu Magazine followed this 2001 story with a series of cover stories on what one author called "government schools" (Heckathorn 2001, 8). I examined the *Honolulu Magazine* headlines about public school between 2003 and 2006. Much of the content focused on a ranking of approximately 250 public schools each year using a survey (the Hawai'i state Department of Education's "School Quality Survey") in which teachers, parents, and students indicate whether or not they agree with the statement "I would send my own child to this school" (teachers), or "I would recommend my child's school to other parents" (parents), or "If I could, I would go to a different public school" (students). Return rate of the surveys varied. In 2001, for example, out of 52,000 surveys sent out, teachers returned 73.9 percent, parents 23.3 percent, and students 85 percent. A second measure used in these articles was test scores from the Hawai'i Statewide Reading and Math Assessments. The scores represent the percentage of students whose proficiency meets or exceeds Hawai'i Content and Performance Standards.

In May 2003 the magazine's cover title was "Grading the Public Schools" (Napier 2003), accompanied by an above-the-mast title, "We Rank 256 Public Schools Statewide." The ranking included 77 public schools that were graded "A" or "B" (above average) and 101 public schools that were graded "C" (average). A total of 178 public schools out of 256 were ranked average or above.

Similarly, in May 2004 the cover title was "Grading the Public Schools"

(Napier 2004). The above-the-mast title was "Is Your Neighborhood School Better or Worse?" The ranking included 77 public schools that were graded "A" or "B" (above average) and 101 public schools that were graded "C" (average). A total of 178 public schools were ranked average or above.

And again, the cover title in 2006 was "Grading the Public Schools" (Bolante 2006), with the subtitle, "Update: 'The Death of Public School' 5 Years Later: Is Anything Better?" and an above-the-mast title, "We Rank 259 Schools Statewide." The ranking included 78 public schools that were graded "A" or "B" (above average), and 103 public schools that were graded "C" (average). A total of 181 public schools were ranked average or above. It is interesting that, given the author's point of view that public schools are dead, approximately 70 percent of the public schools, using these measures, are ranked average or above.

In 2005 there was a *Honolulu Magazine* cover story with a unique slant on public schools: "High School: An Inside Story." This story differed from the others in that associate editor Ronna Bolante went to one of the local public high schools to meet the teachers and the students. She then wrote her story based on her interviews and her observations of daily high school life.

Also on the cover page of this issue was the sidebar cover line of a second story related to public schools: "Can Business Save the Schools?" In this second article, "Act 51: Can It Save the Public Schools?" (Heckathorn and Keany), six Hawai'i business executives were interviewed about the potential for public school reform through the implementation of a new legislative bill, Act 51.

Typical words used in the titles of these *Honolulu Magazine* articles about public schools are "death," "worse," "save," "grading," "rank," "failure," and "government school."

Private Schools

In contrast to the type of article and point of view taken in the public school pieces, *Honolulu Magazine* has also been publishing an annual guide to the private schools. Its cover page for the September 2005 issue includes an above-the-mast title, "Inside: Private School Guide," which refers to a glossy fifty-five-page "Hawai'i Guide to Private Schools 2006" that explores "finding the right school for your child through the years" (Quill 2005, PS6), campus visits, and finances. Included is a comprehensive, alphabetical list of 137 private schools and 16 colleges.

The specific subtitles on the front page of the guide itself include the following: "Hawai'i Guide to Private Schools 2006"; "Finding the Right School for Your Child — At Any Age"; "Applying to Private School: A How-to Guide for Parents"; and "Making the Most of Your Campus Visit." The guide provides parents with information about each school's address, grade levels, gender (when applicable, whether the school boys only or girls only), religion, contact person, phone number, student-to-staff ratio, tuition, accreditation, and availability of tuition assistance, as well as a chronological, step-by-step guide for applying to private school, making the most of campus visits, and ways to finance private school. There is no ranking of test scores.

These annual guides reflect the second half of the community's historical authoritative narrative about schooling in Hawai'i: "Private schools are succeeding. Send your children to private schools."

In sum, the information shared in these articles is different for the public and private schools. It is difficult not to conclude that these articles strongly reinforce Hawai'i's historical authoritative narrative about schools. This is the message conveyed to the professional class, both newcomers and local residents.

Local Newspapers

For the newspaper analysis, I started by reading about the general role of newspapers in framing stories and the impact they might have on communities' beliefs. Using Chapin's framework for judging the significance of the newspaper narrative, I looked at story placement, which she said "is almost as important as content. Did coverage appear on the front page above the fold in the most eye-catching place in the upper right-hand corner? Or was the story or photo assigned an inside page?" (1996, 11).

The focus I chose for this analysis is front-page "above-the-fold" newspaper headlines about public schools in the two local establishment newspapers, the *Honolulu Advertiser* and the *Honolulu Star-Bulletin*, from 2004 to 2005. These are the headlines seen in the newspaper boxes on the street corner as we wait for the light to change. These are the headlines seen when we open our door in the morning or afternoon to pick up our home-delivered newspaper. These are the stories that Anderson (1991) would view as part of the collective book the citizens of the community are reading.

I was interested as to whether or not the front-page headlines of the above-the-fold stories about public schools were typically framed as positive, negative, or neutral, especially in the areas of test scores, safety, and facilities, as these are the three topics that parents mentioned most frequently as creating a negative impression of the public schools. I was interested in whether the framing of such front-page, above-the-fold stories also reinforced Hawaiʻi's historical authoritative narrative, embedding the notion that public schools are failing, and citizens therefore need to send their children to private schools.

For this analysis, the headlines were taken from one daily and one Sunday edition from each of the two newspapers. Criteria for inclusion of a headline in the study included the following:

(1) The headline had to be related to public education;
(2) The headline and story had to be above the fold on the front page;
(3) Photo captions were excluded unless the headline story was also above the fold.

To minimize bias, I invited a member of the professional class who did not participate in the study to rate the newspaper headlines independently. This individual does not have children in either public or private schools, but lives and works in Hawaiʻi. This independent rater was given charts with the dates and titles of headlines, as well as the following directions: "If you read this headline in the newspaper stand while you were waiting for a bus, would you think the headline stated something positive about public education, negative about public education, or neutral about public education? Check the appropriate column on the chart."

I rated the same headlines separately using the same criteria. When we had each completed our separate ratings, I counted the number of headlines for which we were in agreement and the number on which we disagreed. I converted these numbers to percentages of the total. I then shared my results with the independent rater to ensure accuracy. The percentage of agreement is reported under each category in the following pages.

Overall, I analyzed 154 front-page, above-the-fold headlines about public education — 71 stories from the *Honolulu Star-Bulletin* and 83 stories from the *Honolulu Advertiser*.

Testing

For both newspapers, the most frequent stories relating to public education were on the topic of public school accountability and assessment. I'll refer to this as the "testing" category, which includes articles related to testing standards, testing procedures, test scores, ranking of schools based on test scores, and restructuring of schools based on test scores. Between the two newspapers, 42 above-the-fold headlines fit into this testing category.

For the *Advertiser*, 22 above-the-fold headlines out of 83 were about testing. Out of these, 18 headlines, or 82 percent, were rated as negatively framed. Two headlines were ranked as positive, and two as neutral. The independent rater and I agreed 95 percent of the time, meaning that the ratings were the same for 21 out of 22 headlines.

For the *Star-Bulletin*, 20 above-the-fold headlines out of 71 were about testing. Fourteen, or 70 percent, of the testing headlines were rated as negatively framed. Five headlines were rated as positive, and one headline as neutral. Again, the other rater and I reached a high rate of agreement — 90 percent of the time — indicating that the ratings were the same for 18 out of 20 headlines. (See table 6.1, pp. 178–179.)

Looking Closer. Most of us are in a hurry today, and it's difficult to take the time to analyze the headline stories about public schools to see how the dots are connected from one story about public education to another. For example, if a citizen read the *Star-Bulletin*'s front-page, above-the-fold headline from Martin's March 29, 2005, article, "Isle Schools Fare the Worst," how could a reasonable person not conclude that the master narrative is right; indeed, the public schools are failing?

But after reading a subsequent *Star-Bulletin* front-page, above-the-fold headline from Essoyan's May 13, 2005, article, "Isles Sixth in School Standards," a reasonable person might conclude that the public schools' academic standards are rigorous, which is a positive outlook. Perhaps, then, the public schools are not failing.

But would a reader realize these two stories are connected? In the first story, the first sentence reports how the public schools in Hawai'i are ranked at the bottom nationally with regards to meeting the annual targets for No Child Left Behind. If one kept reading, however, one would see that on page 6, in the eighth paragraph, researcher Todd Ziebert, who compiled the report, said state comparisons are unreliable because states have standards of varying rigor.

And that leads to the second story, written two months later, in which the first sentence reports that Hawai'i's state tests (used for No Child Left Behind) are among "the toughest in the country." The article goes on to explain that if states use easy tests, their students can appear to be doing well, and "those with challenging ones can appear to be failing." Thus Hawai'i's public schools are ranked "low" because the public school testing standards are so "high."

That's the difficulty with headings about test scores. They can be misleading.

Table 6.1. Articles about Hawai'i Public Schools: Testing

Honolulu Advertiser Front-Page, Above-the-Fold Headlines, 2004–2005

Date	Headline	Positive	Negative	Neutral
1/04/04	Income a factor in test score disparities			✓
2/16/04	School audits a "wake-up call"		✓	
5/06/04	Educators check tests for errors		✓	
5/07/04	Educators brace for big changes		✓	
8/20/04	Students improve test scores	✓		
9/03/04	Schools to get second chance: Individual students must show progress to avoid sanctions		✓	
10/08/04	52% of island schools meet "No-Child" goals		✓	
10/24/04	"Failing" hardly means it's bad: 37 criteria daunting for high schools and challenged students		✓	
1/06/05	Schools showing progress	✓		
2/07/05	Test-score gap remains for low-income pupils		✓	
2/27/05	Lagging schools face change		✓	
3/03/05	State to take over 24 lagging schools		✓	
3/04/05	Schools brace for take over		✓	
4/09/05	"Cheating" probe halts Wai'anae school tests		✓	
4/10/05	School testing probe expands		✓	
4/15/05	Students must retake tests		✓	
4/16/05	Other schools linked to improper testing		✓	
4/29/05	Restructuring of 24 schools wins an OK		✓	
8/01/05	Schools brace for test scores		✓	
8/05/05	BOE may lower bar to pass No Child test		✓	
8/05/05	Students test scores mixed in fourth year			✓
8/19/05	66% of isle schools miss No Child goals		✓	

Table 6.1. *(Continued)*

Honolulu Star-Bulletin Front-Page, Above-the-Fold Headlines, 2004–2005

Date	Headline	Positive	Negative	Neutral
1/18/04	Isle Asian kids lead in reading and math	✓		
2/16/04	Isle parents stick with underachieving schools		✓	
5/05/04	Errors may void student scores		✓	
5/08/04	School tests widely flawed		✓	
8/17/04	Charter students lag behind, tests show		✓	
8/20/04	Students gain in state test	✓		
8/31/04	Hawai'i below average on SAT		✓	
10/08/04	Hawai'i schools showing big gains	✓		
10/08/04	Isle schools' report card under "No Child Left Behind" law			✓
3/04/05	24 failing schools to revamp		✓	
3/05/05	Control of schools doubted: The state is to take over 24 schools that miss goals under "No Child Left Behind"		✓	
3/20/05	Kāne'ohe kids and teachers feel test pressures		✓	
3/21/05	Parents call state math test too hard		✓	
3/29/05	Isle schools fare the worst: A study puts state public schools at the bottom compared with other states		✓	
5/22/05	Left behind: Special-needs students offer the most challenge to educators		✓	
8/05/05	2 grades break 50% barrier	✓		
8/19/05	Schools cheer test progress	✓		
9/14/05	More schools face overhauls		✓	
10/13/05	Edison schools are only average		✓	
11/26/05	Some schools' exam goals are too low		✓	

But Did You Know? In no front-page headline during 2004–2005 did we read that 169 public schools met or exceeded national Stanford Achievement Test (SAT) averages in 2004 and 2005 (Hawai'i State Department of Education 2004 and 2005). The SAT assesses how well students in Hawai'i are doing compared to students in the rest of the country. Table 6.2 (see pp. 181–183) lists the 169 public schools with scores that met or exceeded national SAT averages in 2004. I included this list to illustrate that if test score headlines reflected the idea that "public schools vary," citizens might view a more balanced picture of public school achievement.

Safety

Private school parents, especially, mentioned safety as a factor in their choice of private schools for their children, so I was interested in how public school safety is conveyed in the media narratives. There are two subcategories related to safety. One is related to student safety, the other to facility safety.

STUDENT SAFETY

Regarding student safety, the *Honolulu Star-Bulletin* published eight above-the-fold headlines. All were rated as negatively framed. The *Honolulu Advertiser* published five above-the-fold headlines, all of which were ranked as negatively framed. The independent rater and I agreed 92 percent of the time, meaning that twelve out of thirteen headlines were rated the same. (See table 6.3, p. 184.)

Looking Closer. Safety is an important issue. Parents do not want to send their children to schools where they won't be safe. Reading these headlines, it is reasonable to see why parents would hesitate when considering public schools for their children. "The Public Schools Are Failing."

In 2003 the *Star-Bulletin* ran a series on public schools titled "Schools Under Stress." In it, they included a couple of front-page stories related to public school safety. The second story ("Safer to Enter?"), written by Susan Essoyan, was accompanied by a photo of a locked gate with police tape wrapped around it. The first five paragraphs were about a terrible incident that happened to a counselor. I was not feeling safe at this point.

By the sixth paragraph, however, the story reported that violent offenses, of which harassment (including verbal harassment) is the most common, had been falling since the 1995–1996 school year. In 2001–2002 these citations were about 15 per 1,000 students. In addition, in the eleventh and twelfth paragraphs the story reported that 9 percent of the 1,080 Hawai'i high school students surveyed were in physical fights on school property. This is about

Table 6.2. Hawai'i Public Schools SAT Honor Roll by District, 2004

School numbers indicate grade levels meeting or exceeding national SAT averages. (Source: Hawai'i State Department of Education, 2004)

Honolulu

'Āina Haina Elementary (3, 5)
'Ānuenue Elementary (3)
Ala Wai Elementary (3)
Ali'iolani Elementary (3, 5)
Haha'ione Elementary (3, 5)
Hōkūlani Elementary (3, 5)
Jefferson Elementary (3, 5)
Ka'iulani Elementary (3)
Kāhala Elementary (3, 5)
Kaimukī Middle (8)
Kaiser High (10)
Kalani High (10)
Kalihi Uka Elementary (3)
Kamiloiki Elementary (3, 5)
Kapālama Elementary (3)
Kauluwela Elementary (3, 5)
Kawānanakoa Middle (8)
Koko Head Elementary (3, 5)
Liholiho Elementary (3, 5)
Lili'uokalani Elementary (3)
Lincoln Elementary (3)
Lunalilo Elementary (3, 5)
Ma'ema'e Elementary (3, 5)
Mānoa Elementary (3, 5)
Niu Valley Middle (8)
Noelani Elementary (3, 5)
Nu'uanu Elementary (3, 5)
Pauoa Elementary (3, 5)
Roosevelt High (10)
Royal Elementary (3, 5)
Stevenson Middle (8)
Waikīkī Elementary (3, 5)
Wailupe Valley Elementary (5)
Wilson Elementary (3, 5)

Central O'ahu

Āliamanu Elementary (3, 5)
Hale Kula Elementary (3)
Hale'iwa Elementary (3)
Helemano Elementary (3)
Hickam Elementary (3, 5)
'Iliahi Elementary (3, 5)
Makalapa Elementary (3, 5)
Mililani 'Ike Elementary (3, 5)
Mililani Mauka Elementary (3, 5)
Mililani Uka Elementary (3, 5)
Mililani Waena Elementary (3, 5)
Moanalua Elementary (3, 5)
Mokulele Elementary (3, 5)
Nimitz Elementary (3, 5)
Pearl Harbor Elementary (3, 5)
Pearl Harbor Kai Elementary (3, 5)
Pearl Ridge Elementary (3, 5)
Red Hill Elementary (5)
Salt Lake Elementary (3)
Scott Elementary (3, 5)
Shafter Elementary (3, 5)
Solomon Elementary (3, 5)
Waialua Elementary (3)
Waimalu Elementary (3, 5)
Webling Elementary (3, 5)
Wheeler Elementary (3, 5)
'Aiea Intermediate (8)
Āliamanu Middle (8)
Mililani Middle (8)
Moanalua Middle (8)
Wheeler Middle (8)
Mililani High (10)
Moanalua High (10)

Table 6.2 *(Continued)*

Leeward Oʻahu

August Ahrens Elementary (3)
Barbers Point Elementary (3)
ʻEwa Elementary (3)
ʻEwa Beach Elementary (5)
Holomua Elementary (3, 5)
Honowai Elementary (3)
Iroquois Point Elementary (3)
Kaleiopuʻu Elementary (3, 5)
Kanoelani Elementary (3, 5)
Kapolei Elementary (3)
Lehua Elementary (3, 5)
Makakilo Elementary (3)
Mānana Elementary (3, 5)
Mauka Lani Elementary (3, 5)
Momilani Elementary (3, 5)
Palisades Elementary (3, 5)
Pearl City Elementary (3, 5)
Pearl City Highlands Elementary (3)
Waiʻanae Elementary (3)
Waiau Elementary (5)
Waikele Elementary (5)
Highlands Intermediate (8)

Windward Oʻahu

ʻĀhuimanu Elementary (3)
ʻAikahi Elementary (3, 5)
Enchanted Lake Elementary (3)
Heʻeia Elementary (3, 5)
Kaʻelepulu Elementary (3, 5)
Kahuku Elementary (3, 5)
Kailua Elementary (3, 5)
Kainalu Elementary (3, 5)
Kāneʻohe Elementary (3, 5)
Kapunahala Elementary (3, 5)
Keolu Elementary (5)
Lāʻie Elementary (3, 5)
Maunawili Elementary (3, 5)
Mōkapu Elementary (3, 5)
Pope Elementary (3)

Pūʻōhala Elementary (3)
Sunset Beach Elementary (3, 5)
Kailua Intermediate (8)

Hawaiʻi (Big Island)

E. B. DeSilva Elementary (3, 5)
Haʻaheo Elementary (3, 5)
Hilo Union Elementary (3)
Hōlualoa Elementary (3, 5)
Hōnaunau Elementary & Intermediate
  (3, 5, 8)
Honokaʻa Elementary (3)
Hoʻokena Elementary & Intermediate (3)
Kahakai Elementary (3, 5)
Kaʻūmana Elementary (3)
Kealakehe Elementary (3, 5)
Kohala Elementary (3)
Konawaena Elementary (3, 5)
Paʻauilo Elementary & Intermediate (8)
Waiākea Elementary (3, 5)
Waiākeawaena Elementary (3, 5)
Waikoloa Elementary (3, 5)
Waimea Elementary (3)
Waiākea Intermediate (8)
Kohala Middle (8)
Kaʻū High & Pahala Elementary (3)

Maui

Haʻikū Elementary (3, 5)
Kamaliʻi Elementary (3, 5)
Kamehameha III Elementary (3, 5)
Kaunakakai Elementary (3)
Kīhei Elementary (3)
Keʻanae Elementary (3)
Kualapuʻu Elementary (3, 5)
  [now a charter school]
Kula Elementary (3, 5)
Lihikai Elementary (3)
Makawao Elementary (3)

Table 6.2 *(Continued)*

Pukalani Elementary (3, 5)	**Public Charter Schools**
Waiheʻe Elementary (3, 5)	
Wailuku Elementary (3, 5)	Hawaiʻi Academy of Arts and Science (5)
Hāna Elementary & High (8)	Innovations (3, 5)
	Ka ʻUmeke Kāʻeo (5)
	Ke Kula o Samuel M. Kamakau
Kauaʻi	Laboratory (3, 5, 8)
	Lanikai Elememtary (3, 5)
ʻEleʻele Elementary (3)	Myron B. Thompson Academy (3, 5, 8, 10)
Hanalei Elementary (3, 5)	University Laboratory (Education
Kalāheo Elementary (3)	Laboratory) (3, 5, 8, 10)
Kaumualiʻi Elementary (3, 5)	Volcano School of Arts and Sciences (3,
Kekaha Elementary (3, 5)	5, 8)
Kīlauea Elementary (3, 5)	Voyager (3, 5)
Koloa Elementary (3, 5)	Waiʻalae Elementary (3, 5)
Waimea Canyon Elementary &	West Hawaiʻi Explorations (10)
Intermediate (5)	
Elsie H. Wilcox Elementary (3, 5)	
Chiefess Kamakahelei Middle (8)	

2 percentage points lower than the national average in the Center for Disease Control and Prevention's survey.

Why were the individual incident and the locked gate leading the story rather than the declining rate of violent offenses?

FACILITIES' SAFETY

The closely related issue of public school safety has to do with the depiction of the public school facilities. This is the third component often mentioned in the master narrative. From 2004 to 2005 there were actually very few stories published above the fold on the front page about public school facilities, and the reporting reflected a slightly more balanced perspective.

The *Star-Bulletin* published five above-the-fold headlines on public school facilities. Three were rated positive and two negative. The *Advertiser* published six above-the-fold headlines on public school facilities, with one rated as positive, four as negative, and one as neutral. The raters agreed 100 percent of the time. (See table 6.4, p. 185.)

Even though there were fewer headlines about safety than about testing, nineteen out of twenty-four safety headlines were rated as negative, reinforcing the authoritative master narrative that "The Public Schools Are Failing." They are not safe.

Table 6.3. Articles about Hawaiʻi Public Schools: Student Safety

Honolulu Advertiser Front-Page, Above-the-Fold Headlines, 2004–2005

Date	Headline	Positive	Negative	Neutral
12/09/04	Schools may use drug dogs: 2 private schools use them; Public schools might get that option		✓	
2/03/05	Isles turn blind eye to racism, some say: Radford High post-game fights highlight question		✓	
2/08/05	Students, police clash in Nānākuli		✓	
2/15/05	School violence difficult to assess		✓	
8/17/05	School waits long for traffic safety		✓	

Honolulu Star-Bulletin Front-Page, Above-the-Fold Headlines, 2004–2005

Date	Headline	Positive	Negative	Neutral
12/18/04	Standoff cuts fanfare for principal: The situation with machete-wielding man shuts ʻIliahi Elementary		✓	
2/01/05	Threat of violence paralyzes Radford		✓	
2/02/05	Racial factor weighed in brawls at Radford		✓	
2/05/05	Campus fighting strikes 3 schools		✓	
2/08/05	Nānākuli students continue brawling		✓	
5/08/05	Suspicious school fire displaces Kauaʻi kids		✓	
5/27/05	School bans 5 from grad ceremony		✓	
12/01/05	Kids in bus crash all out of hospital		✓	

But Did You Know? Interestingly, on September 16, 2004, the *Star-Bulletin* published an article related to public school facilities. It was not a front-page, above-the-fold story; it was titled "Most Isle Schools Pass Facility Inspections." The first sentence reads, "More than 99 percent of the state's public schools passed their facilities inspections last year, with only two out of 255 campuses rated unacceptable, according to a report released yesterday" (para. 1). Schools were rated in six categories: grounds, building exteriors, building

Table 6.4. Articles about Hawai'i Public Schools: Facilities

Honolulu Advertiser Front-Page, Above-the-Fold Headlines, 2004–2005

Date	Headlines	Positive	Negative	Neutral
6/05/04	2nd city celebrates its first grads [new school]	✓		
6/07/04	School restrooms "pathetic"		✓	
5/23/05	School repairs in budget crunch		✓	
6/05/05	Politicians pick which schools to fix, not DOE		✓	
11/28/05	State converts school cesspools			✓
12/02/05	Schools await fixes: $525 M and growing		✓	

Honolulu Star-Bulletin Front-Page, Above-the-Fold Headlines, 2004–2005

Date	Headlines	Positive	Negative	Neutral
9/01/04	Lahaina school gets new trailer for classrooms	✓		
10/08/04	Schools face strain with Strykers' arrival		✓	
1/15/05	Kailua school ceiling falls		✓	
6/02/05	Isle schools get roomier as nation's classrooms bulge	✓		
12/15/05	Program expedites isle school repairs	✓		

interiors, furniture/equipment, safety, and maintenance/sanitation. The ratings were are as follows: "Thirty-four schools received perfect overall scores, 94 were rated very good, 125 were acceptable and two unacceptable. Altogether, 50 percent of the schools, or 128, were rated very good or higher, an increase of 14 schools over the previous year" (para. 5). This evidence would indicate that public school facilities vary.

In addition, the conversations and the front-page, above-the-fold newspaper headlines do not highlight new, modern, public school facilities such as those listed in table 6.5 (see p. 186). One example is the fully air-conditioned Ocean Pointe Elementary School, which will have a state-of-the-art library facility. Part of the library will have the latest technical equipment for video production, with closed-circuit TV equipment to broadcast within the school. The Student Services Building will house counselors, speech pathologists,

Table 6.5. New Hawai'i Public Schools, 1995–2007

(Source: Creamer 2006a, A6)

School	Location	Opened
Ocean Pointe Elementary	O'ahu	2007
Pōmaika'i Elementary	Maui	2007
Mililani 'Ike Elementary	O'ahu	2004
Nānāikapono Elementary	O'ahu	2004
Chiefess Kamakahelei Middle	Kauai	2000
Kapolei High	O'ahu	2000
Kona Waena Elementary	Big Island	2000
Kapolei Middle	O'ahu	1999
Kea'au High	Hawai'i (Big Island)	1999
Kea'au Elementary	Big Island	1998
Mililani Middle	O'ahu	1998
Waikele Elementary	O'ahu	1998
Kapa'a Middle	Kauai	1997
Kealakehe High	Big Island	1997
Kamali'i Elementary	Maui	1996
Holomua Elementary	O'ahu	1995

and second-language resource specialists, and will also include a room for the student council and a small student store. Between every two classrooms there will be a computer room, allowing students to work on projects in a glassed-in room under supervision without having to go to a computer lab or library. In addition, four outside playing fields will separate the students by age groups for safety reasons, and an outdoor assembly lawn as well as play court for basketball will be constructed (Creamer 2006).

But publicizing information on modern public schools does not negate the attention needed by those public schools in disrepair, some desperately so. Working on the Leeward Coast, Heather Harris (2005, A18) shares in the *Advertiser* her dismal experiences of teaching in a subtropical climate with no air conditioning for her classroom. As a result of open windows (critical for ventilation and relief from the heat), she and her students have to cope with the "quarter inch of red dirt that blows through daily, covering every surface in the room," not to mention the noise from jets flying overhead during her lessons.

Table 6.6. Articles about Hawai'i Public Schools: Staff(ing)

Honolulu Advertiser Front-Page, Above-the-Fold Headlines, 2004–2005

Date	Headline	Positive	Negative	Neutral
7/01/04	DOE 500 teachers short		✓	
9/25/04	Educator wins national honor (photo with article)	✓		
10/20/04	Photo: Moanalua Elementary takes pride Article: Teacher named national winner	✓		
12/10/04	Lingle plan cuts special-ed teachers		✓	
2/02/05	Teachers' wishes come true at Windward Borders Shop	✓		
3/19/05	Coaches fired after drinking		✓	
4/27/05	Kaua'i educator gets year in jail for abuse		✓	
7/01/05	Some will add staff, others will subtract			✓
7/11/05	Home and away, state recruits for teachers		✓	
7/13/05	Applicants for principal drop despite higher pay		✓	
7/24/05	Shortage of top-rank teachers		✓	
8/02/05	DOE short 400 teachers		✓	
10/30/05	Increased workload, double the stress		✓	
11/3/05	Teachers: Halt new report card		✓	
11/27/05	1 in 10 teachers absent each day		✓	
12/17/05	Substitute teachers awarded back pay	✓		

Honolulu Star-Bulletin Front-Page, Above-the-Fold Headlines, 2004–2005

Date	Headline	Positive	Negative	Neutral
7/03/05	Applicants for principal drop despite higher pay		✓	
12/17/05	Substitute teachers due $22 M		✓	

Mrs. Harris also spoke of the condition of Waiʻanae Intermediate School, where her husband teaches in classrooms with "myriad broken tables and chairs discarded in the corners. Wood is splintering off the cabinets, and the shelves are held . . . with bent nails." Lee Cataluna (2005) writes of similar Leeward Coast public school conditions at Nanakuli High and Intermediate schools.

Staffing

There were a number of front-page headlines related to public school staffing, which includes teachers, principals, coaches, and the superintendent. These headlines tended to be negative as well. The *Advertiser* printed sixteen headlines about staffing, of which eleven were rated as negative. The *Star-Bulletin* had two headlines about staffing, and those headlines were rated as negative. The raters agreed 89 percent of the time. (See table 6.6, p. 187.)

Public Charter Schools

I analyzed public charter schools separately, as they are a recent innovation, and I was curious as to how public school innovations would be framed. Since charter schools allow for more autonomy than the mainstream public schools, and since they are an example of moving in the direction of public school choice, I was surprised to find that out of nine above-the-fold headlines from the two newspapers, six were rated as negative. Two headlines were rated as positive and one as neutral. One *Advertiser* headline, "Charters Top Public Schools on Exam," and one *Star-Bulletin* headline with the same title are misleading, as charter schools are public schools. The raters agreed 89 percent of the time. (See table 6.7, p. 189.) Chapter 7 has additional information on charter schools and other public school choices.

More Balanced Coverage: School Governance Policies at Large

The category of public school topics that generated the most balanced coverage was the broadly defined one of school governance, which includes headlines about the policies and decisions of the Board of Education, the legislature, the state Department of Education, and the governor, but excluding those headlines related to testing, safety, and staffing.

Between the two newspapers, there were thirty-two above-the-fold headlines related to school governance policies. Thirteen were rated negative, ten positive, and nine neutral. The raters agreed 94 percent of the time. (See table 6.8, pp. 190–191.)

Table 6.7. Articles about Hawai'i Public Charter Schools

Honolulu Advertiser Front-Page, Above-the-Fold Headlines, 2004–2005

Date	Headline	Positive	Negative	Neutral
6/22/04	Charter school director resigns		✓	
9/3/04	Charters top public schools on exam		✓	
1/13/05	Charter schools' troubles audited		✓	
1/22/05	Charter school head guilty in son's beating		✓	
11/11/05	Kona charter school received great honor [West Hawai'i Exploration Academy is one of the ten high schools across the nation to be chosen to receive the distinguished award from Intel and Scholastic Schools of Distinction for its science achievements]	✓		
12/25/05	Military charter school urged			✓

Honolulu Star-Bulletin Front-Page, Above-the-Fold Headlines, 2004–2005

Date	Headline	Positive	Negative	Neutral
4/23/04	Isle charter schools to receive fall funding	✓		
8/17/04	Charter students lag behind, tests show		✓	
9/03/04	Charters top public schools in exams		✓	

Other topics also rated as more balanced or leaning toward positive include community- and union-related topics, and academics.

Community-related headlines included stories about parents, citizens at large, the business community, and student demographics. Of the eleven articles analyzed, four were rated positive, three neutral, and four negative. The raters agreed 91 percent of the time. (See table 6.9, p. 192.)

Union headlines refer to stories related to the teacher and principal unions. There were ten above-the-fold headline stories concerning unions between 2004 and 2005. Six were rated as positive, one neutral, and three negative. The raters agreed 80 percent of the time. (See table 6.10, p. 193.)

Surprisingly, there were only a total of seven above-the-fold headline stories related to academics from the two newspapers. The academics category

Table 6.8. Articles about Hawaiʻi Public Schools: School Governance Issues

Honolulu Advertiser Front-Page, Above-the-Fold Headlines, 2004–2005

Date	Headline	Positive	Negative	Neutral
1/22/04	Session spotlight stays on schools			✓
4/25/04	Most DOE priorities bypassed		✓	
3/01/05	New class schedule sought			✓
4/25/04	Lingle supports teachers' contract	✓		
4/28/04	Two-tiered kindergarten proposed			✓
5/12/04	Middle school standards raised	✓		
6/10/05	Unified school schedule OK'd			✓
8/10/05	DOE hopes to deter dropouts	✓		
10/21/05	DOE softens changes in school money plan			✓
11/16/05	DOE pays price for report card		✓	
11/18/05	Choice of report card left up to each school	✓		
12/10/04	Lingle plan cuts special-ed teachers		✓	
12/06/05	DOE loses $2.28 M in pension deposits		✓	
12/19/05	Lingle: Extra $82 M for DOE	✓		
12/27/05	Middle school merge on track	✓		

includes headlines connected to academic standards, curriculum, and tutoring resources to promote academics. Five of the stories were rated as positive and two as negative. The raters agreed 78 percent of the time. (See table 6.11, p. 194.)

Finally, there was only one above-the-fold front-page headline I could locate specifically related to achievement—academic or extracurricular—and it was rated as positive. (See table 6.12, p. 194.)

But Did You Know? The newspaper analysis revealed that both newspapers run many positive articles about public schools' achievements, but such articles are typically not on the front page and "above the fold"; rather, they are placed in various locations within the newspapers. Table 6.13 (see pp. 195–198)

Table 6.8 *(Continued)*

Honolulu Star-Bulletin Front Page, Above-the-Fold Headlines, 2004–2005

Date	Headline	Positive	Negative	Neutral
1/10/04	BOE funding request gets mixed reactions		✓	
2/07/04	Senate panel OKs textbook fees	✓		
2/18/04	Research fails to back gov on school boards		✓	
4/14/04	Plan adds 2 courses to grad requirements	✓		
5/19/04	BOE set to approve school surf teams	✓		
7/14/04	New law raises age for kindergarten			✓
12/04/05	Left out of equation: Small, rural schools face funding crunch		✓	
1/25/05	Gov urges boosts for schools	✓		
1/26/05	Study lists $278 M in needs for schools		✓	
2/11/05	Isle school officials dread budget cuts		✓	
6/08/05	School board set to unify calendar			✓
6/10/05	Schools given shared calendar			✓
6/19/05	BOE considers ads in schools			✓
6/23/05	Board members lash out against ad proposal		✓	
6//30/05	Many schools face big cuts		✓	
9/22/05	Budget indecision alarms isle principals		✓	
9/29/05	Land swap proposal creates dilemma for DOE		✓	

lists a number of examples of headlines about awards that public schools or public school educators or public school students won. (The independent rater was not involved in the ratings for table 6.13.). Participants in the study didn't refer to these stories; it was the front-page headlines that were remembered, inside headlines less so. For example, how many citizens are aware that, in a recent school year, public school students accepted $31.7 million in college scholarships, led by Mililani High School and Moanalua High School (DePledge 2004)? This information was not a front-page, above-the-fold headline.

Table 6.9. Articles about Hawai'i Public Schools: Community-Related Services

Honolulu Advertiser Front-Page, Above-the-Fold Headlines, 2004–2005

Date	Headline	Positive	Negative	Neutral
3/04/04	CEOs join school debate: Business roundtable stakes middle ground			✓
3/28/04	Polls finds 74% want say in DOE breakup	✓		
3/28/04	Parents see gap between politics, schools' needs		✓	
4/07/04	Priority to classroom, not boards	✓		
10/26/04	Hawaii optimistic on public schools	✓		
10/17/05	Public school rolls shrinking		✓	

Honolulu Star-Bulletin Front Page, Above-the-Fold Headlines, 2004–2005

Date	Headline	Positive	Negative	Neutral
3/04/04	CEOs pitch schools' plan			✓
5/09/05	Donated supplies pour in for school	✓		
1/31/05	Parents exploit U.S. law for school transfers		✓	
10/09/05	Language barrier		✓	
11/15/05	Supreme Court ruling challenges parents			✓

Connecting the Dots

Evidence exists that the historical narrative "Public Schools Are Failing" is alive and well in Hawai'i today. Budnick (2007) reminds us that public schools have been the target of complaints for a number of years. It's the same old community "story." The narrative is reinforced by both our daily conversational narratives and by our media headline stories. I argue that the narrative is inaccurate because it does not allow for the recognition of the good and excellent public schools that exist.

Given this negative social environment in which Hawai'i's public schools operate, it is impressive that so many of the public schools have been able to thrive. Credence for a modification of the historical narrative comes from this study's parents' experiences with the public schools, their children's experiences, and the positive news stories and statistics (such as the award stories) that are typically buried inside the newspapers. For example, if the editors were willing to consider such a modified version of the historical authoritative narrative, how might the front-page, above-the-fold headlines read? Some of these award stories might show up on the front page.

What might the possibilities be if the modified narrative "public schools vary" were the "talk of the town"? There would continue to be an acknowledgment that some public schools do struggle, some facilities are in disrepair, and some schools have incidents of fighting. However, the narrative would also allow for a celebration and acknowledgment that other public schools are successful, other public school facilities are excellent, and, for many public schools, safety is a non-issue. The narrative could be "Public Schools Vary. Check Them Out." It would be a fair assessment. Parents, as with most of those in this study, might be more encouraged to make school choice decisions based on evidence rather than hearsay.

In either case, good schools can improve. Poor schools can change. Chapter 7 will describe changes suggested by parents, both at the individual school level as well as with overall school governance.

Table 6.10. Articles about Hawai'i Public Schools: Union Topics

Honolulu Advertiser Front Page, Above-the-Fold Headlines, 2004–2005

Date	Headline	Positive	Negative	Neutral
4/28/04	HSTA, State say they're hopeful	✓		
4/29/04	State teachers agree on deal	✓		
4/30/04	Teachers to vote on accord May 13			✓
3/21/05	Substitutes seeking a voice: union only hope in teachers' wage battles with state		✓	
11/24/05	Sub teacher pay raises proposed	✓		

Honolulu Star-Bulletin Front Page, Above-the-Fold Headlines, 2004–2005

Date	Headline	Positive	Negative	Neutral
4/29/04	HSTA, State reach deadline	✓		
4/16/05	HGEA wins 10% state pay raise	✓		
4/24/05	DOE and HSTA settle contract	✓		
4/29/05	Teachers OK raise but say it is only one part of the problem		✓	
11/03/05	HSTA flunks new report card		✓	

Table 6.11. Articles about Hawai'i Public Schools: Academics

Honolulu Advertiser Front-Page, Above-the-Fold Headlines, 2004–2005

Date	Headline	Positive	Negative	Neutral
6/25/04	Graduation criteria raised	✓		
11/30/05	90% of students miss out on free tutoring		✓	

Honolulu Star-Bulletin Front-Page, Above-the-Fold Headlines, 2004–2005

Date	Headline	Positive	Negative	Neutral
4/14/04	Plan adds 2 courses to grad requirements	✓		
6/01/04	Wai'anae helps freshmen focus	✓		
10/13/05	Edison schools are only average		✓	
10/15/05	Cool science	✓		
10/30/05	Education games: Recess is becoming an effective learning tool	✓		

Table 6.12. Articles about Hawai'i Public Schools: Achievements

Honolulu Advertiser Front-Page, Above-the-Fold Headlines, 2004–2005

Date	Headline	Positive	Negative	Neutral
	[None]	—	—	—

Honolulu Star-Bulletin Front-Page, Above-the-Fold Headlines, 2004–2005

Date	Headline	Positive	Negative	Neutral
12/28/05	Banding together: Pearl City High tunes up for the Tournament of Roses Parade	✓		

Table 6.13. Articles about Hawai'i Public Schools: Awards/Recognition

Honolulu Advertiser Front Page, Above-the-Fold Headlines, 2004–2005

Date	Headline	Positive	Negative	Neutral
4/11/04	Students to play at Carnegie Hall [Moanalua High School Symphony Orchestra will play at Carnegie Hall for the second time]	✓		
5/01/04	Farrington, Wai'anae share top new award [Hawai'i State High School Journalism Award Competition]	✓		
6/24/04	Essay on Vikings wins top national honors [Kahuku High School, "Best Senior Entry on an International Theme" Category, National History Day Prize from the History Channel]	✓		
4/03/05	Celebrating science [48th Hawai'i State Science & Engineering Fair]	✓		
4/03/05	Campbell [High School] earns national laurels [2005 Breakthrough high school —50% minority students, 50% qualify for full lunch & 90% accepted into college or other postsecondary programs]	✓		
4/05/05	Nakasone [Pearl City High School band only high school band in Hawai'i to receive the John Philip Sousa Foundation Sudler Flag of Honors, and the first to perform at the prestigious Midwest Band and Orchestra Clinic in Chicago]	✓		
4/21/05	Campbell High standout has her eye on Stanford University	✓		
4/21/05	McKinley gains robotic final [Fifth Annual National F.I.R.S.T. Robotics Competition, Atlanta, Georgia]	✓		
4/29/05	Farrington [High School] has top newspaper	✓		
5/03/05	Kahuku High's "We the People" team earns honorable mention [In top 10 national competition testing knowledge of U.S. Constitution and the Bill of Rights]	✓		

Table 6.13 *(Continued)*

Date	Headline	Positive	Negative	Neutral
5/05/05	Kalihi teenager engineers success [Farrington High School 2005 battle robot team that placed first in UH Mānoa College of Engineering competition]	✓		
5/16/05	Kauai High makes a strong case [Second place in National Mock Trial Competition, Charlotte, North Carolina—the best a Hawaiʻi team has ever done]	✓		
5/21/05	Video by 3 Maui [high school] students wins them a New York trip [Video won two national awards sponsored by Panasonic]	✓		
7/28/05	Moanalua 16-year-olds put a winning face on the Great Depression [Trio wins National History Day contest trip to Maryland]	✓		
9/27/05	Waianae school program inspires students, serves local market [Alumni of Searider Productions, a digital production company at Waiʻanae High School, are working in local media and journalism positions as well as college students in film/video production and music]	✓		
10/06/05	4 to take part in national science fair [Two public and two private school students will participate in a national science project competition to determine "America's Top Young Scientist of the Year"]	✓		
10/13/05	Moanalua sophomores capture national honors for oil-leak project [Students placed first in U.S. Army–sponsored eCYBERMISSION Southwest/Pacific Region competition sponsored by the U.S. Army; students' "Project CHO51" earned them place as national finalists]	✓		
11/05/05	Big Winners: Kauluwela, Lunalilo, Nuuanu Schools [Blue Ribbon Schools for 2005–2006]	✓		

Table 6.13 *(Continued)*

Date	Headline	Positive	Negative	Neutral
11/18/05	169 public schools win SAT honors [169 out of 282 public schools met or exceeded the national average on the 2005 Stanford Achievement Test]	✓		
12/01/05	Database system wins recognition [SSFM International Inc. and the Department of Education have received the honor award for developing the school system's Facilities Project Management and Tracking Database System. The award was granted by the American Council of Engineering Companies of Hawaiʻi]	✓		

Honolulu Star-Bulletin Front Page, Above-the-Fold Headlines, 2004–2005

Date	Headline	Positive	Negative	Neutral
4/30/04	High School Journalism Awards: Farrington, Waiʻanae share honor	✓		
5/08/04	Future filmmakers [Roosevelt High School senior Roberto Angel, Best of Show Award winner, teen video awards]	✓		
6/05/04	Teachers honored for civics initiative [Thirty-five middle school teachers participated in national Project Citizen]	✓		
9/25/04	Campbell principal best in nation	✓		
11/03/04	Mililani [high school] teacher wins national award [Horace Mann–NEA Foundation Award for Teaching Excellence, $18,000]	✓		
3/21/05	Moanalua hits high note on trip [Moanalua High School Symphony Orchestra at Carnegie Hall]	✓		
3/27/05	Ceremony honors 7 leaders [7 best principals were named finalists for the $25,000 Masayuki Tokioka Excellence in School Leadership Award]	✓		

Table 6.13 *(Continued)*

Date	Headline	Positive	Negative	Neutral
5/21/05	Top video awards go to Kapolei High	✓		
9/12/05	Historic Victory—Analytical skills help three girls win a national exhibit contest [Three students earn first-place honors at the National History Day competition in Maryland]	✓		
9/24/05	Nation's top schools include 3 from isles [Aliʻiolani, Hōkūlani, and Kāhala elementary schools have been named among the 295 top schools in the nation by the U.S. Department of Education]	✓		
10/11/05	Kahuku Teacher wins $10,000 Wal-Mart grant	✓		
11/07/05	Debate team hopes for return trip to nationals [Roosevelt High School speech and debate team won the state championship in the Lincoln-Douglas debate and advanced to the national tournament]	✓		
11/07/05	Science fest in D.C. thrills isle students [Two public and two private school students were among 40 finalists in the Discovery Channel Young Scientist Challenge at the University of Maryland]	✓		
11/08/05	3 Oahu schools tapped for 2006 Blue Ribbon Honor	✓		
12/10/05	3 isle math, science teachers named U.S. finalists [Three public high school teachers were chosen as Hawaiʻi finalists in the 2005 Presidential Awards for Excellence in Mathematics and Science teaching]	✓		

7 What Can We Do Better?
Making Public School Changes

> Better schooling will result in the future—as it has
> in the past and does now—chiefly from the steady,
> reflective efforts of the practitioners who work in
> schools and from the contributions of parents and
> citizens who support (while they criticize) public
> education. (Tyack and Cuban 1995, 135)

To strengthen the public school system, parents in this study suggested changes at the individual school level, the state level, and the parental or community level.

School Site and School Complex Recommendations

Recommended changes at the school site or school complex levels are organized into three categories:

1. promoting family identification with their children's public school;
2. ensuring high standards for all children;
3. providing the resources to hire more school counselors, especially at the high school level.

Promoting School Identity

Parents who made the first recommendation suggest that public school educators borrow some of what the elite private schools do well, which is promote family identification with their schools, since family identification, in turn, promotes school loyalty.

The Role of Sports

One suggestion to develop parental allegiance is through extracurricular activities such as sports. This section begins with a father who talked about his ideas of using school complex sports activities more effectively as a means of providing both school identity and community cohesiveness and, therefore, loyalty. He believes that principals are not typically aware of or don't appreciate the potential of using sports activities to promote school identity.

Consulting Firm Executive: See, I think [that what is] missing is community cohesiveness around the public schools. What happens is when you siphon off the top 2 percent or 5 percent—whatever the private schools take—you're not only taking the kids, you're taking the family. You're taking the support for the events at the local public school, and so basically it emasculates the local community. That's why [a certain public high school] is much more cohesive because everything in the community revolves around those schools.

I was telling you about all the kids who live in this suburban community who played basketball, football, baseball. You want to retain those kids because they're natural leaders. You retain them in the local public high school, and that local high school then becomes competitive with all the other schools around them athletically. When you have an athletic team that brings school spirit, people show up on a Friday night. You have something tangible that the parents can rally around.

At the little league level, every parent, every sibling, everybody in the whole family shows up to see Johnny sit on the bench for his little league team, and they have a potluck after. It goes on year after year after year, and then they go away.

Sports as the catalyst are very highly visible, and Hawai'i is so sports-minded. You can do that because you have the feeder system all built into it. I'll give you an example. We had at our public high school a youth basketball league. A lot of those kids ended up going to private schools, and primarily to play sports. Over the past three years, we've recruited five of those top kids back to our public high school.

But the principals don't understand that. They don't understand that what builds community cohesion is something that people want to do. What people want to do is cheer for a team. Once you've cheered for the team, it's not that far of a thing to say, "Okay, we're going to have a band concert, let's everybody show up." Or "We're going to have an art show, so everybody show up." So all of a sudden you become part of the community.

Q: And then it's a science fair?

Consulting Firm Executive: Right. Exactly. And it goes on and on and on. It's like my son's the student body president, right? In the beginning of the year, we mapped out what he ought to do to show leadership. One idea was to use the team spirit of his athletic teams and have them do community projects. So what do they do? They organize and they go down to the feeder schools and conduct clinics. What they do is conduct clinics in athletics, basketball, baseball, and other things like that.

They also do speech and drama, science, and then they get kids from all the other classes to do that with them. Then at half times at some of the high school games, these same students [from the feeder schools] come as guests of the big high school kids to show what they can do — whether it's a half-time basketball thing, or show some of the other projects they've worked on. So all these little kids in the community are growing up going, "I want to be a [certain team name] when I grow up."

That's easy stuff to do, but what it takes is it takes the leadership of the principal primarily, and a couple parents who can then galvanize the roundup. When principals go through their administrative education to become certified, I don't think there is enough emphasis on how to build community cooperation. That's easy stuff. It really is easy because all the ingredients are already built in because these mothers and the fathers have been organizing on their own as volunteers since their kids were five years old.

Business Managers to Support the Development of School Identity

The second suggestion to promote school allegiance is the hiring of a business manager for each public school complex. The idea behind this is that one of the responsibilities of such a business manager could be to partner with principals to develop marketing strategies that promote school identity. Business managers would bring marketing expertise to this partnership that educators might need but don't typically have. One Hawai'i parent, in particular, expressed his frustration at the lack of interest in this idea by the Department of Education.

Attorney: It is a pipeline so the attitudes have to be shaped in the elementary public school, and they have to actually market the next level to these kids to prepare them for the type of middle school that's in their complex. These kids should be identifying with the high school from day one — so that's their school. They should be encouraged to go to school events at the high school. High school ought to be the flagship, and everyone should be adopting a high school. And there can be curriculum developed around, within the complex, about the community they live in.

The Department of Education [DOE] does not think like business. It's so obvious to those in business. For example, a DOE presentation is usually very boring because they don't get to the main point. They don't tell you where they're headed; and they repeat it seven times, or ten times. You got it the first time. It's boring. They don't know marketing. They don't even think marketing is important. Every school ought to be marketing to their clientele. They ought to be marketing to keep their best students there.

Q: This is only a personal observation, but I'm thinking that the types of individuals who get attracted to those kinds of professions [teaching, etc.] are not necessarily the types who are very good with marketing.

Attorney: Exactly. I agree. And you shouldn't put a square peg in a round hole. One of the things that I think ought to be done is that in every complex there ought to be a dual tract. There ought to be a business manager for the complex who takes care of things, like the building, supplies, you know, working within guidelines for the requirements on toxic waste, and marketing. But the marketing is sort of a crossover, then, with the administration on the educational side.

Q: You mean someone who understands how you take the philosophy and the values of the school complex and who can communicate them to the public?

Attorney: But I'm telling you, they don't even see a value in communicating. Internally, within the schools, there's very little marketing — very little. The best schools have good marketing.

Q: It's probably a foreign concept?

Attorney: Yes. And not even foreign — it's like a dirty concept. And it's not a dirty concept. In private schools, it's all marketing. You go to Punahou and you see the "P" and buff and blue and even the napkins at the snack bar. You know where you are. All of the umbrellas at the swimming pool are buff, you know, buff and blue. The branding is there. And yet we pay so little attention to that in public education. People will not accept it. They don't want to go there, and that's because they're educators.

Promoting Public School Choice: Mainland Ideas

In addition to using extracurricular activities such as sports and marketing to build school identity and community-school cohesiveness, the Hawai'i parents talked about the idea of public schools developing particular areas of expertise to promote school identity. The Hawai'i Department of Education appears to be moving in this direction: current options include the Hawaiian immersion schools, a variety of charter schools, and the proposed first magnet school, a partnership between the Department of Education and Bishop Museum. I'll share the details of these recent changes in the last section of this chapter.

Two of the mainland parents in the study shared the various types of public school choices available in their school districts. The first excerpt is from a mother who said her husband, initially leaning toward private school for their children, changed his mind and became a public school convert because of the public school choices available to them.

Mainland Public School Parent: So one of the things that I ended up doing first was something called the Kindergarten Roundup for [a certain urban city's] public schools, and at the Kindergarten Roundup parents can come and visit with various principals, teachers, and parents at a variety of schools. Parents walk around and hear about the different options available. Well, I brought my husband to that because what this [urban city's] public school system offers — which I think many districts don't offer — is a tremendous amount of choice.

So you have your neighborhood schools, and typically, again, here the neighborhood schools are pretty strong, but you also have a variety of what they used to call "magnet" programs, and now they are called "focus option" programs or schools. And so you have an environmental middle school. You have an arts middle school. You have a science and math magnet program. And at the elementary school level you have a lot of language immersion programs. Typically, you get into them via a lottery because there's such a high demand for them.

When my husband went around and he looked at all the options available within the city public schools, he was a convert. He became a convert. And he just couldn't believe the variety of options available. As it turns out, we applied to an immersion program, a Spanish immersion program, and we didn't get in through our lottery. We ended up instead going to our neighborhood school, which had certainly been my intention all along, although the immersion option was a fabulous option. I would have been thrilled if we had gotten into it. But my husband had already made the conversion. Once he saw the variety of options available in public education, he made the conversion already. And then going to our neighborhood school . . . he was completely on board with that. So I think that somehow for him, there was a fear that we'd be stuck with whatever neighborhood school we were in.

If the neighborhood school didn't work out, there's a very easy transfer. If there's room in a neighborhood school, you can just ask to go there. It's a very easy transfer policy within [the urban city's] public school system.

Q: Who do you ask for a transfer?

Mainland Public School Parent: There are two different ways. If it's just another neighborhood school, you just go through the school district and you say "I'd like to go to X school." If that neighborhood school has room, you can automatically get into it.

If you're trying to go to one of these language immersion programs or focus option programs, typically you have to apply, and there's a lottery if there are too many people wanting to get in. So it depends on which one you're looking for. And there are a lot of people in [the urban city] who end up going to a neighborhood school other than their current neighborhood school. In fact, it's a huge percentage; I don't know exactly what it is, but it's a lot.

The second parent from this same urban school district also talked about the school choices available within the public school system, including the K–12 alternative school that his children attend.

Q: What kind of school choices do you have built in to the public schools?

Mainland Public School Parent: Well, the choices originated with our voluntary desegregation program, and so we created magnet programs in each of the high schools. The idea was that that would create enough movement across different parts of the city to meet desegregation guidelines. We now, in addition to those different magnet programs at the high schools, have several specialty middle school programs. Then there's the Metropolitan Learning Center where my daughter goes, and my son went. That is a K–12 public school that draws from all over the city, and has an alternative environment to education.

Q: Is that open admission, selective admission, lottery?

Mainland Public School Parent: Well, it's changed over time. It's going much more toward a lottery. It was an application process initially, and they were looking for congruency with the schools goals and educational philosophy. Now, I think they're relying on that happening much more naturally and just recruiting by explaining the philosophy, and almost assuming that the kids who apply are congruent with it because otherwise you wouldn't apply.

High Standards for All Students

The second category of recommended changes at the school site or school complex level focused on ensuring high standards for all public school children. This specific concern was discussed in earlier chapters.

Parents want teachers to adhere to higher standards for those students viewed as "average." They typically believed that students in the Gifted and Talented (GT), Enrichment, Honors, and Advanced Placement (AP) courses were well served, as were those identified as special-needs students. However, they are concerned about the extent to which the average student is academically challenged. The parents who addressed this issue do not believe that all teachers have high expectations for all children.

College Counselors and Tutors

Providing more college counselors and tutors was also a strong recommendation at the school site level. This issue was first discussed in chapter 3, in which public school parents said there were too few college counselors in the public high schools to help students prepare for the college application process. Parents also reported that the scarcity of counselors could result in inadequate tutoring and other counseling services for those children who need extra help.

State-Level Recommendations

The next set of suggested changes is directed at the state level and is organized into four categories:
1. improving working conditions;
2. improving public relations, especially with the media;
3. considering some form of decentralization of the state school system;
4. improving the relationship between child advocates and the teachers' union.

Improving Working Conditions

There are two recommendations under this category: higher teacher salaries and improved upkeep of school facilities.

TEACHERS' SALARIES

The majority of parents clearly support increased teacher salaries. As a group, they are very supportive of the public school teachers. They know that increasing salaries will improve morale and attract more individuals to the teaching profession. Their children, by and large, have had very positive experiences with their teachers, and increasing support for the key players boosts the reputation of the public schools. Excerpts from the following two parents were typical.

Military Officer: You don't pay your teachers in Hawai'i adequately, so you don't have really happy, happy teachers. Your teachers are really the most important part — the most important pillar. Until the state system recognizes that and pays their teachers adequately, you know, you're not going to get the most out of your teachers. They give an awful lot.

There has to be a real commitment. People speak about how important education is in this state, but that means that the citizenry needs to speak up and to take action, and say, "Hey, we need to put our tax dollars into what we believe." We would pay our teachers the adequate salary that they deserve. We would support what is really needed to provide the resources for our children, whether it's textbooks, or computers, the infrastructure, etc. It's the commitment that's needed.

Physical Therapist: Well, I think within the past year or so there have been newspaper articles that have talked about the salary differences between the teachers here and on the mainland. And I think in order to continue to have the high quality, or the quality that we have in the public schools, we need to try to get the salaries higher to retain those teachers, and I think that we have to increase the public knowledge of the inequity.

SCHOOL FACILITIES UPKEEP

There is also concern for the environment in which teachers, principals, staff, and students work. The parents talked specifically about facilities upkeep. While most school facilities are well maintained and safe, others need improvement. Even given the positive 2004 Facility Report, there are problems with lack of air-conditioning, especially in the Leeward community. There is also too little attention given to quality-of-life details, such as clean bathrooms, in some schools. And the "perception" of a school building in disrepair due to lack of landscaping contributes to the master narrative that "The Public Schools Are Failing." All public schools need to be clean, safe, air-conditioned, and landscaped. For both the staff and the children, going to such a school every day builds morale.

In the next several excerpts, parents discussed the impact of driving by a school site that is in disrepair. Such a view gives a negative impression of the public schools, and it is an obvious sign that the public itself is not engaged in public schools. Maintenance for the schools is inadequately funded, so parents themselves often have had to paint and do repairs.

Attorney: One of the things I try to do is focus on school repair and maintenance just because our schools in this area need that. In terms of what we learn in business, generally, first impressions are the most important. You have formed an impression about me based upon my office, the way I'm groomed, the way I speak, etc. And the first impressions are very difficult to overcome. If you have a negative first impression, it's very difficult to change it to a positive. What is the visual impression that our schools create? It's very negative.

Physician: Well, I guess the only other comment would be going back to — at the top of my head — it would be going back to the facilities. Whether it's sports facilities, or whether it's just painting — having the buildings painted and the vegetation looking halfway decent, and not having trash or junk or old refrigerators sitting around on the property. As I said before, I think it goes a long way towards building the morale of the students and teachers, and that definitely is one of the differences between public and private school.

And if you look at it as a teacher, you've got the best of everything at [an elite private school]. If you're a student there, you've got the best of everything. Well, that doesn't solve all the problems. You still have to teach, and you still have to study and you still have to learn. And you may or may not be a good teacher, but at least you're in a setting where . . . as you look around, you can feel good about it. And that's helpful. You get up every morning and you go to work, or you get up every morning as a student and you go to school. Do you look forward to it? Do you look forward to the drive there? Do you look forward to what it looks like when you get there? All those kinds of things may seem not important, but I think they are important.

Q: Is there a way that, from a grassroots perspective, that the parent of a particular public school can form a coalition and meet with the principal to say, "These are priorities that we'd like to see. How can we work together?"

Physician: That happens, and it happened at our public high school. The school was painted and that was all through parents, primarily through the PTSA [Parents, Teachers and Students Association] working with the principal, and it's looked a lot better. But you're limited in what you can do because you're only allowed volunteer parents with very limited funds. For example, the tennis courts are practically falling off the hillside, yet these kids still play there with cracks on the thing and all that. So what can you do? "Well, you have to wait before we'll resurface it, and that's the way it is."

There was an article not too long ago, I think, in the paper about the maintenance of the schools, and how far behind we are. And why is that? That's . . . something that you cannot solve through PTSA and the principal, no matter how hard you try. It is so frustrating.

Professor: In terms of perception, there is the physical plight of the schools here. I think most people who are middle class or upper middle class just look at the way the buildings look and drive by and don't even consider that this is an environment that they want their children in. I mean, that raises the issue about safety.

One of the reasons why I was not so concerned about my son going to a public school is that [a certain public high school] is a small school. And my son and I even talked about this. He thinks that his getting into [an elite mainland university] was based on [being] a big fish in a smaller pond. I look back at our public intermediate school, and I look at what this one principal was able to do just in terms of getting the community to help paint the school. She made the effort so this school is viewed as a part of the community rather than "this is just a school that sits in the community."

Dentist: We have to market public education better. And a visual perception is very important, and I think that [a certain public school advocate's] idea was to spend the money cleaning up the campus and making it look really nice. And, you know, if it looks nice, then people will perceive that it is nice, and I think that there's a lot of truth to that. I couldn't believe the first time I walked into [a certain public intermediate school], and I thought, "Oh my God, this is dreadful! . . . I would never send my kid here!" And again, [a certain public elementary school] was so beautiful and warm, and the middle school — although it is very good academically — it's very old and dingy, and it's almost depressing from a visual perspective.

Communication: Public Relations and the Media

The second category of state-level recommendations returns to the issue of better public relations, but at the state level, and they are focused on improving the school district's public relations (PR) and the relationship with the media. As noted, private schools in Hawai'i pay attention to public relations. The parents believe that public schools could benefit by doing the same, especially in promoting better media coverage than what now exists. Being attentive to public relations could, for example, lead to better communication with the public regarding the truth and the falsehoods of safety in public schools. It could also help to ensure that public school data presented to the public are disaggregated so that the 284 schools are not treated as "one," thereby allowing the public to have a better idea of the variety of schools that exist and a more accurate picture of the "school system."

Q: What would you say could be done to increase community support for public education?

Professor: Well, I think that there needs to be a lot more PR, good PR about the public schools. . . . [At] the elite private schools, they have people who work on press releases all the time. And you read about the good things the kids do there, but the DOE doesn't really publicize well the honors or accomplishments of the kids in public schools. I think that there needs to be more effort.

Physician: One place to start is to get the help of the media. We see articles in the paper all the time. Take [a certain public high school], for example. A couple of years ago, there was a boo-boo on the part of the yearbook director where there was a caption for a picture that was inappropriate. Well, that just got a lot of media attention, and that makes the public school look bad. All the time, these negative things about the public school [are reported], but when something good happens to a public school, it's not reported. So we've actually taken that personally in our family and we called . . . *Midweek* or the *Sun Press*, when it still existed, and we'd say, "This happened. Put it in the paper."

Q: Do they?

Physician: They do. But that's not the *Advertiser* or the *Star-Bulletin.* They tend to be more like the *Honolulu Magazine,* more interested in the spectacular. I understand why, but I think the media has a certain responsibility, a huge responsibility — a responsibility I'm not even sure they appreciate. I think *they* think they appreciate that and understand it. If you were to ask them, they would say, "Oh yeah, we know what we print is very important." But I don't think they really, really understand the power that they have.

Q: How is it possible to help them to understand?

Physician: I don't know. . . . I know that there are — what is that agency of responsible journalism? . . . There's *American Academy for Responsible*

Journalism, or something like that. They put on conferences throughout the country. And I think that's something that would be good if it were more widespread.

In the newspaper analysis in chapter 6, it became clear that the local newspapers do print a lot of "good news" stories about public schools, but they seldom make the front-page, above-the-fold position. As a result, it appears the "good news" stories don't have the same impact on the readers as do the negative front-page stories, leading to the parents' argument that the DOE needs to make public relations a higher priority in order to help improve media coverage. What exists now? The DOE Communications Office has a staff of four, consisting of an acting communications director, a communications specialist, a secretary, and a clerk-typist. This office provides information about the goings-on of 284 public schools (telephone communication with DOE Communications Office staff, March 17, 2008). In contrast, Punahou, an elite private school, has a staff of seven (one of whom is part time) in its Communications Office. This office is organized under the Institutional Advancement Department, which also includes an Alumni Office and a Development Office (telephone communication with Punahou staff, March 17, 2008). 'Iolani, another elite private school, also has an Office of Institutional Advancement with three directors and four full-time staff members (telephone communication with 'Iolani staff, February 1, 2008).

MAINLAND PARENTS' EXPERIENCES
WITH IMPROVING MEDIA COVERAGE

In this section, mainland public school parents share their experiences with how their public school districts communicate with the public. In the first conversation, a father recommended that the school district give out accurate information, be quick in responding to requests about information, and disseminate the information to the parents and media. He felt it is important to take a proactive position. He also mentioned that part of his district's communication problems resulted from a lack of resources to hire adequate staff; he felt, too, that they needed to be proactive. This problem exists in Hawai'i as well.

Mainland Public School Parent: There's one other thing. We talked about the perception in Hawai'i of the public schools and how that ties in with the media. To a certain extent, that's also a problem here, and one of the reasons we're doing the school celebration is to make the information available and get it out there. We want to invite Realtors who make recommendations on where people, moving into the area, should live to go to a good school. We want Realtors to get accurate information. Parents have heard all sorts of different things from Realtors that don't really tie into what we know about the school district.

Making the information the school district provides more accurate, to a certain extent, depended on underlying computer systems. [The school system] had to replace their computer system that had been the same since the early seventies because it seemed like every time you asked the district a question, you would get a different answer, even if the question hadn't changed. So there was just no consistency, and then the district started losing credibility. There's been a lot of effort to be more open, and to just show the information they have and to be as accurate as possible.

There's also been a lot more coordination of the information. They still have a long ways to go, but I think it was really one of the results of the budget cuts. We wanted to keep the budget cuts away from the classrooms, but then they cut the communications department down too far so that you couldn't get any information out of the district. The only information you would hear was people blasting the district, and the district didn't have the resources to even respond.

Q: And so would you say that it is really important for a school district to have a good communications department?

Mainland Public School Parent: Yes, and an emphasis on getting information out quickly and accurately — and getting information out to active parents and to the media outlets. One of the things we did early on in our PPS [Parents for Public Schools] chapter was we set up a Listserv that became sort of a place people could dial up. People would throw out their rumors they had heard, and they could verify them [or not].

Q: Are you satisfied with the newspaper editorial point of view [regarding public education]?

Mainland Public School Parent: I'm satisfied with the editorial point of view. I'm not satisfied with the reporters. The editorial point of view has been very supportive of public education. I think we're really missing the boat in terms of communication, publicity, and PR because all of the media focus just on the problems. We don't have a balanced view. So if you just read the newspaper, you'd think the public schools are screwed up.

Q: How do you get a balance?

Mainland Public School Parent: You'd have to get into the schools.

Q: Does your coalition have a liaison with the media?

Mainland Public School Parent: We've had ongoing relationships with the media — pretty good relationships with the alternative papers. With the local newspaper we've had kind of mixed relationships with their reporters. That's where I really have a problem. Their reporters have tended — sometimes they've come to interview me, and I'll find out what the story's about. What they've done is they've written their story, and they're coming to me to get the quote that fits into this slot in their story.

And I don't know that you'll ever get it balanced one to one, but right now there's virtually nothing on the positive side. One of the alternative publications did run some negative stories, but I thought they were right on target.

And then a positive story happened and [the editor] wasn't running it, and I called him and complained. I said, "You did a very nice job on those negative stories, but we need some of the positive stories to get out as well." He and I debated for a while, and he didn't cover that one, but the next one, he did a nice story on the positive side.

Q: So that's typical of parents such as yourself? You're likely to call up the reporter?

Mainland Public School Parent: We want to reestablish the relationship. Yes. I'll call them, or they call me. They call me a lot more than I call them. Even when they call me, I use it as an opportunity to talk about things I know about.

Q: Well, how important is it that the media and other businesses in the community are aware that there exists this coalition of parents who support public schools? Has that made a difference, do you think?

Mainland Public School Parent: Well, some. I think the reason the media calls us is that we've made it clear, with our actions, that we are a parent group that's concerned about all the students in the district and not just our own. And they don't have a voice to go to for that perspective other than us, and so they call us. So you may get a parent group who's marching in the board room or doing this or that, advocating for their own kids, sometimes at the expense of other kids, and they get news coverage, but they get the news coverage "on the spot" sort of thing. Then if they're doing any sort of analysis with the issue, there's a tendency to call us to get our perspective.

And we have not been the kind of group that's been out there creating the ruckus, primarily because we have very good relationships with the district, and with the school board. We find it much more effective to just go to them directly with our concerns.

Another mainland public school advocate talked about the role of the media and public education coverage in the city in which her children go to public schools.

Mainland Public School Parent: I think that one of the things that parents of public schools have really been focused on is the whole media perspective. You know, many people in this city have a perception about public schools based on what the media writes, especially our newspapers. We were very successful in getting rid of the educational writer for a local newspaper who would never write about anything unless it had a negative connotation towards the district.

Q: How did you do that?

Mainland Public School Parent: Well, what we ended up doing was a one-year analysis of all the articles that were written about education. We mapped them all out on all of the topics that were written about the schools. We did an analysis on how many were positive and how many were negative, and how many of those had inaccuracies. And we delivered the information to the editor and said, "You know, this is not fair and accurate reporting. There are a lot of really great things that are happening in our schools, and these are the things you're writing about. And look at the headlines, you know? You're talking about 'FBI investigating school district,' and then at the very bottom, you write that it was the new superintendent that called for the investigation. But the public is reading these captions, and you're doing a disservice to the community."

So they moved that educational writer. They brought in another educational writer. When there are stories that come up they use us as a resource for accuracies. It's a whole different dynamic now, where we're really having an impact on how information is getting delivered to the larger community through media.

Our analysis had impact. It really showed the editor, "Oh wow, you know, we really *do* need to be looking at some of the stories that we're writing and what service *are* we providing to the greater community?" If it's only negative stories that you're sharing, then, you know, "What's up with that? Then you guys should be sharing more positive stories." And they have. The change in journalism [reporting] over the last year and a half has been dramatic. You know, now they not only have a writer that's more conscientious, but he's somebody that's in the community. I mean, he's visible. He's not somebody that, you know, just shows up when there's controversy. He does that too, but he's also, you know, right there when things are happening. You know who he is. He's talking to a number of different people. He's not only going to one source, so that's been really great.

A good relationship between the public schools and the media is necessary to promote balanced coverage. The relationship needs to include an effective public relations department in the public schools as well as engaged citizens who call the newspapers when they want to encourage or to question the newspaper stories.

If the media reports both the positive and the negative about public schools in a balanced fashion with front-page articles above the fold, the community's perception of the public schools is likely to become more balanced, and more middle-class parents might be encouraged to reengage by exploring public schools as an option for their children.

Perhaps the basic point of this parental advocacy recommendation can be summed up by Dennis Iwanaga's August 11, 2004, letter to the editor in the *Honolulu Advertiser.* He writes, "Instead of people griping about how bad public education is, they should go to the public school and be part of the solution. Be involved with the school as a volunteer and see what is being done. Then if something is wrong, he can be part of the team that makes it right" (A19).

Decentralization of the Public School System

The third category of state-level recommendations is the decentralization of the state Department of Education. Parents' main complaints are that the system-level bureaucracy does not respond in a timely manner to issues at the individual school site, the school system is micromanaged by legislators and others, and the lines of authority are unclear and cumbersome.

The first parent in this section discussed the frustration that occurs when parents want to improve something at a school, but the DOE bureaucracy is slow to respond or doesn't respond at all.

Physician: It is frustrating. I remember when our kids went to public school, we wanted to try to get a basketball court put out there because they had this big field, but there was nothing to do on this field. So we wanted a basketball court, and my wife was . . . PTA president or something like that. She was working, trying to get a basketball court, and just basically, you know, was just banging her head against the wall.

Q: Was that because it's hard to find the one person with authority to take action?

Physician: Yes. It's just because you have to talk to so-and-so.

"Oh, you have to talk to so-and-so." "Well, we'll put it on the list. And we'll do this and do that." Pretty soon you just say, "Aww, forget it. My kid will be out of there in two years. What do I care?" That's especially true in the intermediate schools. . . . You're there two years. There's very little interest in the PTSA or anything because you've only got two years. If it takes three, four years to effect any change, then why should you bother to try?

When I started to ask about deregulation directly, the parents' point of view seemed to be connected to the bureaucracy rather than directed at the school site. There was frustration with the state Department of Accounting and General Services (DAGS).

Q: What's your view on the issue of deregulation?

Nonprofit Executive: I see that DAGS is kind of foot dragging. I know at [a certain public school] we had a fence that had graffiti all the time, and DAGS would never come out and clean it up. We always had to have our can of paint and do that. I think, even with the playgrounds. . . . I think the private schools take more ownership on their own. They don't have those regulations. If they feel that the playground isn't safe, they'll just go in and fix it. They don't have to wait for someone to okay it.

Q: How would that be possible for the public schools system to have that attitude?

Nonprofit Executive: Well, I think that part of the problem lies in the fact that we just have one school district. Personally, I think that it would be better if we had smaller school districts so that we could focus on the needs of the community.

Q: How do you provide some kind of equity in a deregulated school district?

Nonprofit Executive: I don't know. I don't know the answer to that. But it just seems that the way that it's working right now just isn't working, and there's got to be a better way. . . . I don't know. It's just really hard to have one man in charge of a whole area. I know the district superintendent is busy working too, but . . . I don't know.

I guess it's just because I came from a school district that was one town, seventeen schools, and that was the school district. We had problems, but we did things. I worked for two years on a bond issue because our schools were starting to fall apart. They were fifty to seventy-five years old, and the city came together and came up with this bond issue, and the homeowners were taxed.

That's one thing we don't have here. So what I know would not really happen here in Hawai'i, but I know that it has worked in another state. There's got to be a way. Everyone's intelligent enough that we could come together and find a way that would work for all communities.

Living on one of the neighbor islands (outside of O'ahu), this next parent talked about his frustration with having to sometimes contact DOE personnel on O'ahu to solve a problem on the neighbor island. He felt that this contributes to a sense of disengagement from the public schools.

Nonprofit Executive: What do you do when you have difficulty with the Department of Education? If I'm a parent, and I don't agree with a decision that has been made at the school level, I'll speak to the teacher. And the teacher says, "Well, I made that decision. If you don't like it, go and talk to the principal." And so then you go and talk to the principal, and the principal says, "Well, I stand by my teacher, so if you don't like it, go and talk to the district superintendent." And then you go to the district superintendent, and district superintendent tends to say, "Well, I stand by my principal, so if you don't like that, call O'ahu." So for many people on the neighbor islands, there's this huge disconnect. And although we have most of this great equity because we are this one school system, there is also a large disconnect in that people seem so far away. In the case of the neighbor islander, about the third contact the parent makes is to someone on another island, and that person has no contact with the child, and hasn't ever met the teacher, necessarily, and doesn't really understand what's happened.

Q: Do you think deregulation would solve some of those issues?

Nonprofit Executive: Well, I think that somehow we do need the counties to be more involved. If the goal is to have more parental and community involvement in the schools, I don't know how you can do it without having counties involved somehow. Oftentimes people talk about, "Well, if we do that, then we have to move to a property-taxed base for funding education." And I'm not sure that's true. And I don't know why that would have to be true. I don't believe that we have to fund schools based on property tax. I believe that the current funding mechanisms may serve us well, to keep a more equitable funding apparatus alive. But we certainly have to look at how do we start to involve people at the county level. If you have a problem with the local school in your county, you don't talk to anyone in your county, you have to talk to someone who is a state employee.

Other problems mentioned were having no clear lines of authority and having the state legislators micromanage the school system. The next parent was also frustrated with the current overall bureaucratic DOE structure, but while he was generally in favor of less centralization, he makes the argument that there are places where more centralization would be more efficient.

Military Officer: When you have a school system of this size, it's a huge school system that does not have control. It is controlled by the state, and not only by the state, but by the legislators themselves. During the legislative session, whether you're talking about lunch fees, bus fees, or library books, they're involved — much like the old Soviet Union system that crumbled. And so that's what you're looking at. So you're looking at a centralized, large bureaucracy that is not responsive.

Q: Would you be in support of decentralization?

Military Officer: Oh, the bureaucracy is a mess. It won't survive without decentralization.

Q: With autonomy for each school district?

Military Officer: Oh, it doesn't have to be a school district, but definitely at the school district level, and it probably should be like most businesses. At the complex level, even.

But you know, at the same time, just to throw something out at you really quick — there are other things for which the schools system should probably be centralized. For example, textbook buying. You know, in the school system, my kids don't even have textbooks they can take home because there is a shortage. And that's because, not only does each school decide which schoolbooks they'll buy, you can have four different fourth-grader teachers who are buying totally different sets of books. You're not buying en masse. So the cost is horrendous because there is no coordination. So certain things should be, in a sense, centralized or coordinated.

Q: So we're going back to that same issue about how you get the community reengaged in the public schools. What comes first?

Military Officer: No, you have to break the system off first because, otherwise, if you have the community involved, but the system can't actually respond, then the community is going to become disillusioned. It'll become even worse. So you have to have a system that can actually respond to the community.

Part of it is some of the legislators. The word is out, I think, that the system is meant for the legislators. It should be managed as a separate entity. How valuable is the senator's or representative's time if he [or she] is looking at legislation on raising the price of a school bus fare, or if he's considering the different formulas for raising the lunch fare price? That's not what legislators should be doing. That's what school administrators are doing. If school administrators aren't doing that, what are they doing? So it has to be a separate system. Legislators need to set policy, and the school needs to set its own procedures. And so that has to be broken off. And once the school can take care of itself, and manage itself, then it can respond to the citizens. And there'll probably be a cry from the citizens: "Hey, we want this!"

Next we hear from two legislators who sent their children to public schools. They were sympathetic to the idea of realigning the structure of the DOE so that more of the decision making is at the local level. One legislator mentions Hawai'i's history of centralization as continuing to have an impact today.

Q: Do you support decentralization?

Legislator 1: I often thought about whether or not we should decentralize the school district because I think it would engage — more decision making is supposed to be done locally, right? You have to know your history of Hawai'i to understand the reason why the school system is structured the way it is. Back in the days of the monarchy, the days of the plantations, everything was centralized, and the fact that most of the money was situated here in Honolulu meant the other islands don't have a tax base.

Legislator 2: If we have local school boards, people have to be more accountable, and we would need a tax base. Now Kaua'i has to depend on Honolulu. Counties only have a property tax base. They would need money to build schools and to pay salaries. The liquor taxes and everything else is in the state legislature.

One problem with the current DOE system [is] the unclear lines of authority. What to do? If the superintendent was in the governor's cabinet, it might help with line of authority.

I really do believe that we should decentralize. Right now, it's a very hierarchical structure, and the orders come from the top, and filter down through the schools. I really do believe that the school and the campus should be the focal point of all services, and the bureaucracy should put on a service hat, and really be there to meet the school needs, rather than the other way around, and I don't see that happening too often.

Finally, in this section's last interview, with a husband and wife, he introduced the idea of decentralization, and she, a public school teacher, reaffirmed her support of the idea.

CEO: I really feel that the education system should be broken down like it is on the mainland.

Q: Decentralized?

CEO: Yes. That's the way to do it. So you have the neighborhood and community really supporting the school, and they have a big voice in what happens in the schools, and how much the teachers get paid, and all that stuff. It should really be broken down.

Q: And when you say, "decentralized," you're talking about autonomy for the budget, and accountability at the local district? So no more state DOE?

CEO: No more state DOE. No more all that bureaucracy.

Public School Teacher: It's too big and cumbersome.

CEO: It's too big and cumbersome. It's too political. Just get it down to the neighborhood and the districts.

Q: (*To mother.*) And you agree?

Public School Teacher: I definitely agree with that.

CEO: I find that that works on the mainland. We both went to school on the mainland, so we know that too. I think that the superintendent of education has a tough job. She's got too many people to report to: the Board of Education, the governor, and the legislators. It's just very tough. And then she has to deal with the union.

Q: So would you work and support decentralization?

Public School Teacher: I would definitely support it.

CEO: I would. I would support it.

The Union's Role

The next recommendation is not under the control of the state system, but it does affect it, hence its placement in this section. Parents believe that the teachers' and principals' unions protect "bad" teachers and principals. Incompetent teachers are regarded as a minority, but the parents argue that even one bad teacher at a school contributes to a negative perception of the school system.

Public School Teacher: I don't know anyone who has been fired. Some very good teachers have been lured away to private school.

Nonprofit Executive: I don't profess to know the answers, but I do see some of the problems. I do see that there is a lack of faith in the public education system, partly because everyone knows of the really bad teacher who's still working. It's very, very sad because my guess is that "bad teachers" make up less than one-half of one percent of the people working in the system. What's sad is that the occasional bad seed makes the whole rest of the crop of wonderful teachers and wonderful administrators look bad, and you don't hear about them. You hear about that one problem.

There's also a perception that the only way that you could possibly get fired from the Department of Education job in the state of Hawai'i is to actually commit a crime. And anybody, like myself, who works in the private sector, well, you don't have to commit a crime to be released from your job. You just have to not be performing your job. There is kind of a feeling that people who don't perform their job within the Department of Education, if that's the only thing they're doing wrong, they will be kept forever. Now, unless they're actually convicted of molestation or some other heinous crime, they not only do not lose their job, but they'll probably be moved to another school. So that's the perception — not necessarily the reality, but that is the perception.

So how well the union serves their employees is one question. They probably serve their employees well. How well they serve the cause of public education? How well do their contracts reflect what's best for children? This is the question. Although, common sense would say what would be very good for the child would be good for teachers as well — for example, lower student-teacher ratios, appropriately trained professionals, ongoing professional development for teachers, and administrators and staff. All those things that would naturally lead to a better school environment, better living for children, should also lead to a better school environment and a better environment for teachers. We also just need to value our teachers more, and that's a difficult thing to do when people don't believe that they can be held accountable.

This same parent also recommended that the union negotiation process would benefit from having a child advocate as part of the negotiating team, and he suggested that binding arbitration with a child-centered arbitrator might work as a way to prevent teacher strikes.

Nonprofit Executive: I think that there definitely has to be some reform in the way that contract negotiations are handled. I do not believe that the parties that are affected are in the negotiation room, and I don't think there's fair representation of children. There's not a child advocate in the negotiation room. There's not a fair representation of parents. There's not a parent advocate in the negotiation room. There certainly isn't fair representation of the Department of Education. (*Laughs.*) There are members from the board, and they're the primary negotiators for the state.

And then the question of what is fair for teachers has to be addressed in a broader sense. I'm not suggesting that we need to be educated to the nuances of contract negotiations, but that somebody should be on our behalf, or the children, or the parents, and teachers. The union contract negotiations affect primarily children, and they are not represented when it comes to union negotiations.

Q: So you're suggesting an advocate sit as part of the negotiating team?

Nonprofit Executive: That's one possible solution. There are others. We're one of nineteen states that allow teachers to strike. They're considered essential personnel in every other state. In the state of Iowa, for example, they have the teacher's union, and they have contract negotiations. They cannot strike. Whenever it gets to that point, it comes under binding arbitration. My understanding is that there is a great hesitancy to go into binding arbitration in this state because the state feels it has been dealt negative blows by binding arbitration. I think if the binding arbitration system is set up appropriately, with the arbitrator being child-centered, and looking out for what's best for the child, rather than what's best for any individual party, whether it be the fiscal health of the state or the work conditions of the union, that binding arbitration may be the way to go.

The father in the last excerpt gave an example of how unions, other than the teachers' union, can join a coalition to work to improve public school facilities.

Attorney: We're reached out to the unions with our efforts at [a certain public high school], and with America's Promise [a national volunteer organization]. We now have them working with us. In our last work session, I said, "Look, you've got to do something about the visual effect of the schools. We need to get parents, students, teachers, community, businesses, and unions working together as stakeholders." The carpenters' unions sent seventeen apprentices. They repaired all the termite-eaten windowsills one Saturday morning working alongside students.

And we've now divided the school into zones. We're having stakeholder groups adopt zones. So now the freshman class has adopted a zone. They'll keep it for four years. What happens when they adopt a zone? They start micro-focusing on everything there, saying, "Gee, this gutter is in the wrong place because it dumps the water from the roof right onto the sidewalk. Can we get something to get it under the sidewalk?" Things that when you have too big a focus you don't notice. And they planted palm trees in an area that really improved the looks. They've now created rock gardens. They put mulch in areas they want to plant flowerbeds in their zone.

Community Recommendations

Recommended changes at the community level are organized into two categories:

1. encouraging an "engaged public" via grassroots movements and advocacy;
2. encouraging parental research on individual public schools as well as private schools.

Public School Advocates and Coalitions: Grassroots Movements

The first category involves advocacy for public schools. The role of the public education advocate needs to be expanded so that individual parent advocates can participate in partnerships and coalitions that would create and strengthen a grassroots movement for change. Parents in this study also believe that public school teachers and principals need to be advocates for their public schools as well as serve as agents of change. Legislators need to be advocates for public education. The bottom line is that parents who believe in public schools need to speak up.

While individuals can make substantial differences just by speaking out and actively engaging in their children's public schools, coalitions made up of public school advocates may be one of the most effective means of changing the perception of public schools in Hawai'i. Many parents, such as those in this study, are already public school advocates, and many have already engaged in informal or formal coalition memberships.

Parents in Hawai'i shared some of their experiences with coalitions locally, and public school advocates from the mainland talked about strategies they used while working within a coalition.

PARENTS AS ADVOCATES

We begin with a father who believes that one parent speaking up for public education can have an impact.

Professor: I think word of mouth is — I know I've had an impact on people through discussions about the public versus private schools. And because I've had a good experience with public schools, and my kids have had good experiences there, that has changed the opinion of some people.

In the next three excerpts, we will hear from parents who have initiated or participated in grassroots projects in Hawai'i that are working to improve public schools. The first parent talks about working with America's Promise.

Attorney: There is change taking place in the public schools. I don't want to take the credit. I think a lot of people are doing this. But we've met with our legislators. I met with the superintendent. We continue to work at the public school complex. We got organized. But it takes some parent — when you ask how do you get parents involved — we can do hands-on things: we can volunteer at schools, we can sweep hallways, we can help you paint a building. But the impediments we come up against — you can't paint too much because the unions will be upset. For example, four fathers got together two years ago. We repainted the cafeteria and told the principal to close his eyes. Okay? So what we're doing now is we're getting America's Promise in and we're trying to organize.

Q: How do you make your volunteer work public so another school who wants to do that can talk to you and talk to people [at that school] and see what you're doing?

Attorney: That's why we're linking with America's Promise because they have full-time staff so that if we're short some things, they can go out and ask for businesses to contribute. But their thing is that you try to do it on your own first. Parents come in. We've got the military coming in now. Admiral Glenn came. Senator [Daniel] Inouye came for our kickoff on December 9th. The kickoff was widely publicized.

Q: Is it in the paper?

Attorney: It will be more and more so now. But what we're doing is going to the legislature. You know in the governor's package has a hundred million to restore or renovate older schools. That's us. The governor got a hundred million dollars to repair schools — ninety million dollars for new schools. But the repair and restoration and renovation are something that is only coming about because there is this grassroots movement to get it done.

And so I keep saying that it's got to be a grassroots movement. I will not join with an organization. I don't want to link with any organization because then I can't say what I want to say. And more and more people are doing this. There's a bill next Friday that I have to go and testify on for the restoration and renovation.

Q: Who coordinates all this?

Attorney: We're going to try to coordinate through America's Promise. They get funding from businesses and some federal grant money, I think. Colin Powell is the national head of it. Senator Inouye's on the board. It's really a bipartisan thing about improving communities. And the goal here is to get the communities back into the schools. We would like to have every school in the community resourced. I question things like why aren't our school libraries staffed by people in the neighborhood on weekends and open to kids and grandparents and whomever to come in and use the libraries. Why are they closed? Why can't we open our computer centers to our senior's groups in the neighborhood and have them cross-mentoring, where the kids are teaching the seniors? Why don't we have, you know, student-run convenience stores in every school, where retired businesspeople can come in and mentor the kids? And why aren't there curriculums designed around inventory control, accounting, etc., with computers in those stores?

The next conversation is with another attorney who, with a partner, initiated an advocacy organization to raise grant money to work toward establishing a grassroots network, giving public school advocates a platform so that they can be heard in the community.

Attorney: We established an advocacy initiative. We went off and tried to do it by ourselves. We were really committed to this. We started with the Business Round Table, which is already a mix, right? None of those people send their kids to public school, and yet they've been so supportive. We've written grants and received like maybe two hundred thousand dollars to do different initiatives.

We've done focus groups with parents and asked them, "Why do you send your kids to public school?" and "What was the message you would like them to know about how you feel about public education?" We found that there was a lot of pride in the public education system. Parents wanted to let people know about the pride that they had for public schools. They want people to know how important public education is for the state of Hawai'i. And they wanted to just get involved. They wanted opportunities to network.

So that is one of the things we're planning on doing with some of our funding . . . to get public school parents together, and for me, that's one of my things. How do you give parents a platform from where they can begin to have a voice about what they're thinking about public education, whether it is positive, negative? How do we begin to give those different voices more of a platform for conversation, just so it can begin to influence the way people perceive public education, its role, and how important it is?

So I think . . . the main thing we have to do is to begin to network all of these parents and begin the conversation, going back to the basics, of what is the purpose and mission of public education in the state of Hawai'i. What is the role it plays?

In the third conversation, a parent talked about working with the long-established Parent-Teacher Association (PTA).

Q: How do you think we can get the community, particularly the professional class, reengaged with the public school system?

Nonprofit Executive: Well, we have a presentation called "The Building of Successful Partnerships" and [a certain person] and I were the first two who were trained by the national PTA. We actually go into different agencies and do these presentations. It's actually teaching people in the community that we need to work together in areas like communication, student learning, volunteers, and advocacy. And just because you may not have children in school doesn't mean we don't all have a stake in public education.

Q: And do you find that they are receptive?

Nonprofit Executive: Absolutely. And that's why I was getting involved with kids. We always let children sit on our PTSA boards because one day they're going to be the adults on our board. And I think that the whole community has to come together and support them, and be there for them.

I was curious as to what a private school parent's views would be on the role of coalitions as a vehicle for getting more parents acting as public school advocates. The following parent agreed that parent participation is needed, but she felt parents don't know how to organize at the community level. She suggested parents need "a grassroots manual."

Q: Do the advocates for public education have to form some sort of coalition, which would then get the attention of other groups who say, "Well, maybe I might be interested in working on that"?

Private School Parent: Well, I guess it goes back to the communities around the schools. I don't think it can be tackled at the statewide level. Look at even now . . . the schools that are relatively more successful have a relatively high percentage of parents from that community who are participating. But it's almost a grassroots revolution. Two or three years ago, there was a relatively high percentage of kids dropping out of private schools for economic reasons, and I know, talking with these parents, they became active in the public school system. And now they're beginning to demand quality because it's their children who are there.

We also need . . . resources to know how to go about doing it. If you're in a community and you want to raise the quality of schools, you don't know how many other parents feel as you do. Once you know who some of them are, what do you do next? I mean, for example, you have a principal who is not welcoming parents to participate — then what do you do? . . . Maybe we need a manual. Maybe we need a grassroots manual on how parents can really organize themselves to change the schools within their communities. So maybe, to some degree, it's not knowing "how" as well.

MAINLAND COALITIONS: FORMAL AND INFORMAL

There are already parents in Hawai'i who are successful leaders in promoting public school advocacy. There are also the experiences of the mainland parents who have been involved in public school advocacy organizations. From one of them, I was able to obtain a "grassroots manual" of sorts. As I mentioned earlier, I started to investigate possible ways of contacting parents on the mainland who would agree to be interviewed for this study and discovered the Parents for Public Schools (PPS), a national public school advocacy organization operating at the city level in various states.

This coalition's mission statement reflects the ideas that PPS values public education as an important part of American life and as an essential element of democracy. PPS views effective parent involvement as critical to strong public schools. The coalition values the constructive involvement of parents in the governance of schools and as a bridge between schools and the community. PPS values parents as committed owners of, rather than passive consumers in, public schools, and the organization values the improvement of public education for every child, not just one's own (Parents for Public Schools 2004).

These mainland public school advocates shared how they work in coalitions, including PPS, perhaps giving some direction to the parents who said, "Maybe we need a grassroots manual on how parents can really organize themselves to change schools within their communities."

INFORMAL NEIGHBORHOOD COALITIONS

In addition to the parents involved in the PPS coalition, a colleague who knew about my study put me in touch with another parent who is an advocate for public schools via an informal neighborhood coalition. This public school advocate and her husband decided to form a coalition of parents. These are professionals who were willing to consider "going against the grain" of their peer group and send their children to the neighborhood public school.

The organizer of this coalition, who lives in an urban area on the West Coast, talked about deciding to send her child to the neighborhood public elementary school when, typically, her neighbors sent their children to private schools. She was concerned about the fabric of the neighborhood if everyone's children went to different schools.

Q: When you say that within your state, your city has a reputation as being one of the worst urban school districts, is that reality or perception?

Mainland Public School Parent: Some of both. Very few white families who live in [this urban city] send children to public schools. So on our street, there are about five families on the couple of streets that I consider our neighborhood — all of their children are in private schools.

Q: How did you find that out?

Mainland Public School Parent: There are four families in very close proximity to our house who each have a child the same age as my child. And they play together. So we just got to know each other just by being outside and chatting and talking about, "Oh, what are you going do?" . . . So my neighbor, the closest neighbor, and the woman who lives right next door, her child is at a very elite K–12 private school. And the folks across the street and two doors, three doors down, are with my son at the neighborhood public school. And a fourth family, who live around the corner, who we're pretty close to — they are also at the public school.

So this group of parents — I would say there were about a dozen families that started meeting formally last March with one of my neighbors and me as hosts. My neighbor did it because she had been involved with the school and the PTA, and she was out looking at all the private schools and trying to make the decision to go public or private. And I got involved because of my interest, my day job, because my work is in the [urban] schools. So I thought I should really take a look at it from the parents' perspective. And then, of course, having a personal need to get in the school building and thinking, "Is this a safe place for my child?" and "Will there be learning going on?" and "How is this neighborhood school compared to the reputation of the district?" Which is quite generalized, as you can imagine.

Q: So you and this neighbor conducted research?

Mainland Public School Parent: Actually, I would say, she and I probably did the most print research, but all the families were going out to visit schools.

Q: Oh, they did?

Mainland Public School Parent: Except us. We didn't actually go visit a private school.

Q: You said you were visiting public schools?

Mainland Public School Parent: I visit public schools in my rounds, on my day job, but I did go see our neighborhood school that is not one of our project schools. And I went as a parent. Most of the neighbors in our group that were making the same decision about public versus private did go visit open houses in the private schools in the area.

Q: The private schools? Did your neighbors do an equal amount of research by going to the public schools?

Mainland Public School Parent: Yes. Several of them did go to other public schools because we have this semi-choice situation in this city. If there's availability in a school that's not in your neighborhood, you can request an inter-district transfer. And some of the parents who ended up in my child's school did request an inter-district transfer and were not successful.

Q: So when you went to visit this neighborhood school, what did you find?

Mainland Public School Parent: I found a fairly typical elementary school in terms of my experience as a former teacher and as somebody who's spent a lot of time in a lot of schools in different jobs I've had. It's very small. The enrollment is four hundred K–5 students, which is a small school in this city, and I found the principal had been there three years, either starting her third or fourth year. She was open and willing to talk to my neighbors and me.

In terms of doing the print research, I found that their teacher longevity at that school is high. All the teachers have been there I think an average of fifteen years with only one or two having turned over in the last five. The test scores were fairly low by national standards, but in our district, in the top third, I think. Second-language students may be 20 percent, 25 percent, which for this city is low. The school is at the halfway point economically. It's not in the highest-end district, but it's not in the poorest area. It's in-between. I'd say about a third of the kids to half the kids are neighborhood kids, and that the others are inter-district transfers from poorer neighborhoods.

Q: What is the ethnic mix?

Mainland Public School Parent: It's about 25 percent each, African American, Latino, and Southeast Asian, with the other 25 percent being Chinese, Korean, white.

Q: So when you say your neighborhood group started to meet formally, who initiated these meetings?

Mainland Public School Parent: I think my neighbor did or I did. I can't remember.

Q: And what was that process? Did you go talk in person to these other people? What did you say?

Mainland Public School Parent: Yes, pretty much — a few phone calls.

Q: And what was on the agenda?

Mainland Public School Parent: Public versus private school.

Q: And what did you talk about? I mean, what were the criteria for making a decision one way or the other?

Mainland Public School Parent: Well, we agreed that all of us as families were in the same situation of doing research and making a decision. What drew us together was our concern that if all the children in the neighborhood went to different schools it would disrupt the fabric of the neighborhood. That was one of our concerns, and that's what compelled us to start to talk to each other.

Q: You mean, as far as friends playing with each other?

Mainland Public School Parent: Everything . . . and the fact that parental involvement with school is such a part of community work. And that had been true for those of us who are professionals and work in the field, and for those of us who are not.

So we felt that if we could possibly send our kids to the same school, we would improve our chances to do everything from cooperative day care before and after school. We could be making decisions about some after-school activities for the kids to augment what they would be doing in school. And we also felt that if we could get enough neighborhood, middle-class, involved parents into the building, it would improve the school because there would be people there who were committed to being involved on a more regular basis.

Q: How often did you meet and for how long?

Mainland Public School Parent: I think we met starting in October or November because the open-house season in our community is October through February. The inter-district transfer is about January 30th. So that's the window where people do their looking around.

We met once a month. We met once a month pretty much for about a year.

Q: How many attended these meetings? How many families were represented?

Mainland Public School Parent: We started with about five, and we ended up with about fifteen.

Q: And out of fifteen how many chose to go to this neighborhood school?

Mainland Public School Parent: About two-thirds. I'd say about ten out of fifteen are at the school.

Q: What was the argument that the other third articulated, the third that went to private?

Mainland Public School Parent: (*Pauses.*) Probably, publicly, the argument was test scores and the quality of the instructional experience. People didn't say, "I want my child to be in a school with all kids of his same class and race."

So one of the things we did was bring research back to the group to say, "So let's look at the research on test scores and parenting. What do test scores really represent, and what are the other important factors in children having a positive educational experience?" So when people did say, "This is my concern," some of us tried to respond and say, "Here's some information you might want to look at."

Q: So it was almost also a study group where you would bring in research and share?

Mainland Public School Parent: Yes.

Q: That's really interesting. What do you think would have happened if you hadn't worked with this?

Mainland Public School Parent: I think the people on the fence would have been more likely to go to private. Because one of the things several of us said to each other over the course of the year was, "I'm more confident sending my child to the [neighborhood] school if you send your kid too."

We agreed to take turns at the PTA because it's a burnout job. (*Laughs.*) So rather than all of us trying to flood the PTA the first few years, we've agreed to take turns. So I think that will probably continue to happen. And the second thing is we have looked at the other aspects of volunteerism in the school and sort of farmed out those chores.

So my responsibility is to — there's a process that volunteers at the school, or any school in our district, have to go through that includes literacy training, a TB test, and something else. And any single one of the requirements is not onerous, but as a package they are because working people can't get to the clinic and get to the training. As a result, they don't volunteer.

So I said, well, this isn't a good idea. We should get all those people that they need to see like the public health nurse, the literacy trainer, the fingerprinting people to show up at our school on an evening, and anybody who's interested to show up, and get it all taken care of in one night. One-stop shop. So that's my charge.

Q: What was the response on the part of the principal and the teachers to this involvement?

Mainland Public School Parent: A couple of the teachers have been very supportive and I've copied the principal that I'm trying to do this just so she has a heads-up, so I think she'll be thrilled about it.

My counterpart, my neighbor, who is on the PTA, is the carrier. So I just tell her what I'm doing. I say, "Let the principal know, or tell the PTA." Last Monday night I was out of town, so I e-mailed her before I left and I said, "Here's what I'm working on for HEROS"— that's the project for volunteering —"and, would you take this to the executive committee of the PTA and run it by them?" So we're trying to let people know what's going on.

Q: How does this feel from a personal point of view to have this support group?

Mainland Public School Parent: It's very important. It's critical to the decision-making process and to whether our children will be successful.

Q: The typical dominant belief in your urban community is that if parents have a choice they send their children to private schools?

Mainland Public School Parent: Right.

Q: So your group is going against the grain?

Mainland Public School Parent: It felt like that to me this last year because, as I said, when I looked up and down the street, I wasn't seeing a lot of my neighbors in public school. And so we "outed" ourselves early with our neighbors and said, "We're committed to going to public school." So they got that!

Q: So you were explicitly an advocate right up front?

Mainland Public School Parent: Yes, right up front. And unless something of great concern happens, which we'll be first to report back to you, that's our goal. We don't know if we're going be successful. We can't guarantee it, but that's what we plan to try to do.

A FORMAL COALITION

In the next three conversations, I talked with parents from two other urban areas on the mainland. All three are public school advocates who participate in the national PPS chapters in their cities. These interviews were conducted separately. The first interview was with a father, a businessman, who talked about the PPS chapter in his city, explaining how it got started and the types of activities in which the parents are engaged.

Q: So what role does the chapter of the PPS play in public school advocacy?

Mainland Public School Parent: Well, one of our primary missions is to recruit students to public schools. And in our city, we have a very, very high percentage of students that go to public school, and so the emphasis has been more on keeping them.

Q: What percentage would you say?

Mainland Public School Parent: I think it's in excess of 80 percent of the families here. This is the urban area. I think for an urban area in the United States, we have the highest percentage of students going to public schools. Yes, that percentage doesn't include the suburbs, where it's probably even higher.

But the real issue has been, with the budget cuts, some of the programs that attract the upper-income students have been on the chopping block, and so how do we keep those students in our school system to keep our system full, and prevent the flow to private schools?

Q: What kinds of things has the chapter been doing?

Mainland Public School Parent: Probably the biggest thing that we do directly is called the School Fair, or this year it's going to be called the School Celebration. It has been a two-night event, but it's going be a one-night event this year at the convention location. All the schools will be there to show what programs they have. They're going to show student art, student performances, and talk about the programs in the schools, and we've had a lot of different programs of choice, and specialties within the school district. . . .

The . . . original idea of the School Fair was to target parents whose kids were going into kindergarten, going into middle school [sixth grade] or going into high school [ninth grade] to make them aware of what their options are and what the special programs are. This year, it's going to do that, but it'll also be much more focused on just celebrating all the good things going on in all the different schools.

Q: And how do you communicate this fair to the parents at large?

Mainland Public School Parent: Well, through a variety of means. We're actually stepping up the communication this year because our budget's increased dramatically for it. But in the past, it's been a very limited budget, and we've reached out to day cares so that we can reach the parents who are considering kindergarten. We've used the school district's mailing and just some basic advertising. This year we're trying to reach out even more to those groups, and to really also draw to the event more of the parents whose kids are in public schools already so they can look at what is going on and what's good in our district.

Q: How large is your chapter? How many members does your chapter have?

Mainland Public School Parent: We have about fifty paying members, and then we have a couple hundred people who regularly attend events.

Q: And, how did [the PPS chapter] get started?

Mainland Public School Parent: It got started as a combination of parent groups that were already active [in the public schools], consolidating, and deciding we should connect with this larger national group. So, we had several different groups who were working on similar issues but kind of overlapping, and we decided it didn't make much sense. We should get together and pool our resources and then the national resources seemed very attractive.

Q: Who took the leadership role to get the groups together?

Mainland Public School Parent: Well, it was primarily one woman who got things rolling, but we quickly pulled in leaders of the different groups to all work together. It's not like we were just going in different directions and not communicating prior to that. We each had our different roles, different directions, and some independence, but we also had coordinators, and we worked together on a lot of projects.

Just as now there are a lot of other parent groups operating in the urban public schools that we could consolidate, but there's also something nice about each of us having our independence, and focusing on our individual priorities. But where our priorities overlap, we work together.

Q: What are the priorities? You talked about presenting a school fair.

Mainland Public School Parent: Well, our priorities are built around the strategic plan for the school district and increasing parent involvement in the decision making. One of the emphases in the strategic plan is moving towards less central control and more independence at the school level, while still providing better central control in terms of alignment but not in terms of the day-to-day decisions. There are site councils at each of the individual schools that are supposed to help run the operations at that school. Well, right now, those site councils are not functioning very consistently in schools around the district. So, two of our projects — one we call the Parent Leadership Conference, where we draw parents in for a Saturday from all over the district and put on workshops and trainings on everything from "Who are these different groups that function in the school district? How do you connect with them? What are your roles?" to more sophisticated things about how to run those meetings, how to engage with the principal, and what the issues are on the strategic plan. We've also addressed some of the budgetary issues.

Q: Who does the professional training? I mean, how do people know how to run these workshops?

Mainland Public School Parent: We have not relied on the national organization for the workshops. We've relied a lot on the school district itself loaning us people to help run them. Some of us have run them.

Q: So, you work with whatever talent and expertise you have?

Mainland Public School Parent: Whatever talent's needed. Yes, and in our workshop last year on the budget, the superintendent came and ran the workshop.

So we have a very good working relationship with the district. They're very supportive. Before we merged and became a part of PPS, there were leaders who are in our chapter who helped organize a march for funding for the public schools. And we pulled thirty thousand people out to march for funding. And that gives you instant credibility with the district.

Q: Wow. . . . (*Laughs.*) How'd you do that? How'd you get thirty thousand people to come out?

Mainland Public School Parent: A lot of phone calls. But we did it at a time when there were some impending cuts. We were going lay off over three hundred teachers, and our city felt that our funding had been taken away from us because it was removed from local control, transferred to the state, and then the state wasn't supplying us with the money. So now we would have to lay off three hundred people. The people in our city were naturally outraged about it. And it was really just organizing that emotion.

In the next conversation, another member of the same PPS chapter shared her experiences with the chapter's activities that focus on informing the general public about the public schools in their city.

Mainland Public School Parent: It would be wonderful for you to talk to the Schools Foundation director. One of the things that the foundation sponsors, which I think is incredibly effective, is that they have a "Principal for the Day." And one day of the year, every single urban public school — there are one hundred of them — they set it up so that they've had a businessperson be Principal for the Day.

Q: Oh, I see — someone from the community?

Mainland Public School Parent: They spend an entire day shadowing a principal. And there's more to the program than that where, I think, the businesspeople then give feedback, as a businessperson, as to how you might want to run things differently. I mean, I think there's that perspective. But the main thing is the "wow." I mean, this is an eye-opening experience where these businesspeople have a chance to run a school and realize, "Oh my God, you sit in a class with thirty-five kids? How could I do that?" And I think at some level they're trying to move that into a Principal for the Day, where they're inviting legislators and political decision makers to participate as well.

And it's a fun experience. And it's embraced by the community. It's embraced by local newspapers and the television stations. On that day, you see television stories about so-and-so [is] Principal for a Day here and there. But that's one way, at a real grassroots level, to get people into your building. So that would be certainly one thing that I would suggest.

Q: And how do you get the media interested?

Mainland Public School Parent: Well, it depends on who your Principal for the Day is. I mean, the school can call and make the media contact.

We are going to be involved this year in doing what we call "Celebrate Public Schools," which is a celebration of all the public schools. . . . We're trying to make it a citywide celebration of public schools. We'll have local celebrities there, and we'll have student artwork and performances, like the school fair that I mentioned. That kind of turned my husband around about our decision to send our children to public schools. We've been working on this with PPS for years and trying to make it a bigger and bigger event.

Right now it's a two-night event at a high school. You have elementary schools one night, middle schools and high schools another night. Every single principal shows up, and they have a little booth, and they talk about their program to whomever comes. We've had four or five thousand parents show up — preschool parents, fifth-grade parents looking at middle school options, eighth-grade parents looking at high school options.

Well, we're taking that fair to a whole new level this year, where we've got some grant money, and we're going to be doing it in a huge venue and doing a lot more public relations. We're going to have a Realtor fair associated with it.

And I think even at an individual school level, it becomes the responsibility of the principal and the PTA and the community to reach out constantly to the general public and bring them onto your campus, bring them into your buildings. And there are some very simple things that you can do: for example, publicizing a football game for a high school. At our school we do a book fair where we publicize it to the community. Be thinking about any event that you do with a community focus.

We were out at one of the public high schools, which is one of our schools that George Bush would say is a failing school according to the No Child Left Behind Act. One of the things that they do in their gym class once a week is the kids go out and they clean up litter on the street, and the neighbors are coming out and thanking them. You know, it's community outreach. It's simple stuff. But it makes a difference in the long run. So much of how people choose where they're going to send their children to school is just based on their perception and their reality, not necessarily *the* reality, but *their* reality.

The following excerpt is from a parent in another mainland city that has also organized a PPS chapter. She talks about the role of advocacy and coalitions in her urban school district.

Mainland Public School Parent: The bulk of our work during the fall is going out and doing workshops, to families, mostly middle-class families, and saying, "Look beyond these five [good-reputation] schools." Now there's another group of schools that have made it up to the second level that middle-class families have said, "Oh, I've heard about this school, I'm going go check it out. And then I'll consider putting it on my list of schools that would be acceptable." So schools like the public elementary school, which is where my kids are, families wouldn't even consider it five years ago. And now we have a waiting list.

Fewer kids are getting bused in now because more neighborhood kids want to be at the school. So you still get a mix, but you get families that are invested in the school that live in the neighborhood who have the ability to participate, and you still have kids that are coming out of their neighborhoods into a school that's building up.

The first step, we feel, as an organization, is to get the family to just step foot onto the campus. And they're not as afraid if they go," Oh, there's a great little garden. They have a garden? Do they have a gardener? Oh, it's a parent volunteer? Look at this library. God, I never thought that they would have a library like this."

Q: How do you organize the parent involvement in such a way so that the principal and the teachers welcome them?

Mainland Public School Parent: Well, part of that is bringing more active parents, and bringing more resources to the school. I mean, those are all things that should be appealing to teachers and principals, except some teachers and principals who aren't interested in having parent involvement. The kind who have been there for thirty years and don't want to throw a wrench into anything. Those are the schools that are obviously a lot more challenging for us to get into, but we have developed relationships with many of the principals who call for us to help them out. We'll call them and ask them, "What's going on at your school?" Or the superintendent will say, "You know, Principal A, why don't you give Parents for Public Schools a call and find out what they're working on and maybe they can host something at your school." The work that we do has to be district wide. We don't do school sites. We try not to do site-specific work.

There's got to be a draw for families to want to come to a site. So what we've been using is the whole enrollment process because the enrollment process is very complex.

But middle-class families are willing to figure it out, so what we do is we have these informational sessions at underperforming schools. We have the principal, a teacher, and parents from that school who are hosting be able to do their spiel about their school, and then we have somebody from the district office come and talk about the educational placement center, and how kids will be assigned. Then we have [our PPS], who'll speak on behalf of parents, saying, "We're in the public schools. We're at schools like this, and our kids are doing great." So now they're hearing testimonials from parents like them that are saying, "Don't be afraid. Come on in."

Q: And then is there media representation at these events?

Mainland Public School Parent: Mm-hm, right. We invite them to the larger ones. Like there are certain schools that we know will draw a larger group of parents, or there are certain workshops that parents are more interested in than others. We were the ones that started the school fairs. So three years ago we worked with the district to have all of the elementary schools meet in one location on one day so that parents can come and visit all of these different schools. So that they weren't all over the city trying to drive to get to all of these schools.

Q: How do parents find out about this fair?

Mainland Public School Parent: Well, we do a tremendous amount of outreach and marketing. So we as an organization said, "Let's get the district to support our efforts in this." So the district got all the principals to come out to the event. And then we did everything else. We had some funding to provide childcare, and translation, and food. We had it at a brand-new school that was opening in a neighborhood that is disenfranchised. And a thousand people showed up. Families were hungry for this information. So the following year we did it again but we took a step back and we asked the district to take the lead on it. Then they expanded it to elementary, middle, and high school. And we had it at a large high school. Four thousand people came to that one. So this past year, we completely washed our hands of the whole thing. I mean, that's kind of our objective is to come up with ideas, have them institutionalized, and then move on to the next issue.

So last year we had it at the School of the Arts, and charter schools were part of the school fair and we drew seven thousand people this time. And families that had kids in multiple grades were able to go to one location and find out about different schools. And if you went and you said, "Oh, you know, are there any other Spanish immersion programs?" I could say," Yeah, on that side there's [a certain elementary school], so go talk to the rep over at there, and then go over here, there's [a certain elementary school]." The idea was to have the principal, a teacher, and a parent available to talk to people.

Q: Now what about middle and high school? Any success with middle and high school?

Mainland Public School Parent: The middle school level is not as urgent because there's a handful of middle schools — three or four middle schools — that are really, really popular. And there's capacity for students.

So it hasn't been an issue. At the high school level, though, there aren't as many high schools to choose from. There are high schools that are highly desirable. One of the issues that we come across on a regular basis is the whole idea that there are nine hundred seats available at the ninth grade at [a certain urban public] high school, and there are three thousand applicants. So there's been a lot of protesting about, you know, not being able to get into the neighborhood.

What we've been trying to do is promote those other schools that aren't getting any recognition. The ones that are in, you know, neighborhoods that you may not have considered sending your child — or which the media portrayed as, like, this mean and evil school for the last five years, but in the last three or four of those years there's a new principal. There's new leadership, there are new teachers, and the school has turned around significantly.

We coordinated a group of families that got a school assignment even if that wasn't the school they chose. We brought about twenty families down to a public high school and had them meet with the principal and the vice principal and the counselors. They had a group of teachers and had the staff talk to the parents about the programs. And then they had four of the students from this high school who are going on to college — either through the public university system or going to a private one — of them is going to Harvard — to come and talk about the learning environment and their experiences and how nice it is because it's a small school. And because there's not a high-demand school, they get more one-on-one attention. So those twenty families that went to this tour, half of them are going to the school whereas a year ago, they would've said, "There's no way. We're going private."

And we have a superintendent that really appreciates parents, so she uses parents as partners, you know. I don't think we would have been able to get as much work done as we have if we didn't have her support and, you know, she's very open.

Q: So the superintendent is key?

Mainland Public School Parent: I think it's a very key position because they're going to be the ones pushing forward policy.

We are in the public school system, so we're going to try and make it the best that we can possibly make it, which involves parent participation and getting involved at the district level — just being aware, having information, you know, doing all those things. But we also realize that all stakeholders have to be at the table in order for equity to happen.

We also go into communities that don't traditionally participate in, say, the enrollment process. And we tell them, "You have to participate in the enrollment process. You have to fill out an application." It just doesn't happen like magic, and this is basic information that we're providing to certain communities. We are really making efforts to get to the point where we're delivering the same information to everyone no matter where you are on the socioeconomic scale [SES].

And that really has to be our goal. We really felt like we've mastered the outreach to middle-class families, recruiting them back into our public schools, so now we need to take that same energy of outreach to other [SES] communities.

CONDUCTING RESEARCH

Finally, the parents in this study also suggested that parents who are in the process of deciding where to send their children to school should be encouraged to conduct research on the public schools, just as they would private schools. These public school parents report that their colleagues routinely conduct research on private schools, but seldom conduct research on individual public schools.

If more parents researched public schools, the result, of course, would be that individual schools would have to be prepared to share information and also be receptive to potential parents who inquire about the school.

In sum, both the mainland parents and the public school parents in Hawai'i agree on the importance of public school advocacy, the importance of conducting research on the public schools, the appeal of sending one's children to neighborhood schools, and the need to pay attention to outreach, marketing, and good media relationships.

Changes Occurring

School Site Changes: Public School Choices in Hawai'i

Public school choice is increasingly widespread and widely supported. . . .
It sometimes reduces racial and class separation, it usually increases
parents' satisfaction with public schools, and with fair guidelines, it
is consistent with both individual and collective goals of education.
(Hochschild and Scovronick 2003, 110)

In the last section I report on some of the changes already taking place related to public schools in Hawai'i. At the school site level, for example, public school choices are taking shape in the form of charter schools, immersion schools, a proposed new magnet public school, proposed science and technology academies within existing public middle and high schools, and the approval of the first public high school to offer the International Baccalaureate Diploma Programme.

CHARTER SCHOOLS

There are thirty charter schools listed under the charter school profiles Web page (Hawai'i State Charter Schools Administrative Office [HCSAO] 2006). They are as follows.

Connections
Hakipuʻu Learning Center
Hālau Kū Mana
Hālau Lōkahi
Hawaiʻi Academy of Arts and
  Science
Innovations
Ka ʻUmeke Kāʻeo
Ka Waihona o ka Naʻauao
Kamaile Elementary
Kanu o ka ʻĀina
Kanuikapono Learning Center
Kawaikini
Ke Ana Laʻahana
Ke Kula Niʻihau o Kekaha Learning
  Center
Ke Kula o Nāwahiokalaniʻōpuʻu Iki
  Laboratory

Ke Kula o Samuel M. Kamakau
  Laboratory
Kīhei Public Charter School
Kona Pacific
Kua o Ka Lā
Kualapuʻu Elementary
Kula Aupuni Niʻihau a Kahelelani
  Aloha
Lanikai Elementary
Myron B. Thompson Academy
Nā Wai Ola Waters of Life
University Education Laboratory
  School
Volcano School of Arts and Sciences
Voyager
Waiʻalae Elementary
Waimea Middle Public Conversion
West Hawaiʻi Explorations Academy

Public charter schools are independent public schools. Public school funding follows the students enrolled in the charter schools, and the founders of the charter school (parents, educators, community leaders) have greater independence to decide the school's budget, staff, curriculum, and teaching methods (HCSAO 2006). According to the HCSAO, as of October 2007 over 6,800 students in grades K–12 were enrolled in Hawaiʻi's public charter schools. These charter schools, like the traditional public schools, vary but may include the use of multiple-grade learning teams, multi-discipline project-based learning, mainstreaming special education students, and a focus on Hawaiian culture and language. For example, Innovations Public Charter School on the Big Island has multi-age groupings, inquiry, and a project-based curriculum. The University Laboratory (or Education Laboratory) School on Oʻahu develops innovation curricula like its "Measure Up" elementary math program that simultaneously gives students foundations in numbers, algebra, and measurement. The Ke Kula Niʻihau o Kekaha Learning Center on Kauaʻi is currently working on a historical documentary film intended to be part of an archival record of Hawaiian history.

IMMERSION SCHOOLS

The Department of Education's Hawaiian Language Immersion Program has nineteen public school campuses offering this program, with approximately fifteen hundred students enrolled. Students are immersed in the Hawaiian language and culture while also learning other subjects until the fifth grade, when English is introduced as a formal subject (T. Shapiro 2005b).

NEW PUBLIC MAGNET SCHOOL

The Environmental and Cultural Studies School (proposed name as of 2006), a partnership between the Hawai'i Department of Education and the Bishop Museum, is Hawai'i's first proposed magnet school. The intention is to locate this public school on the campus of the Bishop Museum, and the tentative opening date is summer 2009. High school juniors and seniors with an interest in the environment and the culture of Hawai'i and the Pacific will have opportunities to work with scientists in the museum. The school will focus on both environmental sciences and on culture (Brown 2006).

ATTENDING TO THE "MIDDLE"

Education-First includes a series of programs that targets average students, who can be overlooked in the public school system if attention is focused primarily on those in the honors or special education classes. The initial focus on the program, developed by Asai and Keawe Gilman, will be the Kahuku community on O'ahu. The programs include mentoring, a one-week academy to help eleventh-grade athletes prepare for college entrance requirements, and a specially designed class tailored to help students write and improve analytical thinking (Aguilar 2004).

SMALL HIGH SCHOOL LEARNING COMMUNITIES

Thirteen high schools have received grants to redesign the public high school experience. Whole grade levels are divided into small learning communities referred to as freshmen and sophomore "houses." The students in these communities stay together with the same team of teachers (Creamer 2006c). One purpose of the learning communities is to provide a structure that would allow teachers to become well acquainted with their students, in order to better help them become independent learners and prevent them from "slipping through the cracks" (Martin 2006b, A1).

In 2007 Governor Linda Lingle proposed the creation of science and technology academies in public middle and high schools. Academy graduates who attend college in Hawai'i would have their tuition paid (Brannon 2007).

James Campbell High School is the first public high school in the state given approval to offer the International Baccalaureate Diploma Programme, referred to as an elite college preparatory program with an international focus. In addition, both Niu Valley Middle School and Kaiser High School are currently in the process of seeking approval (Creamer 2007; Moreno 2008).

State System-Level Changes

Power is divided among the Legislature, governor and board of education, with nobody fully accountable for results. (D. Shapiro 2001, A12)

The implementation of Act 51 has also had an impact on local school sites, even though it was initiated at the state level. I completed my interviews in 2003, and in the following year state legislators passed the Reinventing Education Act of 2004 (Act 51). Its purpose is to reshape the public school system to improve student achievement. The "reshaping" is to occur in the following areas and in the following ways.

1. **New Funding Process.** The law mandated a Committee on Weights to determine a weighted student formula that would distribute resources based on student enrollment and student characteristics.
2. **Increased Principal Autonomy.** Principals are intended to have control over a minimum of 70 percent of the DOE operating budget — control that would increase their autonomy over planning and operation decisions at the school site. Principals are also to be provided ongoing staff development to help them conceptualize the role of principal to include their new responsibilities. Further, principal and vice principal positions will now be for twelve months, with accompanying increased salaries.
3. **Increased Community Involvement.** Principals will work with the new School Community Councils, created to represent the interests of all students via "majority rule" voting. A part-time parent facilitator position at each school will be funded to support increased parental involvement.
4. **"Cutting the Red Tape."** A working group is mandated to develop plans for transferring responsibilities such as facilities maintenance, project management, and building inspection from other state agencies (such as DAGS) to the DOE.
5. **Increasing Student Resources.** Examples include $2.5 million for math textbooks for schools whose complexes have an aligned math curriculum; approximately $2.1 million for seventy-five regular

elementary teachers to reduce K–2 class size; and $2 million to improve information technology (Hawai'i State Department of Education 2005).

Increased autonomy is currently evident in parts. Witt (2005) suggests that Hawai'i's Act 51 allows teachers and school principals to "reinvent" their schools by

1. shifting resources and decision making down to the school levels;
2. empowering school principals and local school councils to develop a vision and plan for improving student learning;
3. creating school cultures that reflect the communities they serve, thereby increasing ownership.

Public school principals are also acting to provide the leadership to develop a new kind of public high school that emphasizes (1) small learning communities, (2) freshmen "houses" to support transition into ninth grade, (3) upper-class "academies" and career pathways for eleventh and twelfth graders to allow students to concentrate on areas of career interest, and (4) intensified intervention in ninth grade to provide a better safety net for students at risk (Creamer 2006b).

These measures should increase a community's sense of ownership. And with ownership comes increased school identity and school loyalty.

Part 5 of Act 51 contributes to improved working conditions for some. Money was allocated for the purpose of reducing class size for grades K–12. Additional monies are to be dedicated to align math curriculum and to improve information technology.

How well is Act 51 being implemented? After a two-year period, Tschumy (2006) reported on the status.

1. **Twelve-month contract for principals:** Implemented.
2. **Principal performance contract:** In active discussions between DOE and the principals' union, the Hawai'i Government Employees Association (HGEA).
3. **Weighted student formula:** Unresolved.
4. **Unified school calendar:** Began with 2006–2007 school year.
5. **Seventy-percent control of expenditures by principals:** Started 2006–2007 (incomplete).
6. **De-linking the transfer of repair and maintenance and design and construction of schools from the Department of Accounting and**

General Services (DAGS): Implemented. The "de-linking" of DAGS from the DOE is removing one major source of complaints about the upkeep of public school facilities. Rae Loui, the DOE's assistant superintendent for business services, who oversaw the separation from DAGS, is quoted as saying, "We're in charge of our own destiny now" (Martin 2005b, para. 8).

In addition, the DOE now uses a Web-based order-processing system known as Maximo, also used by military bases. Instead of waiting months or years for repairs, the work crew can respond in a matter of days (Martin 2005b).

Other evidence that the state is trying to cut some of the bureaucracy found in the public school system is the consolidation of programs. Following the recommendation in a PricewaterhouseCoopers audit, the DOE merged thirty-nine of its programs into twelve to reduce duplication and improve use of personnel (Creamer 2005).

Following a second audit recommendation, the DOE agreed to create a chief financial officer (CFO) position to oversee the $2 billion school system. However, some worried that the superintendent would choose a former teacher or principal as CFO, neither of whom would necessarily have adequate business expertise (Martin 2006a). But in April 2007 Randy Moore, a former business executive, became the permanent assistant superintendent for the DOE Office of Business Services (Advertiser Staff 2007), allaying those fears.

Community-Level Involvement

What community-level involvement already exists? There are parents, including many of the parents in this study, who participate in the schools in which their children attend. Both the PTA and the implementation of Act 51's School Community Councils are vehicles by which parents can have a voice in the public schools. Other avenues currently available to parents include the following joint ventures among private and nonprofit foundations, unions, and the military.

Local Advocacy and Grassroots Partnerships

One way a School Community Council can receive wider community feedback on relevant school issues is through something called Speak Out. This is an event at the school site organized around relevant school community issues at various "issues stalls"— booths where parents can drop by to "speak out" about their ideas and concerns, say, for example, about the school curriculum, or about moving sixth grade to middle school. Comments are recorded and used for discussion and community council decision making (Yamauchi 2006).

There are also a number of local advocacy and grassroots partnerships currently in operation in Hawai'i. For example, the Hawai'i "Three Rs" (Repair, Remodel, and Restore) started in 2001 with an initiative from U.S. Senator Daniel K. Inouye. Its purpose is to push forward work on needed repairs in the public schools. The program works by matching state, federal, and private money with work from volunteers. Private funding has come from the Hawai'i Community Foundation, the Estate of James Campbell, the James and Abigail Campbell Family Foundation, the AT&T Foundation, and the Harold K. L. Castle Foundation. The program awards grants to public schools that can match the grant amount with private contributions and professional volunteers (Advertiser Staff 2005). Using the Three Rs, one local high school had its athletic complex improved with the help of partnerships with the Honolulu Fire Department's Battalion 1, the Painter's Union, and the Painters Industry of Hawai'i (*Investing in Our Community* 2004, 2).

The Joint Venture Educational Forum (JVEF) is a cooperative venture between the U.S. Pacific Command (USPACOM) military community and the DOE, facilitating active military participation in Hawai'i's public schools (Honolulu Advertiser 2007).

These reported changes are examples of what is occurring to provide more public school choice, parental involvement, principal autonomy, and deregulation of the public school system bureaucracy.

If citizens can recognize that Hawai'i already has good to excellent public schools, and if additional changes continue to occur to strengthen the public school system, will it be enough to change the master narrative about public schools in Hawai'i? Perhaps. More likely, however, a stronger grassroots advocacy movement is necessary to develop an "engaged public." Hawai'i needs an advocacy movement that will work to ensure that the proposed changes are implemented in the public educational system, that the media represent all aspects of public schools in a balanced fashion, and that the financial support for the public schools is stable. As other parents join with the parents in this study to demonstrate their willingness to become public school advocates, the master narrative could finally be modified to become one that reflects a community in which its citizens imagine two viable choices for schooling: public and private.

Why should we care whether or not this happens? The final chapter discusses the role of public education in the economic and civic life of the community.

Why Should We Care?

Public Schools and Healthy Communities

> One article of faith among the founding fathers was that a republic could survive only if its citizens were educated. School has continued to shape our national identity. "The free common school system," Adlai Stevenson once said, is "the most American thing about America." (Mondale and Patton 2001, 1)

> Education for democracy must educate us not only for economic fitness or for the ability to make decisions in a voting booth, but also for a shared social life and the pursuit of human possibility.... A key function of public education is to form a public that can talk, work, and make decisions together. (Darling-Hammond 1997, 42, 44)

Using as a measure whether the public makes decisions together, American democracy is now weak. The practices of citizenship — such as voting and working across diverse groups to solve community problems — do not engage many Americans. And support for public institutions, including public schools, has lessened. Yet good public schools are one of the few remaining institutions where diverse members of the upcoming generation may develop not only the ability to think critically, but also empathy with others despite conflicts of interests and differences in character. Such traits strengthen American civic life, and they are compatible with meeting economic goals in an increasingly globalized world (Westbrook 1996).

An Apathetic "Public"

An argument can be made that Hawai'i has an unengaged civic life in that it had the lowest voter registration and lowest voter participation in national elections between 2000 and 2006. The highest level of national participation (60.7 percent) since 1968 occurred during the 2006 presidential election.

However, Hawai'i has generally had the lowest state (48.9 percent) turnout (Kellman 2005). The Aloha State also ranks near the bottom nationally in the number of citizens who volunteer (approximately 25 percent) (Nakaso 2006; Da Silva 2006). David Shapiro, a *Honolulu Advertiser* columnist, wrote in his October 23, 2002, "Volcanic Ash" column, "Most non-voters are just plain apathetic; they don't think government is about them and won't make time in their busy lives to keep up with public affairs and vote." He goes on to say that "Hawai'i's poor voter participation reflects a failure to teach this most basic act of citizenship in our homes and in our schools over the last generation" (A18). It may be that people don't think their vote makes a difference. In Timothy Hurley's article "Hawai'i's Voter Roll at Bottom" (2004, 1), Grace Furukawa, president of Hawai'i Clean Elections, is quoted as saying, "The people don't think voting matters. . . . They don't feel represented. They don't feel they have much of a voice in the decisions made by the Legislature." In addition to skepticism, perhaps some people find voting a difficult process. The results of a *Honolulu Star-Bulletin* newspaper survey of seventy-five lobbyists, legislators, and neighborhood board chairmen (Borreca 2006) indicated that cynicism and an unfriendly voting system are the two main reasons more of Hawai'i's citizens do not bother to vote.

One example of how such civic apathy is directly connected to the health of the public schools is demonstrated by indifference toward those who run and serve on the public school's Board of Education. Citizen Bryan K. Mick wrote in a letter to the editor, "The biggest problem is not the current statewide board versus the seven local boards, but rather voter apathy toward the people who run."

Civic apathy was not always present in Hawai'i. Hurley reported, "In the early 1960s, when the Democrats were working to push the Republicans out of control, union officials drove field workers to polling sites in pineapple and sugar towns across the new state. The 1964 election saw an astounding turnout of 96 percent of registered voters." This was also a period when citizens were more engaged in public education (2004, A4). Perhaps the recent 2008 primary, with its high voter turnout, indicates the beginning of a renewal of citizenship engagement.

In an article commemorating Law Week in Hawai'i (2002), Ronald T. Y. Moon, chief justice of the Hawai'i Supreme Court, stated, "The right to vote is one of the most important rights and privileges in our democratic society; yet we have failed to engage our citizenry, especially our young people, to participate in this most fundamental exercise of citizenship. . . . Statistics indicate that voter turnout percentages have dropped more than 30 percent over the past approximately 20 years" (A14). He goes on to say that "we must start focusing on conveying to our children the importance of community involvement, being informed and performing our civic duties, such as voting and jury duty." He believes that civics education in our schools has to be reintroduced to enhance public-spiritedness.

But as the parents in this study might argue, it is more than civic education in our schools that should be reintroduced; civic engagement of our citizens is needed as well. Regarding the role of public schools in developing future citizens, parents have also argued that a two-tiered school system does not create in the younger generations the concept of a shared community.

Two-Tier School System and Community Fragmentation

In this new, multicultural America, mutual accommodation will be more important than ever. To make that happen, students should as much as possible be educated with one another. (Hochschild and Scovronick 2003, 198)

As discussed in earlier chapters, the separate schooling for different groups has been part of Hawai'i's history for a very long time. Only periodically have there been movements driven by community passion or by the passion of individual leaders in support of Hawai'i's public school system. The period following the Hawai'i Democratic Revolution in 1954 is one example.

If public schools had more across-the-board community support, they would be better positioned to provide opportunities for both parents and the next generation of citizens to learn how to work across groups for the benefit of the entire community. A healthy public school system is one of the "publics" that support the development of a healthy public civic life.

Parents talked about a two-tier society that they believe currently exists in Hawai'i, made up of the "haves" and "have-nots." They believe that this fragmentation is partially the result of students not having regular opportunities to mix with students from groups other than their own, which in turn leads to a lack of identity, as adults, with the idea of a cohesive community. As the father quoted below indicates, a two-tiered school system breeds resentment and impedes democracy.

Q: How important do you think a strong public education system is in a democracy?

Physician: I think it's vital. I really do. I think it's undeniable that our children have succeeded in public school, and we're happy that we stuck with public school, but I also think it's undeniable that they would have had more opportunities in private school—academically, facility-wise, those kinds of things. But if you have a weak public school system, you create a two-tiered system, and that's very much what is presently in Hawai'i.

I'm the only physician parent at my local high school. You have a two-tiered system, and that creates divisiveness in the community, creates resentment in the community, and that detracts from the ability of a democracy to govern itself effectively.

Q: A them-and-us kind of thing?

Physician: Yes.

Private school parents in the study shared the same concerns. The following parent told a story about two cousins—one who attends private school and the other a public school. The mother of the public school child said her son feels he is "not as good" as his cousin. This private school parent connects that feeling to a sense of disenfranchisement among citizens. The danger, she believes, is that disenfranchised citizens don't participate in civic responsibilities. Two separate groups—the "haves" and the "have-nots"—make it difficult to build a shared sense of community.

Private School Parent: I think the other aspect is that this issue is not a personal issue, but this is a societal concern. I just heard this in a focus group of parents where a mother said, "My nephew goes to a small private school, and my son goes to a public school. My son is very aware that he has to just go to regular public school." The [public school students] feel badly. They feel like her son. I think she said that he was seven or eight. He felt that he was not as good as his cousin, who's about his same age. And that's a terrible thing! Terrible!

I mean, I think that's another issue that does reinforce the sense of disenfranchisement among a population segment that is already socially or economically [or both] disenfranchised. And I think that's the long-term danger.

Q: And why do you see that as the danger?

Private School Parent: Well, the danger is that if we evolve into a rigidly hierarchical society between the "haves" and the "have-nots," then there will be no "buy-in" by these students who feel that they haven't had the same opportunities. They will feel that they don't have the same opportunities or the same level of participation in society. And I think that—again, this is an extrapolation — but how does it lead to community building, voting, the commitment to society, and the laws of our society? . . . You know, we all have our cultures, but we all have to agree that the law is above us all.

The second private school parent connects Hawai'i's history of holding private schools in higher regard as a contributing factor to its two-tiered school system.

Private School Parent: During my older sister's time, there were English Standard schools, and their purpose was to assist promising local students, and not only them — but I think it was for the military also. The military wanted their children to be integrated into a school that was at a higher standard than the local schools. And so if you got into that school by passing an [English-language] test, it was a status thing. There has always been something to do with privileged versus nonprivileged in Hawai'i, even in the public school system.

Q: And do you think that it matters to the community if public schools are not held in high regard?

Private School Parent: Oh, I think so, because then it's like a hierarchy, or a two-tiered system. Those who went to private school versus those who went to public — if you went to public school, it wasn't your choice, but because you couldn't get into a private school, or you couldn't afford a private school, or whatever.

In the next interview, a professor talked about the difference he sees between private and public school students in Hawai'i. He has observed the students who graduated from Hawai'i's elite private schools disengaging themselves from the local higher education institutions and considering themselves failures if they must attend a local public university instead of a mainland one. He also connects the disengagement to the impact of Hawai'i's long history of separate schooling for different groups.

Q: Do you think it's important as a democracy to have strong public institutions?

Professor: First of all, I think you could argue that it's absolutely indisputable that the most important school on O'ahu, historically, is McKinley High School. See, if you actually look at whose graduates have contributed to the making of modern Hawai'i, hold the major political positions, and the business positions — other than those who inherited positions — look at the

Hall of Honor at that public high school, and you'll see all the names that you identify with the transformation of Hawai'i in the twentieth century.

So in terms of democracy, public schools better be there. And I think that in terms of civic life and a contribution to the society, they're absolutely crucial. Students should be feeling that one of their responsibilities is to create the society they live within. Now it might mean that they end up moving somewhere else, but there should be that notion. And one of my problems with the private schools is the initial impetus placed on the students is you must perform in such a way that you will go away. And that what you want to do, or what's of value, is not here in Hawai'i.

I think it has a lot to do with Hawai'i's history. You have an educational tradition here that schools are, in fact, supposed to be ways that make your children go away—the founding of [a certain private school], where the mission was set up to make sure their children would be able to instantly operate in the environment of Yale or the University of Vermont.

I certainly know it works that way because I frequently end up dealing with students from the private schools in my university classes, and fairly regularly get students whose sense is that by being at [a local public university], they have somehow or other failed. They have real difficulties with motivation. You also have that phenomenon of the students that go away for one or two years—one year at [a mainland private university] and then come back and it's seen as a character flaw, and it's their fault.

We just had a student graduate who did incredibly well here at the [local university] as an undergraduate, and who had graduated from [an elite private school]. She just got a huge scholarship to go to a mainland university graduate program in creative writing—huge scholarship. Well, when it was announced in the newspapers, they cut out where she went to undergraduate school.

Q: Oh, really?

Professor: Yes. (*Laughs.*) And I've gone and talked to high school classes at a private school about what expectations they might have for classes at the university. Students come up—in one case this student came after me, and she asked if she could phone me to ask about what the program would be like because she was going to [the local university]. The college counselors [at this private school] were so busy with the students going to the mainland that this student couldn't seem to get any information about [the local university].

Another public school parent spoke about the idea of fragmentation creating "haves" and "have-nots" in a society not only here in Hawai'i, but also on the mainland as well. He pointed out that, nationally, Americans have been disengaging themselves from all public institutions. This is the same message that Putnam (2000) shares as a result of his study, in which he found that "more than a third of America's civic infrastructure simply evaporated between the mid-1970s and the mid-1990s" (43), "partially because those activities that brought citizens *together* . . . have declined most rapidly" (45).

Q: Do you think it matters whether or not we have good public schools or not? Does it make any difference to a democracy?

Professor: There are so many factors going into that equation. I think that I support public schools as a principle, and I think that good education is a right for everybody.

I think that one of the reasons why public education is going nowhere is the lack of support. What is happening in Hawai'i is being duplicated in other places. Instead, the more well-to-do are trying to get out of the public school system, and it's a vicious cycle. The more that people leave, the worse it's going to be, the less clout it has, the worse it gets, the more that people want to leave.

So, I think that the problem is not the public school system per se. I think it's an evaluation of a lot of public institutions. It's a trend, whether it's public schools, or criminal justice, public universities. I think that the splitting of the "haves" and "have-nots" is increasing, and it's fueling other stuff. And it's not just in the public school anymore. I am very worried about the divide between the haves and have-nots becoming larger and more unbridgeable, and I think it's happening.

Both in Hawai'i and on the mainland the concern is that, today, the gap between the affluent and the working class is growing, with the middle class also losing ground. Class disparities among school districts are growing as communities and even whole regions become more economically homogeneous. In 1970 the typical affluent American lived in a neighborhood where 20 percent of the residents were also affluent; twenty years later, that figure had climbed to more than 50 percent. Conversely, the proportion of poor people living in poor neighborhoods and inner cities has increased. In the decade after 1982, economic disparities between school districts rose (Hochschild and Scovronick 2003, 26). In addition, today citizens are less likely to participate in civic activities that bring different groups together to work for the benefit of the entire community.

Minimizing Community Fragmentation

In earlier chapters, parents spoke in some detail about the opportunities provided by a public school education, including the life lessons learned by "mixing" with groups other than one's own. They believe that a public school education promotes the development of traits such as empathy, respect for differences, flexibility, and the ability to communicate comfortably with individuals from diverse groups. The next father returned to this idea as a means of minimizing fragmentation within a community.

Attorney: I think it's a fragmentation of our society. But I look at those kids out there in public schools, and they're doing it. For the most part, there's a lot of mixing [among different groups] going on that doesn't happen even in regular society. That's happening in our public education system. So good public education has to be there because that's maybe our only core of hope for [mixing of different groups] ever happening. Once that starts to go, then you're just going to have everybody fragmented. More than any other place in our society, I think, public school is where there's that mixing going on.

In Honolulu, I think the fragmentation is more prevalent. You have the urbanization where people are very scattered, and there isn't that sense of community around their school, so the neighborhood just becomes a place. The public schools could become a place for the community to gather, whether it be sports, academics, whatever.

The following military officer continued the conversation about the opportunities provided by public education when he, too, spoke of "the mixing." Learning how to get along with others who are from all walks of life is good practice for learning how to participate as a citizen in a democracy. He also discussed the limitations of higher-status private schools to fully develop a community. His own family could not have afforded to send him to a private school, and without good public school education for all, his talent would not have been developed. Underdeveloped or "wasted talent" undermines the potential contribution of citizens in developing a healthy community as a whole.

Military Officer: The public schools system is a very good system, by the way. Public schools are what give everyone an equal—supposed to give everybody an equal start. I know, across the board, that doesn't happen, but for the most part, it's probably the best system that we can come up with right now. I think we just need to tweak it a bit.

The talk about giving people vouchers for sending their kids to private schools just drives me crazy. It's not fixing the situation. If there are problems with the public school system, then we should put money into fixing those problems in the public schools system.

Public school is the way to do it. Children need to learn how to interact with [people from] all walks of life, and what better way to bring a mixture of the community into a place and work together and learn and grow. And I'm sure there's some of that in the private schools system too, but I don't know. I just think the public school is probably the best institution we got going if we want to keep a democracy going. I just wish that we could interject a little more time and money into it, and bring up some of the areas that really need help.

Q: Could you talk a little bit more, too, about why you think it's important in a democracy for a person to have experiences with different groups? How does that help when they are adults and working?

Military Officer: Well, just to be a productive citizen, they really have to understand their entire community. A lot of different people face lots of different challenges in their life. I try to instill that in my kids. Never, ever judge anyone from what you see on the outside because you don't know their situation. Learn about them. Learn about your community. Learn about the culture that you are involved in. And be the better for it.

If people in a democracy don't know different groups, and only the rich folks can go to school, or only the people with means can make it in life, then it isn't a democracy at all. It's very important for everyone to have some kind of equal chance. I think that having public schools and being involved with the community is the only way that we're only going to have a chance at some kind of democracy.

If America is going to work the way that we hope that it does, you have to be an involved citizen, a good citizen.

Q: To what extent do we still talk about the role of citizenship?

Military Officer: I don't think we talk about it enough, and especially as students get older, and they're looking into going to college. I think it's so important that they have good grass roots of what it is to be an American citizen. You can't just be out for yourself. You have to give something back to your community if you want it to have a thriving environment.

And you know, if the school system were just based on family status, then I wouldn't have gone to school, I'm sure. There's no way that my family would be able to pay for me to go to a private school. And I just think the public university is a great institution. That's where I got my bachelor's degree, and that's where I'm getting my master's degree, and I have a lot of faith.

This next legislator also addressed the "wasted talent" concept when public schools are not supported by the community as a whole.

Legislator: Clearly, democracy is only as good as the public school system. I don't think that anybody would really be able to show otherwise. And I really think that the public schools in Hawai'i are a lot better than the media portrays them. I mean, I can name a number of public high schools [for which] I would put graduates on par with private school graduates.

Q: Could you talk a little bit more about your statement that a democracy is only as strong as its public schools?

Legislator: You know, I think a fundamental democratic principle is that anybody can be anybody, anyplace, any occupation. I think that what makes democracies vibrant and active, and working for the social good of everybody involved, is that everybody knows that they have an equal chance. People might argue about whether they have an equal chance or not. I would be shocked if a larger proportion of doctors and lawyers didn't choose to send their children to private schools. I mean, my parents couldn't afford to send me to private school when I was growing up, and if the public schools had not been able to challenge me, or get the best out of me, then society and the community in general have lost something. They've lost the opportunity for somebody to contribute beyond what they might be otherwise.

And I think that societies and democracies in general can only achieve the most if all of their citizens are participating and engaged and able to contribute the most and the best that they can. And you know, you can't get that unless the public school systems are preparing children and students to be active and engaged and contributing.

The "real world" benefits gained in a public school education came up during the next interview. This couple talked about how, in their view, the "real world" experiences in public education offer students an opportunity to understand firsthand the impact of government's decisions on its citizens.

Q: Shifting to the last category, how important do you feel it is to have a strong public education in a democracy?

Public School Teacher: Oh boy, very important.

CEO: Very, very important.

Public School Teacher: I think that is the key to our understanding of what a democracy is. Democracy is knowing not only the outline of your government, or government's expectations, or how your government is set up, but it's also how you can participate. So I think that public education offers that opportunity.

Q: And so you're saying that public school students are participating in a democracy by being in public schools?

CEO: Private schools are so much more insulated from the real world, whereas, in a public school, you are going to be affected by what happens because what happens to the government affects you. And what happens to the government is what happens in the real world. For example, if revenues are down, and the budget can't be balanced, and cuts are going to happen, it just trickles all the way down to the public school. It gets right down to the grass roots. A private school can be insulated from all that.

Public School Teacher: Last year, when the teachers went on strike, our niece was in the second grade. But she got an education as to what all this was about. She had to deal with it, and she had some strong feelings about what they had to say (*laughs*), so—

CEO: It's the real world.

Public School Teacher: Yes, these are experiences that help you to make decisions about how you feel about these issues.

Q: I don't find much discussion in the newspapers about the citizenship role in the public schools. Most of the focus seems be on academic competency determined by test scores.

Public School Teacher: Right.

CEO: Because we don't measure "the real world"—street smarts—the kind of things you can learn besides getting educated purely by the books.

Public School Teacher: If your study included a sampling of children who graduated from public schools and then children who graduated from private schools, and measured how their lives were, that might be very interesting. Yes, that might give parents perspective because, definitely, in our experience, once they're out of high school, and they're all the same in the college environment, it doesn't matter.

CEO: Because our kids went to the mainland colleges with some of the private school kids, and they did just as well or better.

To strengthen the support for public schools and thereby neighborhoods and communities, this next mother believes that community leaders need to send their children to public schools.

Q: Oh, I'm glad you said that word "citizen" because that reminded me—do you feel that it's important to have strong public education in a democracy?

Vice President: Yes. Well, the reason that you need to have a strong public education in a democracy is that the theory behind democracy is that everybody has an equal chance. If the children don't have a very good chance at a good education, then you'll always have a problem with classes. The people with the means are always going to give their children — send them to, say, a private school, which is believed to be better than a public school. And if you take the brightest kids out of the public school system and put them into private schools, that in itself is going to cause a separation of classes.

I believe if professional people start sending their kids to public schools, I think the public schools are going to get better. And I think you're going to have stronger communities because I believe that if the community leaders have their kids going to the public schools, they're going to start supporting the public schools, and supporting the kids' activities. Right now, they're all supporting activities somewhere else in another geographical location.

I think if all the kids in the community went to a public school, I think the community would be stronger. [A certain neighborhood] is an area where a lot of kids go to the local high school. When they win the state championship, the whole community is celebrating. When a private school wins a championship, the community doesn't celebrate. The school celebrates, but nobody else celebrates with them. It's not like the family atmosphere that you have in the neighborhood. I think it's very important for communities to feel like a family.

The issue of two-tiered school systems and fragmented communities was also discussed by mainland parents. One of them talked about believing in and taking responsibility for helping to strengthen her neighborhood elementary school as a way of fortifying the neighborhood and community, thereby minimizing fragmentation.

Mainland Public School Parent: The school-community partnership is strengthened by the community members also having relationships so that we don't just see each other at school, but we also see each other at home. And so it's the basic idea that when you see somebody else's kid doing something wrong, you tell 'em, "You know, I know your momma." The neighborhood kids know that all the parents are in the loop. For example, my husband had an eight o'clock meeting. He had to farm our two kids out across the street — one to go to day care, the other to go to kindergarten — with another family who goes to the same day care and the same kindergarten. And last week, one of our neighbors was out of town and I picked up some of the slack for her because she was a single mom and couldn't be two places at once.

So there's the most simple chore level of getting the kids moved around. Then there is the in loco parentis work that we do. So that her children know that when they're with me, I'm in charge. I tell them what they need to be doing when they're five, so that when they're fifteen and when I see them doing something they're not supposed to be doing, that I have the kind of relationship with them and with their parents . . .

Q: So this is really community building.

Mainland Public School Parent: It is, yes. It's pretty deliberate, too.

Q: How would this neighborhood be different if you were all going off to different private schools?

Mainland Public School Parent: We would still have some of the fabric in place because my neighbor, whose child had been in a different day care and is now in an elite private school — we have a good relationship with her. Our kids play together and they're both five years old. I speculate by the time the kids are a little older, unless they're in some after-school activity like music or sports, that we will have less and less to do with them just because of the time. The families on our street whose children are in private schools — I literally don't know what the children look like. They live within eight houses of me.

And somebody said, "Oh, they have three kids."

And I said, "What do you mean they have three kids? Like, grown up kids?"

"No, no, they're in high school."

I've never seen any kids there. I literally never see them on the street.

There are two other families who have kids in private school — one two doors down on one side, and one across the street. I do see those children and those adults. And I'm not as close to them. We wave, "How's it going." We know each other's names. If I saw a strange vehicle in front of their house I would call the police.

I feel that if our schools are going to improve, then we have to send our kids to them. I mean, you can't go to your day job and try to improve your schools and then not engage with the schools as a community member. To me that doesn't make any sense.

Q: Why do you feel that's so important?

Mainland Public School Parent: Well . . . schools are the community. If only part of the community is engaged in schooling, then there's a whole part of the community that's not. I see it as resources. If all the resources in the community were available, rather than only half, the schools would improve.

There's also an accountability factor. The more that educated people send their children to public schools, the more accountability there will be because educated people — and I mean, they've had a formal education in this country — they know what should happen in the school. A lot of immigrant parents don't. They're smart, but they're not formally educated in this system, and so they're working without all the information. They don't have the personal experience with the schools to know that when they go see something going on that is not acceptable, they should not allow that to happen to their child. Whereas, people who have had a formal education, people of color and whites, they are down there right now saying, "This is not acceptable for my child."

In the next interview excerpts, three professors all build on this connection between the community and a well-supported public school system.

Professor: I think it's very, very important for a democracy to have a strong public education system. I think better-educated people make better decisions. So if you've got a democracy and you're asking people to make decisions, it'd make sense to educate them well. Better-educated people also tend to be healthier, to make better decisions about themselves, and that makes for healthier communities in general.

To me, it's kind of a no-brainer, you know? You get what you put into an education system, maybe. One of the main functions of any society is reproducing itself, in terms of making the next generation healthy, competent individuals, particularly in a democracy where those individuals are also supposed to be actively involved. It's not just a matter of bringing them up and making sure they survive. It's a matter of giving them the tools to find out what they're good at, and tools to decide what, rationally, they think is in the public interest. I think the public educational system is one of our best bets.

Q: So you include a role for citizenship?

Professor: Yes, right. I think better-educated people have a better chance of making good decisions in the public interest and they are less easily swayed by demagoguery or simple self-interest. For example, I don't think education wipes out racism, but it's certainly a move in the right direction. If you've had a better-educated populace, you're more likely to get what I would call enlightened social policies.

The next father shared his personal experience in a community in which a two-tiered public school system did not exist. He spoke about community loyalty to the high school attended by all segments of the community.

Q: Does it matter to the community if private or public schools are held in higher regard?

Professor: On the basis on my own growing up, it matters a great deal. Because if the public at large doesn't respect the public school system, especially the high school system, it seems that something is lost in the community. I mean, if a portion of the population says the schools are not good enough for my children, then that prevents something important from happening in our community.

Q: What is that something important?

Professor: Well, it's a sense of community and well-being. I keep thinking of my old high school [on the mainland], which just recently got torn down. A new high school is being built on its place. I went for my high school reunion and it was held in connection with the dedication of this new building. And there was such an outpouring of the community. I mean, there was such a thirst for the way it used to be that the alumni have contributed this enormous amount of money to make this new school like the one that we remember.

We had a real sense of community with the high school as a kind of center. And that just doesn't happen here in Hawai'i. I mean, maybe it happens in [a certain local neighborhood] or some other places, but it doesn't happen the way it happened, and is happening, in my hometown now.

Q: So the citizens of that community are supporting the new high school financially in order to make it in a certain way. They have a sense of shared ownership?

Professor: Yes, yes. And now it's more interesting because it's very ethnically and racially diverse now.

Q: And that sense of shared ownership is being passed on to a new generation?

Professor: It is in the process of being passed on now. And partly it's got to do with money, I think. That city is prosperous now, and even though a lot of the people have moved out of the area — not all of them have — and yet they still feel a loyalty to the public high school, a connection with it, you know? That's the legacy, I suspect, of going to high school there.

Q: What causes that loyalty to continue? Is it leadership at the school level? Is it leadership by the civic officials in the community who encourage that involvement? Do your newspapers support public education in that city? Do the professionals support public education?

Professor: I don't know enough to answer all those questions, but I know that there's a lot of community support. And they had a very charismatic superintendent of public education. He made big changes. He really did well, I gather, for the school system. He started things going. It's probably a lot of things coming together at the same time — with the prosperous condition of the city, the fact that people of my generation [the 1950s and 1960s] are in a position to support the schools financially and otherwise. A number hold positions of leadership in the community.

Q: And what intrigues me is that those graduates choose to give back to the public education system rather than giving money to a private school system.

Professor: Yes, and that seems to be missing here to some degree — although I have friends who went to [a certain urban high school] who are incredibly loyal.

Q: So it might be occurring at the school site. It might be in different schools in the state in which there is that kind of loyalty as well?

Professor: Yes. I think it's got to be the school site, actually. I don't think about this a lot, but you've got me thinking about it now with charter schools where people come from all over the area. I wonder if you could have the same sense of community.

Q: Because it's not in your neighborhood, you mean?

Professor: Yes.

Similar experiences are shared in the following interview by a third professor. Again, in his experience, all classes of society went to the same public school system. The impact, he believes, of everyone going to the public schools was a commitment to high standards for all.

Q: So you had a much closer tie to your childhood neighborhood school?

Professor: Yes. You thought of neighborhoods in terms of the schools. And often they were named the same. The schools usually established the whole identification of the district. So at least when I was going through, I had no sense whatsoever that education was being underfunded or undersupported. And I think — I'm tying into one of your later questions — that was because everybody was using it. And the pressure on making sure that the schools would train people for universities, that the schools would be able to handle the very brightest students possible, and that they would also have the vocational training or whatever. There was a real commitment to the notion that the schools really did have to be all things to all people because all people were in them.

Q: You used the word "commitment." There was a commitment because everybody was going to use the public schools. There was the expectation that the schools would have high standards and they would provide a good education?

Professor: Yes.

Q: And then you said that the local taxes went to support the schools. Different than the centralized system we have here in Hawai'i?

Professor: Yes, there would be a Board of Education, and that would be administered by a kind of mayor, and a council was elected just for that area. There was a school board just for that area that was apportioned out by districts. The sense of them being immediately accountable was very strong there.

A Two-Tiered School System and an Inequitable Economy

An apathetic public is not the only result of a fragmented society. The parents in this study also believe that a two-tiered society that doesn't support strong public education also has an impact on the state's economy. For instance, the community's master narrative about schools suggests to outside businesses that there exists in Hawai'i a lack of commitment to good public schools. This reputation in turn discourages companies from moving to Hawai'i. Also contributing negatively to the economy is the brain drain of private school students who feel they need to leave Hawai'i to be successful, and the potential self-perception of a number of public school students who live in an environment in which they have to fight against a view that they are second-class citizens.

Hawai'i parents, in the next several excerpts, expressed their concerns about limiting economic possibilities as a result of a failure to provide the entire community's children with adequate resources and funding for the public school system. The first parent talked about his experience on the mainland when his professional work involved encouraging corporations to relocate to a particular county. He said that if a county's public school system had a good reputation, it played an important role in convincing corporations to relocate.

Consulting Firm Executive: [Two wealthy mainland counties] were probably the two best public school systems in the country. Now, even those counties have suffered economically lately. Our job was to increase economic development in one county, basically recruiting major corporations to establish regional or corporate headquarters. And we were able to move several major corporations. They all came to this county. And you know what the number one issue was in terms of convincing the senior executives?

Q: Public education?

Consulting Firm Executive: Yes.

The next two fathers spoke about the idea that as members of a community, we need to be concerned about the education of all the community's children and not just one's own. When that value is weak in a community, and the community's master narrative is "The Public Schools Are Failing," public school graduates are suspect as potential employees, and that reputation has an impact on the types of companies that want to invest in Hawai'i. In other words, Hawai'i's reputation for not supporting public schools hurts business.

Nonprofit Executive: When the day comes that I can walk into a major hotel, or a group of them, and speak to the general manager of each hotel in Hawai'i, and find out that this manager was raised in Kalihi, and this one was raised in Kahuku, and this one was raised in Kapa'a, that's going to be a lot more important to me than today when I walk through and find that this manager is from Seattle, and this one's from San Francisco, and this one's from British Colombia. The reality is that we're not training our children to seek the very best in their jobs. Not that everyone is going be the general manager of the Marriott (*laughs*), but that they at least have the opportunity to strive for that.

Part of the question is, "Do we have private business supporting public education to the level that it should be?" When a potential employee turns up and says, "Well, I graduated from a public high school," there's a kind of underlined, "Well, I hear that's not a very good school." So what is the impact on this student? Even if a child graduates with good marks from a school that's perceived as not being good, how does that affect his or her future? We have a long ways to go. The public education in this state can stand out. I look to places like Menlo Park, California, and Cambridge, Massachusetts, as models.

When you look at any town that surrounds a public university, whether we're talking about the Mānoa area, whether we're talking about the university area in Albuquerque, New Mexico, or in Boulder, Colorado, these cities have their own economic structure that's built by having a great public education institution. And so if we can have that kind of reverence, not only for our universities, but also for our public schools, I think it makes a tremendous difference.

Military Officer: Well, I guess we all need to be on the same team and to realize that your neighbor's children across the street should have the same education — at least a very good education — and to not just be concerned about ourselves. So I think a lot of it has to do with the fact that a lot of people need to take the responsibility for the community. Not just take the responsibility of educating their own child, but be a citizen of this state and community and make the decision that we want all of our children to receive a high-quality education.

Q: If you were talking to a parent who was sending their children to private school, and you were talking from a philosophical point of view, what argument would you make for supporting public education?

Military Officer: The majority of the people look at things in a very economical way. So you obviously have to target what affects them, what interests them. You need to bring up the argument that if you're going to have a future, it's not just their child but it's also all the other children who make up the future of Hawai'i.

Today's citizens are making the decisions about Hawai'i's future every day by the choices they make. By encouraging them to see that by investing in an educated Hawai'i, they are investing in a prosperous Hawai'i — they will be supporting the development of students who are happy, who have friends, and who can take care of themselves.

You have to bring in the community, and talk about jobs and the economy. What is Hawai'i going to be like ten years from now? Is it going to be very similar to the way things are now? Things don't usually stay the same. So it's going to either creep ahead a little bit, which would be rather unsatisfactory, or — God forbid — will it slide back and become even worse? Will there be more "haves" and "have-nots?" So pretty much the argument is, What type of future does Hawai'i want? Does Hawai'i want a future of educated citizens — you know, people who know how to vote to make the right choices?

To be honest with you, I think the public schools make a tremendous effort, but the schools have to take care of so many problems. I don't think that the base is the problem here. It's not that the school doesn't have control of itself. It's that the community doesn't support the school. And it doesn't support public schools with dollars. Anybody can say, "We need good schools" and "We need good teachers." Well, when a manager in business says, "I need a good employee," and — if he really wants that good employee, he's going to pay for it. And the community hasn't made that commitment with public schools.

This state has such potential. It is a very beautiful state. It has roots. You mentioned someone who said, "The price of living in Hawai'i is poverty." The state has to move beyond a service economy. There's such great potential. You know, this state could be a great place for think tanks or for high-tech industry, but there's no company that is going to come here.

I came from [a particular continental state], which is the opposite of Hawai'i. There are more start-ups there than any other place, and there's a lot of different set-up types, especially in the large metropolitan areas, and it's because the community supports that growth. They realize that your [public] school system is your feeder to your employee base. Well, if the community wants more than someone to cook and clean, and vacuum your rugs and make your beds, then it needs to invest. It needs children for the future. And that's where this community hasn't made that decision yet.

Economic Inequities

Robert M. Rees reported in his article "Wealth, Poverty and Taxes" (2003) that the patterns of income distribution suggest inequities in Hawai'i. Based on income reported in residents' tax returns in 2000, the top 2.7 percent of residents accounted for 20.1 percent of adjusted gross income. The next 14.1 percent accounted for 45.6 percent of adjusted gross income. The bottom 52 percent of residents accounted for only 17.9 percent of adjusted gross income. Rees complimented the Republican governor of Hawai'i, Linda Lingle, for not rushing to make substantial tax cuts, which would have exacerbated the economic inequities. He wrote, "Lingle senses the stress of two seismic plates — the verticality of wealth and the horizontality of democracy — pulling in opposite directions" (B4).

In "Report Points Out Inequities in Quality of Island Life" (2005), Karen Blakeman noted that the data collected by the University of Hawai'i Center on the Family indicate that the poorest 20 percent of the state's population have lost 7 percent of their income since the 1970s, and the richest 20 percent have seen a 31 percent increase.

Dan Nakaso also reported in his article "Hawai'i's Workers Struggle with Low Pay, Low-Level Jobs" (2004) that Alex McGehee, executive vice president of Enterprise Honolulu, an economic development agency, talked about

Hawaiʻi being one of the leading states in which citizens hold multiple jobs and in which these job holders include the college educated. Salaries are low, and the workforce remains largely based in tourism and the military.

Allison Schaefers (2005) confirmed this picture in her article "Average Hawaiʻi Paychecks Rank 19th," in which she reported that while blue-collar workers in Oʻahu's hottest industries — tourism and construction — lead the nation in wages, the state's average wage ranks nineteenth nationally, just below the U.S. average. "The bulk of Hawaiʻi's employment is in lower-paid occupations," according to Charlotte Wee, a regional economist for the federal Bureau of Labor Statistics (A1). James Hardway, special assistant to the state labor director, said, "More higher-paying positions will be created in Hawaiʻi when the states' work-force initiatives begin to produce better-educated and skilled workers" (A6).

The idea that investing in public education is a solution to these social and economic problems is echoed by Dean Uchida (2005) and Glenn Miyataki (2005); they state, in essence, that education is the key to economic and social prosperity in today's global economy. During a visit to Hawaiʻi, Irwin Jacobs, co-founder of Qualcomm Inc., a San Diego–based wireless technology company, recommended that "Hawaiʻi should concentrate on building a sound K–12 public education system" (Duchemin 2003, D2).

Unfortunately, the historical master narrative that "Public Schools Are Failing" is so entrenched that, like some residents, outsiders such as Jacobs would, unsurprisingly, become aware of that perspective and paint all 284 public schools with the same brush. This historical narrative hinders the economy.

A corollary issue is the impact of the unusually high enrollment in private schools. Hawaiʻi has one of the highest percentages of parents who send their children to private schools. Hochschild and Scovronick (2003, 60, 85) noted the following.

> Parents of children in private or parochial schools [are] less likely than the median voter to support tax increases on bond issues for education. . . .
>
> Businesspeople in cities hesitate to get involved with schools. . . . Many . . . send their children to private schools so their personal commitment to public school reform is low. When they do become involved, their efforts tend to focus on making schools run more efficiently rather than helping them educate students better.

Educating all of the community's children well necessitates, at least in part, financially supporting good public schools. When a high percentage

268 Going Against the Grain

of parents with means are disengaged from the public schools because their children are in private schools, it is difficult to get that support.

A Double Whammy: Hawai'i and the Mainland

While Hawai'i's recent history lends itself to the development of a two-tiered school system, the related issues of public apathy and citizens retracting their support of public institutions is occurring now not only in Hawai'i, but also at the national level. In the well-known, defining work *Bowling Alone* (2000), Putnam documented the change in America from the civic behavior of its citizens during the first two-thirds of the twentieth century, when Americans became increasingly connected to each other and to community activities, to the ongoing reversal of this behavior beginning in the last third of the twentieth century, during which, as Putnam subsequently wrote with Feldstein and Cohen, "Americans in massive numbers began to join less, trust less, give less, vote less, and schmooze less. . . . Involvement in civic association, participation in public affairs . . . all have fallen by 25 to 50 percent" (Putnam, Feldstein, and Cohen 2003, 4).

What are the causes of this increasing lack of national civic participation? Putnam mentions a number of factors; the most important one, he believes, is "the slow, steady, and ineluctable replacement of the long civic generation, by their less involved children and grandchildren" (2000, 283). The environment in which these less-involved generations have grown up include electronic entertainment, especially television, which keeps citizens at home rather than out participating in community activities; the increased pressures of time and money on families; and increased urban sprawl and commuting. The end result of less civic involvement, Putnam argues, is a lack of social capital that, in turn, helps to create unhealthy communities with voter apathy, economic inequalities, and lack of support for public institutions, including public schools. In Hawai'i, these generational changes meet the historical legacy to create a "double whammy" of compounded difficulties and effects.

Social Capital: What Is It?

Come to our breakfast, we'll come to your fire. — Fund-raising T-shirt slogan used by Gold Beach, Oregon, Volunteer Fire Department (Putnam 2000, 21)

Social capital refers to the connections among individuals within community networks that provide a structure for developing the reciprocity and trustworthiness necessary for healthy civic life. Reciprocity, in this context, means "I'll do this for you without expecting anything specific back from you, in the confident expectation that someone else will do something for me down the road" (Putnam 2000, 21). Reciprocity implies a certain level of trustworthiness among citizens of a community.

People who trust their fellow citizens are likely to volunteer more often, contribute more to charity, participate more in politics, and enjoy an economic advantage. Conversely, disengaged citizens who don't trust their fellow citizens feel less constrained to be honest. "Have-nots" are less trusting than "haves" (Putnam 2000).

Putnam, Feldstein, and Cohen (2003) are among the researchers who view face-to-face horizontal interactions among diverse groups of citizens as key to producing reciprocity and trustworthiness within a community. Working across diverse groups is referred to as bridging social capital. Bridging social capital is tough but necessary for healthy civic communities. This type of social capital is defined as inclusive, with members from diverse groups engaged in face-to-face conversations in community activities. It is more likely to develop when there exists in a community horizontal structures that provide opportunities for citizens to connect with people different from themselves. In other words, we get to know each other and discover areas of common ground. This is the type of social capital that has declined in America (Putnam 2000; Putnam, Feldstein, and Cohen 2003).

Especially worrisome is the disappearance from community meetings and from community conversations the ideologically "middle of the road" citizens (Putnam 2000) — worrisome because this type of organizing within a neighborhood or community is about building relationships first rather than pushing special interest agendas. Participants need to be open to changing their minds as a result of the conversations they have with members from diverse groups. Rather than being imposed ahead of time, the agenda emerges from these meetings (Putnam, Feldstein, and Cohen 2003).

Face-to-face conversations are "more effective at building relationships and creating empathy and understanding than remote, impersonal communication. . . . The more extensive interchange that is possible in smaller groups make it possible to discover unexpected mutuality even in the face of difference" (Putnam, Feldstein, and Cohen 2003, 276). To develop social capital beyond small groups, the authors refer to a type of federation in which small, horizontal structures are nested within larger groups (Skocpol 2003), allowing for the benefits of both intimacy and breadth.

Rather than the repetition of an "incessant conversation" that reinforces an authoritative community narrative, conversations in these horizontal structures are used as thinking devices. The goal is to have the participants begin with what they care about, discover areas of commonality, and develop a collective agenda out of overlapping personal stories (Putnam, Feldstein, and Cohen 2003).

What Might This Look Like?

Using the research by Grisham and Gurwitt (1999), Putnam, Feldstein, and Cohen (2003) describe Tupelo, Mississippi's economic and community-building success, quoting the *Wall Street Journal* report on March 3, 1994: "Tupelo's proven track record [in attracting new firms] without handing over the keys to the city and leaning on local tax payers has made it the envy of corporate recruiters across the U.S." (101–102). In addition, Putnam, Feldstein, and Cohen quoted Federal Reserve Bank of Atlanta economist Sheila Tschinkel, who said, "Tupelo is what we always come back to in economic development circles" (102). In 1940 Tupelo was one of the poorest cities in America. Nearly seventy years later, it is thriving. Much of the credit has been given to George McLean, the owner of the *Tupelo Journal,* the local newspaper. As Putnam, Feldstein, and Cohen documented, McLean adhered to the broad principle that "treating town and region as an interdependent community would be more productive than focusing on narrower interests, that community development is the sturdiest foundation for economic development" (2003, 102).

How did McLean do it? He initiated the idea of Rural Community Development Councils (RCDCs), modeled after the New England town meeting in which everyone is expected to participate. Neighborhood groups of ten to twelve families met once a month to have one-on-one conversations about local issues as well as to share meals and participate in group singing. McLean also recognized the need for the city and its rural areas to be interdependent, so each rural development council was paired with a Tupelo civic club.

A second innovation resulted in the formation of the Community Development Foundation (CDF), which replaced the Chamber of Commerce. The CDF was broader in scope, and its mission was focused "first on the community with the expectation that successful commerce would follow." As an organization, it helps to coordinate "government, business, and educational entities that need to work together to foster community and economic development" (Putnam, Feldstein, and Cohen 2003, 104).

Today the *Tupelo Journal* is the *Northeast Mississippi Daily*. The current editor, Lloyd Gray, stated, "Newspapers help give a community its self-definition." He believes that "no community ever rises above its newspapers. . . . A newspaper mirrors a community, and if that image is distorted and fractured, members of the community will find it hard to rouse enthusiasm for shared endeavors" (Putnam, Feldstein, and Cohen 2003, 113). The *Northeast Mississippi Daily* carries stories about serious problems. The editorials are strong and focused on resolving issues (Putnam, Feldstein, and Cohen 2003).

Social Capital and Public Schools

Mathews (1996) takes a perspective similar to Putnam, Feldstein, and Cohen in that he, too, is concerned about the current lack of engagement with and support for public institutions. His focus, however, is public schools. The thesis of his book *Is There a Public for Public Schools?* is that the relationship between communities and public schools is in need of repair. For the better part of two centuries, he notes, there existed a national consensus that public schools were meant "to create and perpetuate a nation dedicated to particular principles, such as freedom and justice; to develop a citizenry capable of self-government; ensure social order; equalize opportunity for all . . . ; [and] provide information and skills essential to both individual economic enterprise and general prosperity (1996, 12).

Public schools have also garnered support for being one of the few institutions that provides the possibility and opportunity for students of diverse backgrounds to come together (Harwood Group 1995a). This value is evident in this study, with parents discussing the benefit of life lessons as their children interacted with diverse groups. To them, the public schools provided not just an academic program, but also enabled their children to develop a sense of comfort working with others different from themselves and encouraged the development of traits such as empathy and flexibility. These traits, in turn, are useful in minimizing the separation between the haves and have-nots. An issue, if not addressed, as the parents note, contributes to the development of community fragmentation.

Mathews takes a similar perspective on the process of community rebuilding in that he, too, focuses on the civic health of the community in which public schools reside, and not on the public schools in isolation. In the long term, he believes that community development and "strengthening our ties as citizens can pave the way for sustainable school improvement" (1996, 27). He also believes that face-to-face community conversations — what he calls "deliberative dialogues" (34) — play an essential role. Deliberative dialogues are used as thinking devices. Naming the problems and framing the issues is an important part of this process. And the people who name the problems are important as well. Professionals might use technical terms, while your neighbor might respond to problems described in everyday language based in their everyday experiences. Problems worded such that citizens understand them to be shared problems can lead to a sense of shared fate and can help to encourage trustworthiness (Mathews 1996). Together, citizens from various backgrounds can consider what they might do to resolve such problems.

The next level of deliberative dialogue might be to increase the number of inclusive civic organizations, such as community foundations in which representatives from various neighbor alliances can participate. Community foundations can also act as umbrella organizations, called "boundary spanners," which take on the role of making connections among the neighborhood alliances, foundations, and other, more local organizations. Umbrella organizations encourage community-wide discussions, help to develop a sense of interrelatedness among local issues, build networks, and promote resource sharing. In Grand Rapids, Michigan, for example, thirty to forty civic and educational organizations convene in the community each year to deal with three major issues. They have been doing this for more than fifteen years (Mathews 1996).

Conversations within deliberative dialogues must go both ways. It's not a case of community leaders showing up with an agenda and their own solutions. And public action isn't the same as the action of special interest groups. Communities with vigorous and healthy populaces have leaders who function "not as gatekeepers but as door openers, bent on widening participation. They also insist that others take ownership" (Mathews 1996, 68). They are not preoccupied with protecting their turf.

Mathews also believes it is important for the public to protect schools from special interests. To do that, a community needs a supportive public with interconnected purposes and a mutual sense of direction.

High Social Capital and Good Public Schools

According to Mathews and the Harwood Group, communities with high social capital usually have strong support for public education, whereas "schools are seen quite differently where public life is failing. People talk about them as being detached from the community. The dominant concern is 'taking care of *my* child' rather than educating every child. In this atmosphere, public schools find it virtually impossible to garner the support they need to be successful" (Mathews 1996, 74; Harwood Group 1995b, 4). And Putnam reports that states with high social capital have measurably better educational outcomes than do less civic states. He notes, "The Social Capital Index is highly correlated with student scores on standardized tests taken in elementary school, junior high school (middle school), and high school" (2000, 299). Communities where people connect with one another have a positive effect on the education of children.

A very important characteristic of civically engaged communities with healthy levels of reciprocity and trustworthiness is the loyalty of the educators to the public schools. Where there is a high level of trust among teachers, parents, and principals, these stakeholders are more committed to school improvement. When teachers are in high-trust settings, they "feel loyal to the school, seek innovative approaches to learning, reach out to parents, and have a deep sense of responsibility for the students' development." Trust remains a key ingredient for school reform (Putnam 2000, 305; Bryk and Schneider 1998).

Communities with high social capital are typically viewed as also having strong community support for public schools. Tupelo, Mississippi, and Portland, Oregon, are two examples. In Tupelo, the scholar Vaughn L. Grisham refers to the public school system as one of the city's finest achievements. And Mathews provides examples of community support when he writes, "A community foundation created to provide private funds for the public schools has received donations larger than the state universities have had in some years. Supporting the public schools is a strong community tradition" (1996, 74).

Putnam, Feldstein, and Cohen (2003) present Portland, Oregon, as another example of a community with high social capital and high civic engagement. Recently, the Bill and Melinda Gates Foundation and the Meyer Memorial Trust announced a three-year investment of $8.9 million in the Portland public school system. The investment is a major joint initiative between the Portland Schools Foundation and Portland public schools. Foundation executive director Cynthia Guyer said, "The decision to invest here now is testimony to three things: the strength and leadership of our superintendent and school board; the incredible talent of our principals and teachers; and the unwavering commitment of Portland's citizens and civic leaders to create one of the finest urban school systems in the country, right here in Portland" (Guyer 2005, 1).

Grassroots Advocacy:
Providing Horizontal Conversations

Public school grassroots coalitions may be one place to begin strengthening the community's horizontal structures. Public school advocacy itself needs to become stronger. And grassroots coalitions, either those that currently exist in Hawai'i or the formation of new coalitions like Parents for Public Schools (PPS) — or both — could facilitate face-to-face conversations that could help bridge the divide among diverse groups interested in education but who have very different perspectives.

One member of the PPS grassroots coalition describes (below) the impact of a strong and active community with high social capital that worked to overcome financial issues at the city and county levels. This example illustrates, as well, how horizontal community structures connected to an umbrella organization can facilitate different citizen groups' efforts toward meeting a common goal. In this case, the common goal was to obtain adequate financial support for the urban public school system.

Mainland Public School Parent: We have been able to maintain class sizes of thirty or less. We have tremendously strong community support in general for our schools, both business support and community support. In the last year, when it looked like state funding was not going to come through, our county passed a one-and-a-quarter percent income tax in the middle of a recession to support schools. So I think we have a tremendously supportive city and county, and a supportive business community as well.

Q: And could you talk a little bit about that? How does the business community support public education and why?

Mainland Public School Parent: I think that the business community in general understands that to attract families and workers, we need to have good schools. And if you don't, you're going to end up probably having to compensate your employees another ten thousand dollars a year per child for private education. So I think this city is known around the country as being a wonderful place to live. But ultimately what will attract a family here is the fact that it also has strong public schools. And so I think our business community understands that, and therefore understands that if they want to attract and retain employees here, they need to support our schools. It doesn't mean they don't grumble about it. But they are generally supportive. (*Laughs.*)

Last year, when the public schools were looking at cutting twenty-five days off of its school calendar and having the shortest year in the nation, the way that was resolved was that our teachers agreed to essentially work for free. Now, that's not the term you would use, but they took a pay cut that was equivalent to working for free for ten days — unheard of. And our city council imposed a business income tax — temporary for the year — to cover the rest of the funds. So it was a twenty-five-million-dollar gap, and businesses ended up paying for fifteen million dollars of that. This year, we have a three-year temporary county income tax that is being partially paid for by business, but it's primarily a personal income tax. But again, even with that, the business community was on board and at the table supporting it.

To give you a sense of how supportive this community is of public schools, in 1996 there was a big issue regarding teacher layoffs because cuts were coming from the state level, and a march was organized here in support of schools. It was primarily driven by businesses and the community foundation. Thirty thousand people showed up.

More recently, on this most recent county tax that passed, it became very clear that the governor wasn't going to step up and try to fill the void in state funding to make sure that education was left whole. Most of our legislators — a good portion of our legislators — had signed "no new tax" pledges. And so it was pretty clear that we were going to be facing class sizes of forty-five next year, or, you know, cutting the equivalent of forty-five million dollars, or forty-five days off the calendar for this school year if something wasn't done. And a group got together — of about five of us; I was one of them — and then with a larger group in January of about sixteen parents, we formed a group called HOPE — Help Out Public Education. Our mission was to basically face the reality that the state wasn't going to come through with funding and what could we do on a local level? And so we went public on Super Bowl Sunday, and in January, within two to three weeks, we probably had two thousand to three thousand parents signed up — parents and community members signed up on an e-mail Web site.

Q: How did you go public?

Mainland Public School Parent: First of all, we worked through groups like community Parents for Public Schools. We basically blasted e-mails out through every avenue we could think of. And our goal was to lobby —

Q: So you used the Internet?

Mainland Public School Parent: Yes, and our goal was to lobby city commissioners and the mayor and the county commissioner to get the city and county to step up to fund schools. And we talked to the media constantly. We did parades. I mean, we did signs on the bridges. We did all kinds of things.

The three things that we were asking for were not wild things. They were: a full school year, thirty kids or less per class, and a decision by the middle of March because that's when we felt that parents would be making decisions as to whether or not they would leave the public schools. And those were our three mantras throughout.

After our first meeting with the mayor, she got together a group representing businesses, city representatives, county representatives, parents, and school district representatives. This group met twice a week from the end of January through March acting as an ad-hoc committee that was figuring out how are we going to save schools. And then the measure was put on the May election [ballot] and it passed.

I mean, when you can amass two or three thousand people in a period of two or three weeks to start lobbying the city and the county — we would have different groups of people who would go in every single day to talk to different city and county commissioners. And then we had e-mails coming in, and we had phone calls coming in, and there was a sense of absolute desperation and despair during that time, and so the media was all over it.

There were articles were in *Education Week* and the *New York Times*. I think there was a real sense of understanding by city and county leaders and business leaders that what was happening in terms of public education in this city was hurting them too on a much bigger, bigger level than just local politics.

Believers Needed

The public school parents in this study are part of an "engaged public" in Hawai'i. They point out what is right with the public schools, and they suggest changes that will make them better. They make these suggestions based on firsthand experiences, offer an alternative perspective on the public schools in Hawai'i, and offer a counter-narrative to the master narrative. This is a perspective not typically considered a point of discussion by their fellow citizens. Yet an appreciation of others' perspectives provides the foundation for the development of community trustworthiness and reciprocity that would, in turn, encourage a larger civically engaged community with higher social capital.

Budnick (2007) reminds us that people in Hawai'i have been complaining about public schools for many years. The same issues of inadequate funding, overcrowding, separate tracks for different groups, and teacher pay are discussed over and over again. Perhaps the uneasy relationship between public schools and the community will not be resolved until we can imagine change, as Anderson (1991) might suggest, and until we can consider counternarratives about schools.

Rather than "pointing the finger," perhaps we need to "look in the mirror" and ask ourselves the question that Mathews (1996) asks in his book title: *Is There a Public for Public Schools?* Can we imagine a "public" in Hawai'i that believes in public schools as a worthy institution and as a viable alternative to private schools? Underlying the willingness to participate in deliberative dialogue and in grassroots coalitions — or just showing up for a meeting — is often a believer: a believer in democracy, in public schools, in creating healthy economies, in safe neighborhoods.

The 180,000 children who attend public schools in Hawai'i need passionate citizens who believe in public education. They need parents to believe. They need their teachers and their principals to believe. They need their legislators to believe. They need the members of the Board of Education to believe. They need the business community to believe. In addition, these children need to believe that the grown-ups in their community will do their best for them.

Yoon Jee Kim, a 2001 Roosevelt High School graduate, reminded us when, as a student in a public high school, she wrote in a letter to the *Honolulu Advertiser* (2001) that "the first step we need to take as a state in improving public education is to believe our students can achieve, expect the most out of our students and support them when they ask for help." Yoon Jee graduated from Yale University in 2005.

References

About us. 2006. *Honolulu Magazine,* http://www.honolulumagazine.com/about .html. Accessed June 16, 2006.

Aguilar, E. 2004. Program benefits "academic middle"; education-1st also infuses Hawaiian values into lessons. *Honolulu Advertiser,* June 17, B4.

Anderson, B. 1991. *Imagined communities: Reflections on the origin and spread of nationalism,* Rev. ed. London: Verso.

Bakhtin, M. M. 1981. *The dialogic imagination: Four essays,* ed. M. Holquist, trans. C. Emerson and M. Holquist. Austin: University of Texas Press.

Benham, M. K. P. A. N., and R. H. Heck. 1998. *Culture and educational policy in Hawai'i: The silencing of native voices.* Mahwah, N.J.: Lawrence Erlbaum.

Bertaux, D., ed. 1981. *Biography and society: The life history approach in the social sciences.* Beverly Hills, Calif.: Sage.

Blakeman, K. 2005. Report points out inequities in quality of island life. *Honolulu Advertiser,* August 13, A1.

Bolante, R. 2005. High school: An inside story. *Honolulu Magazine* (May), 82–87, 106–109.

———. 2006. Grading the public schools. *Honolulu Magazine* (May), 58–68.

Borreca, R. 2006. Isle nonvoters don't seem to care, but why? [Commentary, "On Politics."] *Honolulu Star-Bulletin,* July 16, F5, F10.

Brannon, J. 2007. Plan for innovation unveiled; public school "academies" would grab student interest; $30 million project may help diversify economy reliant on land tourism. *Honolulu Advertiser,* January 13, A1.

Brown, W. 2006. Bishop Museum will open magnet school; curriculum will blend sciences with cultural expertise. ["Island Voices" commentary.] *Honolulu Advertiser,* March 9, A10.

Bryk, A. S., and B. Schneider. 1998. Social trust: A moral resource for school improvement. In *Rebuilding the village: Social capital and education in America,* ed. G. G. Wehlage and J. A. White. London: Falmer Press.

Budnick, R. 2007. History repeats itself in Hawai'i education; since the early 1900s, people have grumbled about public schools. *Honolulu Advertiser,* February 9, A18.

Cataluna, L. 2005. Harsh reality of 'making do' in Nanakuli. *Honolulu Advertiser,* September 11, A31.

Chapin, H. G. 1996. *Shaping history: The role of newspapers in Hawai'i.* Honolulu: University of Hawai'i Press.

Chun, M. N. 2006. *A'o: Educational traditions.* Honolulu: University of Hawai'i at Mānoa, College of Education, Curriculum Research and Development Group; and the Hawai'i Department of Education, Office of Curriculum, Instruction and Student Support, Instructional Services Branch. Pihana Nā Mamo Project, Ka Wana Series, Book 3.

Creamer, B. 2005. DOE consolidates 39 programs into 12. *Honolulu Advertiser,* October 26, B2.

———. 2006a. New model for isle schools; Ocean Pointe Elementary to include state-of-the-art, hands-on learning features. *Honolulu Advertiser,* March 12, A1, A6.

———. 2006b. Principals plan high school overhaul. *Honolulu Advertiser,* April 23, A1.

———. 2006c. Public school's redesign gets DOE support, some resistance to creating small learning communities expected. *Honolulu Advertiser,* September 13, B1.

———. 2007. Niu Valley Middle to pilot elite curriculum; no other public schools here have International Baccalaureate program. *Honolulu Advertiser,* January 1, B1.

Creamer, B., and T. Shapiro. 2005. Students' test scores mixed in fourth year; youngsters made gains; upper grades show less progress. *Honolulu Advertiser,* August 5, A1, A2.

Darling-Hammond, L. 1997. Education, equity, and the right to learn. In *The public purpose of education and schooling,* ed. J. I. Goodlad and T. J. McMannon. San Francisco: Jossey-Bass, Inc., 41–54.

DePledge, D. 2004. Good fit for your child is most important goal. *Honolulu Advertiser,* August 29, A1, A2.

———. 2005. Business consultant to fill vacancy on BOE; Paul Vierling has daughter attending Kailua public school. *Honolulu Advertiser,* May 7, B1.

Dotts, C. K., and M. Sikkema. 1994. *Challenging the status quo: Public education in Hawai'i, 1840–1980.* Honolulu: Hawai'i Education Association.

Duchemin, J. 2003. Qualcomm chief [Irwin Jacobs] puts focus on schools. *Honolulu Advertiser,* January 21, D1.

Elam, Stanley M., L. C. Rose, and A. M. Gallup. 1991. The 23rd annual Gallup poll of the public's attitudes toward the public schools. *Phi Delta Kappan* 73.

Essoyan, S. 2003. Safer to enter? Despite a few bad incidents, teachers and students say they feel secure. *Honolulu Star-Bulletin,* July 6. http://starbulletin.com/2003/07/06/news/story2.html. Accessed July 9, 2003.

———. 2005. Isles sixth in school standards; Hawai'i's tests for proficiency in reading and math are among the toughest in nation, an educational journal says. *Honolulu Star-Bulletin,* May 13. http://starbulletin.com/2005/05/13/news/index1.html. Accessed May 14, 2005.

———. 2008. The private school pull. *Honolulu Star-Bulletin,* January 13, A4–A5. Also available online from http://starbulletin.com/2008/01/13/news/.

Feirer, G. 1983. Interview with B. K. Hyams. Honolulu: University of Hawai'i at Mānoa, Hamilton Library, Hawai'i Collection, Tape 7.

Gon, S. M. 2001. Pols should send their kids to public school. [Letter to the editor.] *Honolulu Star-Bulletin,* April 21.

Grading the public schools. 2006. *Honolulu Magazine,* http://www.honolulumagazine
.com/Honolulu-Magazine/Schools/Grading-the-Public-Schools/. Accessed June
16, 2006.

Grisham, V. L. 1999. *Tupelo: The evolution of a community.* Dayton, Ohio: Kettering Foundation Press.

Grisham, V., and R. Gurwitt. 1999. *Hand in hand: Community and economic development in Tupelo.* Aspen, Colo.: Aspen Institute.

Guyer, G. 2005. National foundations place confidence in Portland schools. *Connections* 6(2): 1–2.

Harris, H. 2005. Leeward Coast school conditions horrible; many classrooms are
hot, dirty, noisy & rundown. [Commentary.] *Honolulu Advertiser,* October 28,
A18.

Harwood Group. 1995a. *Halfway out the door: Citizens talk about their mandate for
public schools.* Dayton, Ohio: Kettering Foundation.

———. 1995b. *Forming public capital: Observations from the communities.* Dayton,
Ohio: Kettering Foundation.

Hawai'i 3Rs grants, volunteers sprucing up 11 schools. 2005. *Honolulu Advertiser,*
November 24, B4.

Hawai'i guide to private schools 2005. 2004. Supplement to *Honolulu Magazine*
(September), PS1–PS56.

Hawai'i guide to private schools 2006. 2005. Supplement to *Honolulu Magazine*
(September), PS1–PS56.

Hawai'i State Charter Schools Administrative Office. 2005. History of charter
schools in Hawai'i (table). http://www.hcsao.org/hicharters/history.html. Information also available at http://www.hcsao.org/hicharters. Accessed March 31,
2006.

———. 2006. The charter school experience; What are public charter schools?
http://www.hcsao.org/hicharters/profiles. Accessed March 31, 2006.

Hawai'i State Department of Education. 2004. 2004 SAT honor roll: Public schools
meet or exceed national SAT averages. [News release.] http://lilinote.k12.hi
.us/STATE/COMM/DOEPRESS.NSF/a1d7af052e94dd12oa2561f7000a037c/
9b3a10b55c120b260a256f21000ad35d?OpenDocument. Accessed February 9,
2006.

———. 2005. *Na Lono Kula: The News of the School* 2(7). Also available online:
http://doe.k12.hi.us/periodicals/nlk/0405/nlko207.pdf. Accessed February 9,
2006.

———. 2007. JVED: A partnership of the Military Community and Hawaii Public
Schools. [Advertising supplement to the *Honolulu Advertiser.*] September 12.

Heckathorn, J. 2001. Government schools. [Foreword.] *Honolulu Magazine* (May), 8.

Heckathorn, J., and M. Keany. 2005. Act 51: Can it save the public schools? *Honolulu Magazine* (May), 88–93, 110–112.

Hickey, S., and S. Mendelsohn. 2003. Where senators send their children for
school. KITV4 education Web page: http://www.thehawaiichannel.com/
education/1959035/detail.html. Accessed July 21, 2005.

Hirata, T. T. 1988. Interview with E. H. Tamura, June 30. In The struggle for core studies: Miles Carey at McKinley High School in the Territory of Hawai'i, by E. H. Tamura (1996). *Pacific Educational Research Journal* 8(1): 19–38.

Hochschild, J. L., and N. Scovronick. 2003. *The American dream and the public schools*. Oxford: Oxford University Press.

Hurley, T. 2004. Hawai'i's voter roll at bottom; registration level, participation lowest in nation in 2002. *Honolulu Advertiser,* July 29, A1.

Hurley, T., and T. Shapiro. 2005. BOE may lower bar to pass No Child tests; superintendent says new "realistic" standards are likely. *Honolulu Advertiser,* August 5, A1, A2.

Hyams, B. K. 1985. School teachers as agents of cultural imperialism in Territorial Hawai'i. *Journal of Pacific History* 20(4): 202–219.

Investing in our community. 2004. Newsletter of Senator Carol Fukunaga, Hawai'i State Senate (Winter): 2.

Iwanaga, D. 2004. Letter to the editor. *Honolulu Advertiser,* August 11, A19.

Kamehameha Schools. 2006. The legacy of a princess. http://www.ksbe.edu/about /facts.php. Accessed February 8, 2006.

Kellman, L. 2005. Voter turnout best since 1968; 60.7% of electorate cast ballots in presidential race. *Honolulu Advertiser,* January 15, A3.

Keone'ula Elementary opens today in 'Ewa; new public school has computer labs, closed-circuit TV. 2007. *Honolulu Advertiser,* January 12, B3.

Kim, Y. J. 2001. Students must believe that they can succeed. [Letter to the editor.] *Honolulu Advertiser,* August 8. [Surname printed as "Kimph."]

Koyama, E. 2006. Busting the big myths about the DOE budget. [Commentary, "The gathering place" (editorial column).] *Honolulu Star-Bulletin,* http://starbulletin .com/2006/03/12/editorial/commentary.html. Accessed March 13, 2006.

Lotman, Yu. M. 1988. Text within a text. *Soviet Psychology* 26(3): 32–51.

MacIntyre, A. 1984. *After virtue: A study in moral theory.* 2nd ed. Notre Dame, Ind.: University of Notre Dame Press.

Malo, David. 1996. *Ka mo'olelo Hawai'i: Hawaiian traditions.* Trans. Malcolm Nāea Chun. In Educating the new leadership of young chiefs, by series author Malcolm Nāea Chun (2006), in *A'o: Educational traditions.* Honolulu: University of Hawai'i at Mānoa, College of Education, Curriculum Research and Development Group; and the Hawai'i Department of Education, Office of Curriculum, Instruction and Student Support, Instructional Services Branch. Pihana Nā Mamo Project, Ka Wana Series, Book 3, 16–19.

Markrich, M. 2000. The crumbling of our public schools. [Opinion; Focus section.] *Honolulu Advertiser,* October 8, B1, B4.

Martin, D. 2005a. Isle schools fare the worst; a study puts state public schools at the bottom compared with the other states; researchers and officials caution that national comparisons are unreliable. *Honolulu Star-Bulletin,* March 29. http:// starbulletin.com/2005/03/29/news/index1.html. Accessed March 30, 2005.

———. 2005b. Program expedites isle school repairs; staff reassigned to the education department cut the red tape that let problems linger. *Honolulu Star-Bulletin,* December 11. http://starbulletin.com/2005/12/11/news/story02.html. Accessed December 17, 2005.

———. 2006a. DOE seeks financial officer post for schools: Officials hope it will improve fiscal and program monitoring. *Honolulu Star-Bulletin,* January 21. http:// starbulletin.com/2006/01/21/news/story10.html. Accessed February 2, 2006.

———. 2006b. Small school groups lauded; Isle educators urge the BOE to fund and expand the "learning communities" concept. *Honolulu Star-Bulletin,* September 13, A1.

Mathews, D. 1996. *Is there a public for public schools?* 1st ed. Dayton, Ohio: Kettering Foundation Press.

Menton, L. 1992. A Christian and civilized education: The Hawaiian Chiefs' Children's School, 1839–50. *History of Education Quarterly* (32)2: 213–242.

Mick, B. K. 2004. School boards are not issue; public apathy is. *Honolulu Advertiser,* February.

Mink, L. O. 1978. Narrative form as a cognitive instrument. In *The writing of history: Literary form and historical understanding,* ed. R. H. Canary and H. Kozicki. Madison: University of Wisconsin Press, 129–149.

Miyataki, G. 2005. Education has become the No. 1 economic priority. [Commentary.] *Honolulu Advertiser,* February 8, A7.

Mondale, S., and S. B. Patton, eds. 2001. *School: The story of American public education.* Boston: Beacon Press.

Moon, T. Y. 2002. Civic education is critical; most Americans have a woeful understanding about government, manifested in voter apathy. *Honolulu Advertiser,* May 2, A14.

Moore named DOE deputy. 2007. *Honolulu Advertiser,* April 6, B7.

Moreno, L. 2008. Campbell High lands international college-prep program. *Honolulu Advertiser.* http://the.honoluluadvertiser.com/article/2008/Jan/07/ln/ hawaii801070360.html. Accessed January 9, 2008.

Most isle schools pass facility inspections. 2004. *Honolulu Star-Bulletin,* September 16. http://starbulletin.com/2004/09/16/news/index8.html. Accessed March 3, 2005.

Nakaso, D. 1999. Island schools' history a matter of class. Millennium Hawai'i 2000 series, Special section. *Honolulu Advertiser,* September 27, S1.

———. 2004. Hawai'i's workers struggle with low pay, low-level jobs. *Honolulu Advertiser,* October 2, A1.

———. 2006. Ranking surprises Hawai'i charities; study says residents volunteer at nation's eighth lowest rates. *Honolulu Advertiser,* June 13, A1.

Napier, A. K. 2001. The death of public school. *Honolulu Magazine* (May), 56–61, 77–78.

———. 2003. Grading the public schools. *Honolulu Magazine* (May), 34–43, 70–76.

———. 2004. Grading the public schools: The grades. *Honolulu Magazine* (May), 32–42.

Ochs, E., and L. Capps. 2001. Living narrative: Creating lives in everyday story telling. Cambridge, Mass.: Harvard University Press.

Orr, B. J. 2004. Letter to the editor. *Honolulu Advertiser,* February 2, A9.

Otake, M. 2001. Make public schools requirement of job. [Letter to the editor.] *Honolulu Advertiser,* March 28.

Parents for Public Schools. 2004. www.parents4publicschools.com./mission.htm/.

Patton, M. Q. 1989. *Qualitative evaluation methods.* Tenth printing. Beverly Hills, Calif.: Sage.

Putnam, R. D. 1993. Making Democracy Work: Civic Traditions in Modern Italy. Princeton University Press.

———. 2000. *Bowling alone: The collapse and revival of American community.* New York: Simon & Schuster.

Putnam, R. D., L. M. Feldstein, and D. Cohen. 2003. *Better together: Restoring the American community.* New York: Simon & Schuster.

Quill, J. 2005. Age of opportunity. *Honolulu Magazine* (September), PS6–11.

Rees, R. 2003. Wealth, poverty and taxes. *Honolulu Advertiser,* March 2, B4.

Reiziss, Stan. W. 2005. Schools offer option to lousy public ed. [Letter to the editor.] *Honolulu Star-Bulletin,* August 18, http://starbulletin.com/2005/08/18/editorial/indexletters.html. Accessed August 21, 2005.

Rod Mcphee leaves vast educational legacy. [Editorial including a tribute to Miles Carey, principal of McKinley High School.] 2005. *Honolulu Advertiser,* March 4, A16.

Sakoda, K., and J. Siegel. 2003. *Pidgin grammar: An introduction to the Creole language of Hawai‘i.* Honolulu: Bess Press.

Schaefers, A. 2005. Average Hawai‘i paychecks rank 19th; Isle wages statistics reveal a shortage of high-paying jobs. *Honolulu Star-Bulletin,* August 5, A1, A6. Also available online: http://starbulletin.com/2005/08/05/news/index3.html.

Schultz, M. 2005. Kona charter school received great honor. [Letter to the editor.] *Honolulu Advertiser,* November 11, A19.

Seidman, I. 2006. *Interviewing as qualitative research: A guide for researchers in education and the social sciences.* New York: Teachers College Press.

Shapiro, D. 2001. Politicians are finally getting it. [Volcanic Ash column.] *Honolulu Advertiser,* November 21, A12.

———. 2002. Not voting is just a cop-out; low voter turnout only makes it easier for self-serving candidates and the special interests that back them to maintain control. [Volcanic Ash column]. *Honolulu Advertiser,* October 23, A18.

Shapiro, T. 2005a. Latest student test results a mixed bag; Despite gains, state fails to rise from bottom of pack. *Honolulu Advertiser.* October 20, B1.

———. 2005b. Renaissance waiting to bloom, Programs hampered by lack of teachers and course materials. *Honolulu Advertiser,* November 7, A1.

Shoho, Alan R. 1997. The ethical leadership of Miles Carey: Dare a school principal build a new social order at McKinley ("Tokyo") High School. Unpublished manuscript. Department of Educational Leadership and Policy Studies, University of Texas at San Antonio.

Sikkema, M. 1997. Early Hawai'i schools fought anti-democratic social values. [Commentary.] *Honolulu Advertiser,* April 20, B4.

Skocpol, T. 2003. *Diminished in democracy: From membership to management in American civic life.* Norman: University of Oklahoma Press.

Strauss, A., and J. Corbin. 1998. *Basics of qualitative research: Techniques and procedures for developing grounded theory.* Thousand Oaks, Calif.: Sage Publications, Inc.

Stueber, R. K. 1982. An informal history of schooling in Hawai'i. In *To teach the children: Historical aspects of education in Hawai'i; A publication accompanying the exhibition commemorating the 50th anniversary of the College of Education and the 75th anniversary of the University of Hawai'i,* ed. A. L. Pickens and D. Kemble. Honolulu: Bernice Pauahi Bishop Museum, 16–36.

Tamura, Eileen H. 1994. *Americanization, acculturation, and ethnic identity: The nisei generation in Hawai'i.* Urbana: University of Illinois Press.

———. 1996. The struggle for core studies: Miles Carey at McKinley High School in the Territory of Hawai'i. *Pacific Educational Research Journal* 8(1): 19–38.

Tehranian, M. 2001. Dual school system reflects ethnic, class differences. Letter: Elite content with low level of public education. [Letter commentary.] *Honolulu Advertiser,* March 18, B1, B4.

Tschumy, Ruth. 2006. State public education reform proceeding much as planned under Act 51. [Education Matters column.] *Honolulu Star-Bulletin,* March 5, F1, F10.

Tyack, D., and L. Cuban. 1995. *Tinkering toward utopia: A century of public school reform.* Cambridge, Mass.: Harvard University Press.

Uchida, D. 2005. Shift housing focus to educated workforce; increasing income would be influence on Hawai'i's market. [Island Voices commentary.] *Honolulu Advertiser,* September 29, A14.

Volunteers wanted; Hawai'i ranks near the bottom when it comes to residents giving up their limited free time. 2006. *Honolulu Star-Bulletin,* June 13, A1, A6. Also available online: http://starbulletin.com/2006/06/13/news/story03.html.

Vorsino, M. 2007. Punahou has come long way from missionary-school roots. *Honolulu Advertiser,* March 1, B4.

Watanabe, Eiko Otsuka. 1962. The McKinley High School core program. Master's thesis, University of Hawai'i, College of Education.

Watanabe, J. 2001. Many public school teachers put own kids in private school ["Kokua line" help column]. *Honolulu Star-Bulletin,* October 10. http://starbulletin.com/2001/10/10/news/kokualine.html. Accessed October 15, 2001.

Wertsch, James. V. 1998. *Mind as action.* New York: Oxford University Press.

———. 2002. *Voices of collective remembering.* Cambridge: Cambridge University Press.

Westbrook, R. 1996. Public schooling and American democracy. In *Democracy, education, and the schools,* 1st ed., ed. R. Soder. San Francisco: Jossey-Bass, 125–150.

Williams, Shirley JoAnn. 1991. The educational theory and philosophy of education of Miles Elwood Cary: Implications for democracy in a global civic culture. Ph.D. dissertation, Northern Illinois University.

Wist, Benjamin O. 1940. *A century of public education in Hawai'i: October 15, 1840–October 15, 1940.* Honolulu: Hawai'i Educational Review.

Witt, R. M. 2005. NCLB won't work, but Act 51 just might. *Honolulu Advertiser,* November 27, B1.

Yamamoto, K. 1979. An oral history of Miles Cary and McKinley High. Unpublished article prepared for Education Foundations. In "The ethical leadership of Miles Carey: Dare a school principal build a new social order at McKinley ("Tokyo") High School" (1997), by A. R. Shoho. [Unpublished manuscript, Department of Educational Leadership and Policy Studies, University of Texas at San Antonio.]

Yamamoto, L. 2000. *Tidbits on raising children: Making our most important job easier by doing it better; an online parenting book.* Version 1.0. Bloomington, Ind.: 1st Books Library, The International Online Library. Also available online from http://www.hawaii.edu/medicine/pediatrics/parenting/parenting.html.

Yamauchi, L. 2006. *Using a Speak Out to gain family and community perspectives.* Paper presented at Speak Out Mānoa 2006, Mānoa Elementary School, Honolulu.

Index

ased against public schools, 1, 32, 85, 92–95; bias toward private school, 69, 86, 87; inaccuracy of, 5, 62, 90–91, 134; lack of first-hand research, 19, 85, 90, 134, 142; in the media, 99, 134–141, 143–144; unsubstantiated, 19, 85, 92–93, 126, 128–129, 133–134. *See also* narrative

core studies, 18, 35, 37, 42, 43–44, 53, 64, 69, 71, 121, 160, 241

counselors: changes proposed for, 199, 205; general, 76–79; high-school college counselors, 76–80, 199, 205, 239, 252

culture: Asian influence, 152; elitist influence, 158; European/Western influence, 152, 156–157; Hawaiian, 9, 241–242; positive school culture, 35, 120, 158; private school culture, 107, 119–120; public school culture, 48, 71, 80–81, 115, 116, 158; tools of, 167

curriculum, 44, 65, 83, 116, 137, 143, 161, 240, 256; advanced/honors, 53; challenging, 9, 26, 31, 35, 49, 52, 60, 73, 98, 151; recommended changes, 205, 243–244; unchallenging, 76, 79–80, 105, 111–112

decentralization, 205, 214, 217–219, 244–245

de-linking. *See* decentralization

democracy, ix, xi, 4, 155, 158–159, 160, 161–162, 226, 247, 249–258, 260, 266, 277

Democratic Revolution, Hawai'i, 249

Democrats, 152, 162, 258, 259

Department of Accounting and General Services (DAGS; Hawai'i). *See* changes, state level; facilities

Department of Defense (U.S.) schools, 40, 104

DePledge, Derrick, 100, 154, 156, 172, 191

deregulation. *See* decentralization

dialogues: community, 165; conversa-

tional narratives, 169; deliberative, 272, 277

disadvantages of private schools, 15, 66–67, 86–87, 90, 264; crime or misconduct, 142, 146–148. *See also* variability of schools

disadvantages of public schools. *See* belief, community-held; conversation, incessant; negative experiences in public schools; variability of schools

diversity, 150; advantages/benefits of, 8, 11, 14, 26, 57–59, 66, 74; celebrating, 9; in communities, ix; ethnic, ix, 9, 29, 53–54, 61, 68, 157; issues, 54, 145; lack of, 13, 14, 57, 66, 112, 115, 142; of parents interviewed, 1, 2; race, 150–152; socioeconomic, ix, 6, 10, 26, 29, 38, 53–54, 61, 68; of student population, ix, 6–13, 26, 37, 40, 66, 73. *See also* culture; empathy; friendships; realism; values

Dotts, Cecil K. and Mildred Sikkema, 157

drama, 67, 71–72, 201

economy: and good public schools, 135; inequities, 263–268; and the role of public education, 4, 263–268

educational forum. *See* joint ventures

educators, innovators. *See* Cary, Miles; innovation; MacCaughey, Vaughan; teachers, public school; Townsend, Henry S.; Yarberry, R. Burl

elementary schools, 16, 20–21, 23, 31–48, 51–53, 61, 63, 72, 81, 83–85, 118, 124; and community, 258–260, 273; mainland, 203, 227–228, 236–238; private, 13; programs, 241, 244; quality, high, 94–98, 116–117, 130, 143–144, 164, 185, 208; teachers recommending private school, 107–109, 111–112

elitism, 131–132, 158. *See also* English Standard Schools; stratification, social